REGAINING THE LEAD

REGAINING THE LEAD

Policies for
Economic Growth

by

Herbert E. Striner

PRAEGER

PRAEGER SPECIAL STUDIES • PRAEGER SCIENTIFIC

New York • Philadelphia • Eastbourne, UK
Toronto • Hong Kong • Tokyo • Sydney

Library of Congress Cataloging in Publication Data

Striner, Herbert E.
  Regaining the lead.

  Includes index.
  1. United States—Economic policy—1981–
2. Germany (West)—Economic policy—1974–   . 3. Japan
—Economic policy—1945–   . 4. Economic policy.
I. Title.
HC106.8.S77   1984   338.973   83-17787
ISBN 0-03-069772-7 (alk. paper)

Published in 1984 by Praeger Publishers
CBS Educational and Profession Publishing
a Division of CBS Inc.
521 Fifth Avenue, New York, NY 10175 USA
© 1984 by Praeger Publishers

456789 052 987654321

Printed in the United States of America
on acid-free paper

To Professor Broadus Mitchell, economist and teacher. He introduced me to economics and set a standard for concern, good-humored probing, and an eager, honest sharing of efforts to understand. No student has ever had a better teacher, nor teacher a better exemplar.

Acknowledgments

The patience of, and the most helpful editing and reediting, by my wife, Iona, were in turn amazing and critical in moving through this work's many versions and my many moods. My son, Richard, gave me the able editing and intellectual insights that come only from a first-rate historian with a deft feeling for just the proper phrase or reference, all with a touch of love. My daughter, Deborah, was the schedule task-master. Chiding me when the output timetable was lagging, her kind prodding was essential. Nanette Brown, whose dexterity with the word processor, at the Business College, the American University, was equalled only by her morale-building comments on the content.

A grant from the Pittsburgh Plate Glass Foundation (PPG), of the PPG Corporation, aided me greatly during the summer of 1982. This support permitted me to flesh out my research in West Germany and spend the necessary time writing, free of other commitments.

Kurt Kruger, of Darmstadt, West Germany, was of major help to me in arranging interviews, accompanying me in meetings, performing as a first-rate interpreter, and otherwise making my research in West Germany both productive and enjoyable.

Finally, the numerous business, government, and labor leaders with whom I met in West Germany and Japan were of tremendous help; far too many to list, I am nonetheless much in their debt. Their patience and concern in showing how their democratic societies have been able to develop highly effective economies is only partly a reflection of national pride. Knowing full well how dependent their nations' economic health is on that of the U.S. economy, each of these individuals acknowledged a stake in the development of more realistic and effective U.S. economic policies.

Table of Contents

List of Tables

Introduction

"What has gone wrong with America?" is the question most of us have been asking since the late 1970s. Democrats and Republicans, conservatives and liberals, were, by the end of 1982, increasingly concerned about a recession that was far worse than any since the Great Depression of the 1930s. This sense of frustration and anxiety appeared in an excellent article in the *Washington Post* in October 1982. Lou Mervis, a Republican business and civic leader of Danville, Illinois, was discussing the effects of the recession on his hometown and its people:

> They are at their wits' end. They don't know who to blame or what to blame. They are just withdrawing into themselves. And now we're seeing the old problems, the worst in people, coming out: the latent anti-Semitism, the blacks, the Puerto Ricans. . . . Those are the kinds of things that are starting to hit. I'm seeing more and more of it.[1]

The recession of 1981–82 did not arrive without ample warning. Since 1975, every indicator of economic well-being said the United States was in trouble. This happened while the economies of competitive industrial nations like Japan and West Germany were performing at continuing high levels with low unemployment and inflation. Even during the worldwide recession of 1981-82, the problems of unemployment, low productivity and economic growth, and high interest rates were more severe in the United States than in these other countries. What was happening? Answers coming from political leaders, Democrats and Republicans, were correctly perceived by most Americans as both self-serving and without meaning. For many in the United States who could recall the 1930s, the recurring promise by political leaders that "the recession was bottoming out" was reminiscent of the 1930s' slogan that "prosperity was just around the corner" — a corner that took ten years to get around!

By the late 1970s, it had become apparent to both Democrats and Republicans that something was sorely amiss with the Great American Dream. The 1960s had been the decade when the "War on Poverty" had been launched. We were all partners in an unprecedented national effort to use our great wealth and abundance of economic resources to bring to all of our citizens a decent life. Few doubted this could be done. By 1975, with 9 percent unemployed, low productivity, and equally low economic growth, there was growing doubt.

But by 1982 there was no longer doubt, only a sense of failure and despair over our nation's future. Levels of unemployment higher than any time since the 1930s, zero productivity increase, and almost zero economic growth had produced a sense of bewilderment and a predicament with which most Americans had never been confronted. As Lou Mervis put it so well, the questions in the minds of most Americans were what had happened and why were our leaders not able to deal with the situation?

In reality, these questions were not new. They first began to be asked in the late 1970s, when cracks in our economic structure became apparent to the average concerned citizen. The answers provided by business and union leaders and government officials were of little help; indeed, they were misleading and counterproductive. The once highly lauded American worker was accused of being unmotivated, greedy, and unproductive. Industry was viewed as selfish, if not incompetent. Our corporate leaders were accused of mismanagement not found in Japanese or West German executive suites. And our government was accused of blundering, heavy-handed and excessive regulation of once-efficient industries.

Although all of these concerns did, and still do, contain some elements of truth, they do not provide the real answer to the question, "What has happened to the economy of the United States since the late 1960s?" The truth, and the answers, go much deeper. The reasons are many and complex. They grow out of changes that took place in the world after the chaos and destruction of the 1940–45 wars in Europe and Japan. The Europeans and Japanese understood the nature of these changes and organized their basic institutions, such as labor, industry, and government, in a way calculated to deal with the needs of the new post–World War II economy. They approached economic problems differently than they had before 1940. Much of this was unplanned and grew out of a desperation that could only attend economies that were in shambles. These countries had to move quickly and pragmatically, with little time wasted in arguments over economic ideology.

During this heroic effort to rebuild, a new approach to a more effective form of capitalism developed. This new form of capitalism has provided the basis for the economic competition that has so eroded the position of United States industry, both at home and abroad. And this new form of capitalism has also provided these countries with a greater ability than exists in the United States to deal with economic recessions.

With an economy undamaged by war, as the supplier of help to the war-torn countries, the United States proceeded after 1945 along its path of economic growth with the same set of values and institutional relationships forged during the late 1930s and immediate post–World War II years. We didn't have to change—we thought. But we really should have.

By mid–1983, there was grave danger that an economic recovery would mask the basic flaws that still existed in our economy. Political leaders in the Reagan administration cautioned that though the recovery from the recession of 1981–82 had begun, a continued level of 8 to 9 percent unemployment may exist for several years. Reports from basic industries such as steel, auto, and electronics confirmed that as their output began to climb back to normal, only a relatively small percentage of their former employees would be called back to work. In the midst of the joy of a recovering economy, the continued signs of fundamental economic problems are ignored. Continued high interest rates, high unemployment, and, still, in early 1983, productivity gains only a quarter to one-third those of Japan, West Germany, and France are seen as problems that will shortly succumb to a broad recovery "on all fronts."

But such a recovery will not happen. It will not happen because we must marshall our resources and learn to use these resources in a manner far different from the patterns of the past. We must begin to develop an industrial policy. But, contrary to the models being suggested by most political leaders and economic advisers in mid-1983, an industrial policy that is based on some superordinate "Council of Advisers" or a single "Super Department of Trade" will not be up to the task. Our culture, our values, and our history dictate a different approach. As capitalism has matured in our nation, it has developed institutions and relationships that call for an industrial policy that cannot be imposed from above. We must develop an industrial policy that is a product of leadership as well as nurturing at lower levels.

Unless we develop an industrial policy that reflects a building of new relationships between government, industry, and labor, as well as formally charging new organizations with policy development, the economic recovery of 1983 will prematurely abort and develop a two-track society. This two-track society will consist of the majority who will share in the benefits of recovering industries, people equipped with the skills called for by those businesses capable of competing with foreign firms, or with foreign-owned firms expanding into our own economy. But there will also be a very large minority—black, white, and brown—who will remain unemployed. Those who lack sufficient educational and vocational skills will also be unemployable. This minority and their families, representing perhaps 20 to 25 percent of the United States adult population, will not only not share in our recovery but they will represent a very significant part of our nation that will drain society of funds, motivation, and a sense

of national purpose. This underclass will co-exist with industries unable
to compete with their counterparts in Japan and West Germany, where
industrial policies have harnessed all of the resources of industry, labor,
and government in a more effective form of capitalism than exists in the
United States.

We must now rethink our basic economic philosophy and our fundamental economic institutions. Past success has never been a guarantee of
a similar future. History is full of discouraging examples. Ancient Egypt,
Greece, and Rome were followed by more recent examples of political
and industrial empires, such as Austria-Hungary and Great Britain, which
also have gone their way. No one of them ever thought it could happen to
them. It did. And it can happen to us.

This book is about what has happened to the United States that has
caused it to begin to lose its sense of being able to give to each new generation something more than the preceding generation. It is about how other
countries, industrial countries like Japan and West Germany, have been
able to surpass us in attaining their economic goals. Finally, it is about how
all of us, workers, managers, and government officials, must change—begin to think and act differently. How we must think differently about what
an economic system is, how it must now work, and how we must now
work together in very different ways to make a very different type of economic system operate effectively based on a dynamic industrial policy.

Old terms like "liberal" or "conservative" are passé. We are where we
are because neither those espousing liberal nor conservative economic
philosophy have truly comprehended the changes that took place after
World War II. We had better understand that we must be ready to move in
a different direction, or America, as we have known it, will no longer exist.
My hope is that once Americans are aware of alternative economic policies, which have worked in other nations that have the same democratic
values as we do, we will be willing to adapt our institutions and ways of
doing things to these new directions.

The United States simply must alter its underlying economic philosophy and the policies that emerge from it. The key to the world economy is
the United States of America. The world recession of 1981–82 in a way
mirrors the experience of the 1930s. But there is a significant difference.
The flows of technology and the rapidity with which industries move
among countries make the economy of the modern period far more inter-
dependent than the world economy of the 1930s. The United States economy must change to reflect the realities of this new interdependence or
we will continue to be a force of economic stagnation. This stagnation
will, in turn, continue to limit the recovery of the other major nations with
which we trade. Without their full recovery, ours will continue to fail, re-

covering incompletely only to fail again. Economic, rather than political, philosophy must drive us in the direction of a concept of one world.

The clear way to produce the jobs, the competitive industries, and the economic growth we need for the sort of future we want for ourselves and our next generation can be ours only if we are willing to change fundamentally. The old form of our capitalist system, with its outmoded economic policies, doesn't work any more. A new type does. We must change!

Note

1. Lou Mervis, "Danville Civic Leader: People Are at Their Wits' End," *Washington Post,* October 3, 1982, p. A11.

What Can
Economics Tell Us?
====1====

Adam Smith is dead. Karl Marx is dead. And John Maynard Keynes is dead. They are dead not only physically, but also intellectually because their insights are no longer relevant to the economic problems confronting the industrialized nations since World War II.

Economic theories must relate to the real world. We Americans pride ourselves on our traditional practicality and often with reason. In the field of economics, however, we are now among the most dogmatic people in the world. In part, the professional economists are heavily to blame for this, with their rigid and highly theoretical models, based so often on a false pretension to science. But even more to blame are the ideological rigidities that, in the form of conventional or folk wisdom—however decked out in intellectual elaboration—bind our view of the economic world into terms so limiting they tend to weaken or paralyze.

We are past the time when a further rehashing of conservative, liberal, or radical dogmas will do our economy good, and we are past the time for palliative, myth, and fantasy. It is time for a new approach, a new economic synthesis.

This is not to argue for an "end of ideology" or to claim that liberal, conservative, or radical approaches to social analysis lack meaning. Rather, it is to claim that American conceptions of terms like "liberal," "conservative," and "radical" are frequently one-dimensional, static, and essentially rigid. By the same token that scientific theory has evolved within a framework of culture, with its terms adapted to and drawn from the spirit of its times, by the same token that the academicians in the field of economics must adjust theories to the terms of human reality, so, in the realm of political and social theory, which impinge every moment on the terms whereby we interpret economic reality, we must understand that

1

the meanings of liberal, conservative, and radical thought are in a constant state of transition and adaptation.

Could it be that by locking ourselves into rigid definitions of liberal or conservative policy, we lose that same intellectual suppleness lost by the economic scholar whose calculus attains such a life of its own that the view of economic life has become inhuman? A brief recounting of economic thought makes for a fascinating tale that has a great deal to do with our current economic, if not our cultural, predicaments.

In the eighteenth century, Adam Smith provided a much needed economic rationale to understand the factors affecting the use of economic resources in order to increase the well-being of the society. His keen intellect provided much of the new body of knowledge we call economics and shed light on the role of market forces for increasing the economic wealth of a nation. But since his monumental work, *An Inquiry Into the Nature and Causes of the Wealth of Nations*, more than 200 years have elapsed. The society within whose framework Smith was envisioning an economic system capable of serving the needs of that society bears no resemblance to the industrial world of the 1980s. Smith's arguments were those reflecting the prevailing middle class, independent merchants of eighteenth-century England. These were merchants who were reacting against the vestiges of the centralized regulations that were the core of the mercantilist system. Though he was as suspicious of businessmen's motivations as he was of those of government bureaucrats, he nonetheless saw the gains in productivity and output of economic wealth as only available in a system that was based on individual, profit-oriented goals, unhampered by government involvement. But the world of Adam Smith was a world with very little in the way of large-scale multinational firms and governments with legislated responsibilities to provide for many aspects of economic security and stability, personal as well as corporate.

Those who in the 1980s support in the abstract the basic philosophy of Adam Smith would be horrified by the practical implications of an "applied" Adam Smith. Every U.S. business firm enjoying any form of government aid or protection whatsoever, in the form of import tariffs or quotas, would lose that help. Tax subsidies such as depreciation would have to go. Since Smith envisioned the state as partially supporting only basic reading, writing, and arithmetic and for only the "common people,"[1] in a public educational system, without doubt there are many who would object to the dismantling of our state universities or the exclusion of all but the "common people" from our public schools. Indeed, the public schools themselves would have to eliminate all parts of the curriculum except the very basic elements of reading, writing, and arithmetic. No chemistry, literature, geography, or computers would be found in the curricula.

This brief description of an application of Smithian ideas of the eighteenth century to the world of the 1980s is, in a way, "dirty pool." Fair-minded readers will immediately react by claiming that Smith, in the late 1700s, could not envision the values that we in the twentieth century would deem to be so fundamental that on many principles central to the doctrine of a laissez-faire system we would choose differently than he. This is true, and it makes the point that is central to this book. Not only is the field of knowledge we label "economics" not a science, but it makes sense only in the light of a larger system of values in a society.

Why Is Economics Not a Science?

Once we understand the nonscientific nature of most of economic theory, and the fact that what most economists call laws of economics are not laws but usually best guesses or rough estimates, we can understand better how to use economics and economists for achieving national economic goals. To comprehend why economics cannot be viewed as a science, we must understand that any real science must be based upon an ability to observe, hypothesize, quantify, and predict. And the predictions must be consistently correct. The law of gravity correctly predicts that when an apple is dropped on our earth it will fall down—every time. No one has ever been surprised by an apple falling up, at least outside of laboratory experiments simulating a gravity-free world.

In many ways, social scientists, including economists, suffer from a form of professional insecurity vis-à-vis the "hard" sciences. Too many feel that to be truly professional, one must be a scientist in the sense that we think of physicists, chemists, or biologists. This sort of thinking seems to place all of these hard disciplines on the same level of scientific predictability. This is not so. Indeed, even in physics there is still growth of new knowledge, new facts growing out of an expanding body of knowledge. Whereas the use of mathematics to establish facts and theories for accurate prediction expanded during the Egyptian and Greek civilizations, hundreds of years before Christ, physics only began to separate itself from religion and mysticism during the fifteenth and sixteenth centuries. Biology is a very recent arrival on the scene, dating probably from the nineteenth century. But there is a major difference between a "science" such as physics and a "science" such as biology. The difference is such that it is highly probable that the level of understanding and predictability that exists in physics will never be achieved in biology.

In biology, as contrasted with physics, chemistry, or engineering, equations and theories are rare or at least far less prevalent. The simplest one-cell organism is infinitely more complex than our entire solar system.

There always seem to be exceptions to the rule in biology. Though the average, well-educated, intelligent person cannot help but be impressed by the discoveries of the genetic code and tremendous implications of DNA, there are major exceptions to any of our generalizations about DNA and genetics. Genes have been found that use different genetic codes. Life is distinguished by its variety. While we have a theory of evolution, it is only a good working hypothesis. The theory does not provide a mathematical, or certain, rule about the evolution of species. The precision, universality, and predictability of laws of physics are not to be found in biology. Life itself is still the greatest and most awesome of mysteries.

But this does not mean that without the certainty of physics, we cannot use what we have gained, slowly, painfully over the centuries in biology to deal with many of our biological problems. One can have fairly reliable guides to action without having a science. Medicine is not a science. For good reason it is referred to as the healing art. It combines knowledge of a scientific nature with judgment and psychological sensitivity, which we sometimes refer to as a good bedside manner, in order to treat a patient. Though medicine is not a science, it surely beats witchcraft.

In the social sciences, of which economics is one, we are still in the early stages of determining what is soluble. We are still probing to discover which problems can be observed sufficiently in order for us to come up with a hypothesis that can be tested against reality over and over again to determine if we can predict correctly. Above all, to qualify economics as a science, we must be able to repeat these predictions accurately.

The problem is that the tidy equations and mathematical formulas of physics are based on relationships between things that are infinitely less complex than people. The simpler relationships described by laws of physics are linear. That is, a change in one factor causes a predictable change in another. All of the knowledge we have about humanity and what affects it can only be described by nonlinear equations. That is, when there is a change in one variable, it results in a highly complex set of changes in other variables with many, usually unpredictable effects.

Even more dismaying, when one goes from one culture to another, say, from Russia to the United States, rough guidelines that help to understand the Russian "mentality" are not too helpful in understanding the "mentality" of the average U.S. citizen. To worsen the situation, even in the same country, insights and knowledge about how the "average" person thinks and reacts to situations change through time. And the time involved for change need not be long. An institution like the Supreme Court of the United States is a perfect example of how we change our ideas and values with regard to something most of us believe is quite clear and straightforward, the U.S. Constitution. The Supreme Court seems to be continuously clarifying and changing our minds about what the Founding Fathers meant. What supreme impertinence! Franklin, Jefferson, Madison, Washington, and the others knew what they meant and expressed their values in this written document. But as times and values have altered perspectives and goals, we have, politely, said we no longer agree with the particular values of our esteemed forefathers and how they were translated in the past into public policy.

Before relating all of this to the question of economics as a science, and the implications for our society, one last point must be made regarding physics. As much a science as physics is, it too is in a process of continuous expansion of knowledge and new insights. Every theory, every law turns out to have its limits. Though Newton's observation on gravity and apples has been of major significance, there were limitations. Einstein built on Newton, going beyond the theories of Newton, which were themselves based on earlier insights.

Given all of this, and the fact that economics inquires into the factors that affect humanity in its efforts to produce, trade, and increase its physical and social well-being, why do we accept the image of economics as a science? Why do people accept the simplistic homilies of a Karl Marx or a Milton Friedman as though they are eternal truths or laws?

Understanding Economics

To understand why people seem to accept simple solutions to extremely complex poblems in the field of economics, one must consider at least two facts: (1) Most people have not studied much economics. (2) Most people would like to feel that the complicated national economy, with such matters as budgets, expenditures, and so on, is not too different from their own household economy. "What is prudent for the family, must be prudent for the nation." Or "If I have to live on a balanced budget, so must the nation."

Taking the first point first, it is interesting to note that not only do most people know very little about economics but most people whom you think do know a great deal about economics also do not. For example, most business editors or reporters for the newspapers and other media know very little about economics or business. In recent years, efforts have been underway to change this situation. For example, the Brookings Institution has had an educational program for business reporters. The School of Communications at the American University also has had a program to educate reporters in economic matters. The problem is not the reporter. The problem is that the media hire reporters, most of whom are graduates of schools of journalism, who have little or no education in economics or business. You may not have to know about embalming to be able to write obituary notices, but it certainly does help to know about economics when you evaluate federal reserve policy for an article on the supply of money. Schools of journalism do not have economics as a major interest. Editors of newspapers and magazines should hire people who have the proper background. Not many do; it costs too much in terms of what they are used to paying. Only the largest papers and specialized magazines do a really good job in the coverage of business and economics.

With regard to the second point, assuming that what is true of a personal budget, for example, is true of a national budget, is a familiar form of fallacy. It is hard not to fall into this very human form of misunderstanding by simplifying what is a very complicated situation. It certainly seems that no one can go on owing money constantly, and it would seem equally applicable that a country cannot either. As a matter of fact, both can—providing, of course, that someone else, the lender, thinks that the person or country has the basis for paying back at some point and can pay the interest rate. It is hard to believe, as an individual, that in many cases corporate financial stability must be based on a combination of continuous loans as well as ownership. Although our major corporate executives are usually most critical of a government's unbalanced budget, and hence the frequent necessity to borrow money by selling bonds, almost every corporation does exactly the same. Just look at the corporate bonds being sold every day and also being refinanced because neither the corporation nor the lender wants repayment to occur, but for different reasons. The bank or retiree wants to continue to receive interest on a safe loan, which is a ready asset, while the company wants to retain the capital for sound business reasons.

What is interesting is that we do not speak of the private company as having a deficit, but we do of a government if it uses bonds to raise money to balance its expenditures not covered by tax revenues. Why is this? Primarily because of the way we have designed our accounting systems. In the private sector we use a double-entry accounting system. Thus, by definition, every asset has a liability, and vice versa. When General Motors sells a bond for a million dollars, that fact shows up on the liability side of the books as a debt. But the million dollars it received shows up as a cash asset on the asset side. The books balance. When the federal government, or state or county government, sells a million dollars worth of bonds, all that shows up is the debt. There is no double-entry accounting system for government. The money will be used to produce an asset such as a highway or a bridge, but there is no asset or capital budget that tells us that an asset was created. So we continue to gripe about a government spending beyond its means when no family or private firm can, and it all sounds so right. Yet it can be very misleading in terms of understanding the problem of maintaining a healthy economy.

There may indeed be times when we should not borrow, or we borrow for the wrong things. But the process of borrowing is not an inherently sinful process. It often represents the only way a government can obtain necessary investment funds when a need dictates that we do not have enough time to wait for tax revenues or a shift in the pattern of expenditures. Just think of the lunacy if in 1941 we had delayed all expenditure increases for the defense needs of the United States because President Roosevelt felt that until the budget could be balanced by more tax revenues the United States simply could not afford to defend itself. Similar situations arise in recessions, sudden changes in unemployment, and so on.

This whole issue of basing a national economic policy on simplistic personal experiences emerged during the national debate on a constitutional amendment to prohibit an unbalanced federal budget. Though it was impractical and stupid economics, this seemed to have little impact on the general desire for a simple solution to a highly complicated problem. In a *New York Times* editorial on August 1, 1982, a first-rate and succinct answer to the supporters of this amendment makes the point well:

> Why is it ignorant economics? Because the United States should not want to balance the budget every year, it should want to balance the economy. In a recession, spending for unemployment and other benefit programs goes up. That is a desirable counter cyclical effect; it is sensible to run a deficit then. Otherwise the economy would nose dive. If the amendment were in effect now, there would be five million more unemployed.[2]

But there is another problem in understanding economics. The problem is not only understanding the recent theories but also the history of economic thought. Unless one understands how we got from Adam Smith to Keynes, or Friedman, one is likely to miss some very important insights into what is credible. Indeed, we may even accept some terribly incredible stuff as being credible. And most people, including most economists, really do not want to spend too much time on history, especially the history of economic thought. Is it really necessary anyway? About as necessary as knowing what Madison, Jay, and Hamilton had to say about their concepts of a federal structure if you want to understand the U.S. Constitution. It is absolutely necessary.

As we have already discussed, economics is perceived as a body of knowledge, more or less scientific, with a somewhat well-established set of laws—natural laws, if you will—concerning the production, distribution, and use of goods and services. Complicated formulas, curves, and computer programs must be involved in this understanding of how the forces of the marketplace affect prices, sales, consumption, and so forth. This perception is the one held by most of the economists who are usually at the elbow of our public leaders. These leaders usually want recipes or simple, direct solutions to deal with problems that bedevil the society. And these leaders are usually gratified by economic advisers who quickly reassure them that the problem can be dealt with if only "we get government off the back of the private sector," or "have government assume the role that industry is not fulfilling," or "control the amount of money rather than concentrate on fiscal policy," or "control fiscal policy rather than control the money supply" — depending on which party's or faction's ideology is in the saddle. Policymakers look to economic advisers for firm guidelines to achieve clear results.

It turns out that throughout the entire history of economic thought there are disquieting notes raised about economics as a science and the ability of economists to provide such error-free advice. There is even a questioning of the ability to understand economic phenomena without healthy inputs from other areas, such as psychology, sociology, politics, or even philosophy. Little of this shows up in current debates about fiscal, monetary, or economic growth policies. Without going back to the nineteenth century, when such intellectual giants as John Stuart Mill and Thomas Malthus were questioning, and in conflict with, the key ingredients of what emerged as classical theory, let's look at some interesting insights from a few prominent contemporary economists.

In September 1971, in his presidential address before the Royal Economic Society, G.D.N. Worswick stated:

> There now exists whole branches of abstract economic theory which have no links with concrete facts and are almost indistinguishable from pure mathematics. . . . They are not, it seems to me, engaged in forging tools to arrange and measure actual facts so much as making a marvelous array of pretend-tools which would perform wonders if ever a set of facts should turn up in the right form.[3]

Commenting on the lack of relevance of classical economic theory, in her Richard T. Ely Lecture in December 1971, before the American Economic Association annual meeting, Joan Robinson said:

> In the orthodox micro theory, having put Keynes to sleep, perfect competition and optimum firms come back and all the problems of the New Industrial State drop out of the argument. At this very time, when the great concentrations of power in the multinational corporations are bringing the age of national employment policies to an end, the text

books are still illustrated by U-shaped curves showing the limitation on the size of firms in a perfectly competitive market.[4]

In his presidential address before the Royal Economic Society in July 1970, E. H. Phelps Brown struck at a fallibility of economic theory that was observed indirectly by John Stuart Mill and continues to the present. Brown complained that basic assumptions about human behavior as it affects economic decisions, and affects all institutions as well since they are controlled by people, are assumptions that are "plucked from the air."[5] The only way to remedy this failing, and the only way to bring relevance to economic theory, was to remove "the traditional boundary between the subject matters of economics and other social sciences."[6]

A more recent criticism in the same vein came from Wassily Leontief, an Economics Nobel laureate. Referring to an article in *Business Week* (January 18, 1982, p. 124) that stated "A dismal performance. . . . What economists revealed most clearly was the extent to which their profession lags intellectually," Leontief reacted by the following:

> This editorial comment by the leading economic weekly (on the 1981 Annual Proceedings of the American Economic Association) says, essentially, that the "King is naked." But no one taking part in the elaborate and solemn procession of contemporary U.S. academic economics seems to know it, and those who do don't dare speak up.
>
> The central idea of what is now being referred to as Classical Economics attracted the attention of two (turn of the 19th Century) mathematically trained engineers. Leon Walras and Vilfredo Pareto, who translated it with considerable refinement and elaboration into a concise language of algebra and calculus and called it the General Equilibrium Theory. Under the name of neoclassical economics, this theory now constitutes the core of undergraduate and graduate instruction in this country. . . . Herein lies, however, the initial source of the trouble in which academic economics finds itself today.
>
> Page after page of professional economic journals are filled with mathematical formulas leading the reader from sets of more or less plausible but entirely arbitrary assumption to precisely stated but irrelevant theoretical conclusions.[7]

Criticizing the lack of reality orientation by "the great majority of the present-day academic economists," Leontief refers to the fact that this is reflected in "the methodological devices that they employ to avoid or cut short the use of concrete factual information." In a devastating table showing a percent distribution of articles in the *American Economic Review* from March 1977 to December 1981, by relationship to what might be called reality, 54 percent were mathematical articles not based on any data. Another 22.7 percent used empirical analysis, but the analysis used indirect statistical inference based on data published or generated elsewhere. Finally, another 11.6 percent of the articles had analyses without either data or mathematical formulations. Fully 88 percent of the articles published in what is regarded in the economics profession as one of the leading professional journals would be highly suspect in terms of methodology relating them to the real world.

Leontief really says it all when he states in the same article, in exasperation:

> Year after year economic theorists continue to produce scores of mathematical models and to explore in great detail their formal properties; and the econometricians fit algebraic functions of all possible shapes to essentially the same sets of data without being able to advance, in any perceptible way, a systematic understanding of the structure and the operations of a real economic system.

As Leontief was a former faculty member in the Economics Department of Harvard University and is now on the faculty at New York University, his point of view is especially refreshing and meaningful.

One of the few practising economists to have moved in the direction of a broader base of understanding of economic problems was the late George Katona. He stands almost alone in having produced a body of knowledge that brings economics and psychology together in a form relevant to our real-world needs. Katona "considers economic processes as manisfestations of human behavior and analyzes them from the point of view of modern psychology."[8]

Interestingly, if we assume that through history we have observed that values and behavior patterns of people change, then we must accept the fact that what is held to be "correct" in economics must also change. So-called economic laws can only be seen as at best approximations, for varying lengths of time, reflecting the social, political, legal, and cultural forces of the larger society. So-called laws of economics are valuable insights. They are valuable, however, only so long as they are related to the noneconomic variables that can impinge on or affect their validity.

The so-called law of supply and demand depends upon the shifting sands of personal preferences. As we all know, personal preferences are very real, but to categorize and tabulate them as though they are permanent and unchangeable is nonsense. A law of supply and demand is only a good law if the relationships it establishes can truly predict how people will react in their purchasing patterns to changes in price, quality, and shifting income. For gross change, the law of supply and demand is very helpful. The smaller the group one wishes to apply it to, the less helpful it is. But even for gross phenomena, there are times when it can be very misleading. During the 1981–82 period, interest rates simply refused to drop as rapidly as economic advisers predicted would happen, given the supply side policies, high unemployment, and so on. The reason grew out of many noneconomic phenomena. Businesspeople were too uncertain of the future. Uncertainty is a highly subjective factor. There is nothing objective or scientific about it. It is purely personal. In spite of the fact that one of the largest tax cuts in our history provided new sources of investment funds, no one was about to invest if his or her "feeling" did not support an economic policy of spending more money on plant and capital.

The simplistic nonsense of the correlation between lower taxes and higher investment rates, which the Laffer curve reflected, was the foundation for much of Reaganomics. Not only were there no data to support the Laffer curve thesis, but there was also no way that this curve could reflect the importance of psychology in the decision-making process every corporate executive goes through. It was reminiscent of the effort in the early 1930s to rejuvenate the economy by reestablishing a "healthier" price level through the National Recovery Act (NRA) codes. Agreed-upon prices, with no competition, would guarantee a decent profit level! The only problem was that most people did not have the funds to meet any decent price level. Even the frequent playing of "Happy Days Are Here Again" did not mislead the unemployed into believing they were jobholders once again with purchasing power.

Our economic theories must relate to the current values of the society—which means that economics and economists must be willing to see their most cherished theories put to a constant test of relevancy. And if they fail this test, the theorist must be willing to change even the most fondly held concept. This is no new idea. Keynes made this point. He held that his general theory was to be seen as a major rethinking of economics. Indeed, he stated that for him this work was "a long struggle of escape — a struggle of escape from habitual modes of thought and expression."[9] He stated the problem most simply and elegantly, in words that should provide a guide for every economist convinced that the latest theory will indeed remain the last word: "The difficulty lies, not in the new ideas, but in escaping from the old ones, which ramify, for those brought up as most of us have been, into every corner of our minds."[10]

And what were the forces of past economic theory from which Keynes sought escape? He was seeking a model that was not moored to the natural market forces that Adam Smith saw as providing the basis for economic growth. But he was also seeking a model that rejected the Marxist theories consigning capitalism to the scrap heap of history. Keynes did not accept the inexorable evolution from capitalism to the communist economy ordained by Karl Marx. Keynes sought to save capitalism during those years of worldwide depression when the Marxist predictions and theories seemed more than ever to have indeed been prescient.

The Troubled Economy Begins

The so-called Keynesians and non-Keynesians are in reality closer in their basic assumptions than is generally thought. All modern economists believe in the basic tenets of the crucial relationship among investment, consumption, and economic growth. The falling out between economists is over the role of the private sector as opposed to government in achieving a healthy economy. If one uses Walter Heller as an archetype Keynesian and Milton Friedman as his opposite number, the difference is clear. One supports a greater role of government as a stabilizing force, while the other views government as a largely negative force in achieving a healthy economy. Since the late 1960s, however, the economy of the United States has exhibited a major weakness, regardless of whether a Keynesian or non-Keynesian philosophy has been dominant in the design of our public policies.

Until the late 1960s, by and large the U.S. economy tended to perform well. There was no recurrence of depression, and the recessions that occurred periodically were shorter and less severe than had been the case in our earlier history. In fact, as recently as 1969 both the rate of unemployment and the rate of inflation *at the same time* were below 4 percent. Later wringing of hands over the inevitability of the Phillips curve, which preordained that inflation had to go up as unemployment went down, supported presidents, senators, congressmen, and industrial leaders in their position that to lower the rate of unemployment below 5 percent would only cause the rate of inflation to rise well above that figure. Recent history was forgotten. Even worse, no attention was paid to the fact that there was no one Phillips curve. Each country had a different one, with different trade-off points between lower unemployment and higher inflation. What also seemed to escape the notice of most U.S. economists, politicians, industrialists, and labor leaders was that the U.S. Phillips curve was far worse than those of other major industrial countries.

By the early 1970s, something was beginning to happen. Economic indicators were beginning to light up that not only began to cause discomfort for Keynesians but also began to stimulate glances over our shoulders to the "good old days" of an economy with less government spending and less government involvement. Not only in the United States, but in other countries like West Germany, Japan, France, and the United Kingdom, there were signs of major changes in their economies. What were some of these harbingers?

Table 1.1. Percentage Unemployment—United States, United Kingdom, Japan, West Germany, France—1970-73

	United States	United Kingdom	Japan	West Germany	France
1970	4.9	2.6	1.1	.7	1.3
1971	5.9	3.5	1.2	.8	1.6
1972	5.6	3.8	1.4	1.1	1.8
1973	4.9	2.7	1.3	1.3	1.9

Source: Yearbook of Labour Statistics, 1980 (Geneva: International Labour Office), pp. 281-83.

As can be seen in Table 1.1, during the period 1970-73 unemployment had become a serious problem in the United States. During these days of 6 to 9 percent unemployment becoming more nearly the norm, one must remember that as recently as 1969 the unemployment rate was below 4 percent. Between 1966 and 1969 inclusive, the unemployment rate averaged 3.67 percent. But, by 1973, it was apparent that problems were confronting us that did not seem to exist among our major industrial counterparts.

Additionally, for those very few observers interested in comparative productivity statistics, by 1973, it was evident that other major countries had pulled ahead of us in productivity growth rates. Though we were still the most productive industrial nation among the major countries, some voices were beginning to raise questions about the future. Table 1.2 presents the data available to those few who seemed to have been interested in 1975. Though the effects of the oil price increase show the expected impact in 1974, what is most interesting is the fact that the United States, the industrial giant, appears to have been the most seriously affected. As we will see, Japan and West Germany had achieved changes in their economic approaches that permitted them to deal more effectively with this situation than could the United States.

Finally, a third indicator was the growing discrepancy between the U.S. rate of growth of its domestic economy as contrasted with the growth rates of the other major industrial countries. Table 1.3 indicates this devel-

Table 1.2. Annual Percentage Change in Manufacturing Productivity, 1960-73 and 1974

	United States	United Kingdom	Japan	West Germany	France
1960-73	3.0	4.3	10.7	5.5	6.0
1974	-2.4	.8	2.4	6.0	3.5

Source: Monthly Labor Review, Bureau of Labor Statistics, Department of Labor, December 1981, p. 15.

Table 1.3.   Index and Rate of Growth, Gross Domestic Product, in Purchasers' Values, 1968–74 (1975 = 100)

	United States	United Kingdom	Japan	West Germany	France
1968 Index	86.1	86.8	64.7	79.0	72.7
1969 Index	88.5	88.1	72.6	85.2	77.8
Change	+2.8%	+1.5%	+12.2%	+7.8%	+7.0%
1970 Index	88.3	90.0	79.7	90.3	82.2
Change	−.003%	+2.3%	+9.8%	+5.9%	+5.7%
1971 Index	91.3	92.4	83.4	93.2	86.7
Change	+3.4%	+2.7%	+4.6%	+3.2%	+5.5%
1972 Index	96.3	94.5	90.7	96.6	91.8
Change	+5.5%	+2.3%	+8.8%	+3.7%	+5.9%
1973 Index	101.5	101.6	98.7	101.3	96.7
Change	+5.4%	+7.5%	+8.8%	+4.9%	+5.3%
1974 Index	100.9	100.6	97.7	101.9	99.8
Change	−.006%	−.01%	−.01%	+.006%	+3.2%

Source: OECD National Accounts, vol. 1, 1951–80, p. 80.

opment. It is apparent that the economies of the United Kingdom and the United States had the slowest rates of growth between 1968 and 1974, whereas Japan, France, and Germany grew the most, in that order.

By 1975, three major portents, unemployment, manufacturing productivity, and the rate of economic growth told the interested observer that the U. S. economy was in trouble, as was the economy of the United Kingdom, while those of Japan, West Germany, and France were not. This is not to say that the latter three countries did not have problems. They did, and still do. But the trends and degrees of swing in their indicators were far more positive than those of the United States and the United Kingdom. Even in the case of comparative economic growth, during the period 1969–74, the average annual rate was about 2.8 for the United States, 2.7 for the United Kingdom, 7.4 for Japan, 4.25 for West Germany, and 5.4 for France. The United States and United Kingdom were running neck and neck for last prize. What was happening? What was going on in Germany, France, and Japan? Why were the United States and the United Kingdom performing so poorly while their competitors were humming along?

The Economics of the Holy Grail

In June 1982, I met with a senior official of the Ministry of Economics of the Federal Republic of Germany. He had been present at the 1982 Versailles Conference, the so-called Economic Summit for heads of state.

During our two-hour conversation, we ranged over a large series of topics, such as the role of the German government in setting economic policy, relationships between German industry and the trade unions, and worker participation on boards of directors. Finally we chatted about his impressions of the U.S. economic staff members with whom he came in contact while at Versailles. He was obviously circumspect, both in his language and detail of discussion, but in one remark he was most revealing. When he described the philosophy, the attitude, the perspective, if you will, of our economists, he looked unbelieving as he used the word "pure." Though his English was perfect, I asked him to elucidate on this word. His response was that the positions taken by the U. S. staff reflected highly theoretical, almost absolutist stances with very little appreciation of the realities of social and economic systems.

Later in the summer of 1982, as I picked up the Sunday, July 4, copy of the *Washington Post,* the words of that German government economist came to mind. On page 1 was the headline "Reagan's Crusaders Fail to Find the Grail." Key officials of the Reagan administration were resigning. Martin Anderson had left the White House staff to return to the Hoover Institution at Stanford University. Undersecretary of the treasury Norman B. Ture had departed for the Heritage Foundation. Another senior Treasury Department official, Paul Craig Roberts, had left for Georgetown University's Center for Strategic and International Studies. In a telling comment on these departures in the *Post* article, Willa Johnson, senior vice president of the Heritage Foundation, said "This administration has many, many more of these kinds of people. They are convinced their ideas will work but they're not used to thinking in the political terms that an administration has to look at. They become impatient."

As the article continued, it presented to the reader the most marvelous insight into the fact that no problem in nature occurs by a discipline! There is no such thing as a "pure" economic problem. All economic phenomena must be viewed, and dealt with, from the perspectives of the political, social, psychological, historical, and other contexts within which the real world functions. It was best summed up in the article's reference to Steve Hanke. Hanke, who came from the Johns Hopkins University in 1981 to serve as a senior staff economist with the president's Council of Economic Advisors, resigned in order to return to his academic post. In the *Washington Post* article, Hanke observed: "There is a large gap between the rhetoric and the reality."[11] Since Hanke's title is that of professor of applied economics, one cannot help but muse over the need for a truth-in-packaging law for academic titles.

The economic policies of the Reagan administration only serve as an excellent example because of the matter of degree. Previous administrations, including those of Democratic presidents, have exhibited equally costly flights from reality. The Reagan administration serves best as a prototype of what ails the economic policies of this country only because its belief in what can only be described as economic revelation is so starkly apart from reality.

Back to the Garden of Eden, and Other Fantasies—Part I

What is disconcerting is that most often those who should be most pragmatic, our industrial leaders, are so frequently in the vanguard of those seeking quick, simplistic answers to what they should know are terribly complicated problems. The "darling" of the conservative community, business as well as economic, is Milton Friedman. Generations of Friedman's students have carried the message of the need to return to a world of less government and unfettered economic enterprise and the simplicity of a world where economic stability can be achieved if only a relatively fixed rate of growth of the money supply can be assured. But the degree to which Friedman is in a cocoon of simplistic unreality is hard to understand unless one reads, and thinks about, what he has written.

For example, one of Friedman's recent best sellers is *Free to Choose*,[12] which he wrote with his wife, Rose Friedman. The book was praised by President Reagan ("superb"), former Secretary of the Treasury William Simon, William F. Buckley, Jr., *Business Week*, *Reader's Digest*, and so on. Leaders of the business community with whom I have talked see it as a clear, precise, and wise appraisal of the problems confronting us as government and business compete for scarce resources. Friedman is seen as brilliant as he holds aloft the banner of free enterprise and points the way to a return to a past more worthy of our national heritage. A past where we had not sold our birthright for the pottage of government involvements, consumer protection, public education, or cradle–to–grave security.

But surely the erudition and practicality of Friedman must have been questioned by those who actually read and thought about this book rather than reading into the book their own conceptions and fantasies of the economic world. What business leader or government official, including those in the last several administrations, who have dealt with the problems of Japanese trade would not have objected when Friedman said: "In the Far East, Malaysia, Singapore, Korea, Taiwan, Hong Kong, and Japan—all relying extensively on private markets—are thriving."[13]

Taking Japan only, anyone really familiar with that country's trade and commercial policies would know the key role government plays in targeting industries for aid through government research expenditures, managed interest rates, and tariffs in order to achieve specific economic objectives. On page 31, Friedman lauds the free trade, both domestic and international, policies that became a part of Japanese policy after the Meiji Restoration in 1867. This must surely be one of the most naive statements made in any study pretending to economic sophistication. Just ask one of the U. S. automobile manufacturers about the foreign trade policies of the 1950s and 1960s in Japan calculated to aid the development of Japanese auto producers via both tariff and nontariff measures. Yet many of the leaders of the auto industry in Detroit have seen in Milton Friedman a man of incalculable insight and veracity.

What is perhaps most humorous, in a way, about Friedman's reference to the free market philosophy of Japan is that collectivist East Germany sees the Japanese model of targeting and investing in industries by government as superior to its own industrial policies. Apparently, the government of East Germany has been impressed by policies of Japan's Ministry of International Trade and Industry and the Ministry of Finance. Both of these ministries have been most successful in targeting such industries as steel, auto, television, microelectronics, and shipbuilding for export growth and designing supportive government programs to help achieve the goal of export growth. According to a *Washington Post* article, East Germany appears ready to adopt similar policies.[14]

Apparently, Friedman never asked Japanese businesspeople about their analysis of what has contributed importantly to their tremendous rate of economic growth and high productivity. He would have been surprised, and even educated, by their response. In a survey of attitudes in five nations, beginning in 1971, about key factors affecting productivity, Louis Harris, of the reputable Harris and Associates survey organization, found that when "We asked Japanese businessmen and workers alike, what is the single most important reason for your success and, as astounding as it sounds, . . . they said 'government. . . .' "[15]

I am referring to this not as a reason for U.S. industry and labor looking to government as the answer to our national crisis in productivity but only to indicate the credibility and professional astuteness of an economist to whom national leaders look for economic insight and guidance. It brings to mind the ill-fated Children's Crusade of the Middle Ages. Revelation and economics simply do not mix.

Where Are We Now?

During the last decade, beginning with the early 1970s, the economic performance of the United States has lagged seriously behind that of other major industrial nations. This situation was evident prior to the mid-1970s, as already shown in Tables 1.1 to 1.3. This poor showing by the United States has continued. Tables 1.4 to 1.6 would appear to indicate

Table 1.4.   Percentage of Unemployed

	United States	United Kingdom	Japan	West Germany	France
1974	5.6	3.1	1.4	1.6	2.9
1975	8.5	4.6	1.9	3.5	4.2
1976	7.7	6.0	2.0	3.5	4.6
1977	7.0	6.3	2.0	3.5	5.0
1978	6.0	6.3	2.3	3.4	5.4
1979	5.8	5.7	2.1	3.0	6.1
1980	7.1	7.4	2.0	3.0	6.5
1981	7.5	11.2	2.2	4.3	7.5

Sources: 1974–80 data: Monthly Labor Review, Bureau of Labor Statistics, Department of Labor, December 1981, p. 5. 1981 data: OECD Observer, no. 115, March 1982.

that in comparison with Japan, West Germany, and France, the United States has continued to lag in productivity gains, rates of unemployment, and economic growth. In comparison with the United Kingdom, the records appear to be fairly close. Finally, in Table 1.7 we can get some comparison of the rate of inflation in consumer prices in these countries.

The pattern that emerges from the tables is that the United States and the United Kingdom seem to be in tandem, neither doing too well. Japan and Germany have consistently bettered the economic performance of the United States. The question is why? We are no longer looking at the immediate post–World War II period when one would expect major jumps in output and productivity as the European and Japanese economies recovered. Why, during the last decade or so, has the U.S. economic performance been declining while those of other nations have performed better with respect to employment, productivity, economic growth, and price stability?

Table 1.5.   Annual Percentage Change in Manufacturing Productivity, 1975–80

	United States	United Kingdom	Japan	West Germany	France
1975	2.9	−2.0	3.9	4.8	3.1
1976	4.4	4.0	9.4	6.3	8.2
1977	2.4	1.6	7.2	5.3	5.1
1978	.9	3.2	7.9	3.8	5.3
1979	1.1	3.3	8.0	6.3	5.4
1980	−0.3	.3	6.2	−0.7	.6

Source: 1975–80 data: Monthly Labor Review, Bureau of Labor Statistics, Department of Labor, December 1981, p. 15.

Table 1.6. Index and Rate of Growth, Gross Domestic Product, in Purchasers' Values, 1976–1980 (1975 = 100)

	United States	United Kingdom	Japan	West Germany	France
1976 Index	105.4	103.6	105.3	105.2	105.2
Change	+5.4%	+3.6%	+5.3%	+5.2%	5.2%
1977 Index	111.1	104.9	110.8	108.4	108.4
Change	+5.4%	+1.3%	+5.2%	+3.0%	+3.0%
1978 Index	115.9	108.4	116.4	111.8	112.4
Change	+4.3%	+3.3%	+5.1%	+3.1%	+3.7%
1979 Index	119.2	109.9	122.8	116.8	116.3
Change	+2.8%	+1.4%	+5.5%	+4.5%	+3.5%
1980 Index	119.1	108.3	128.2	119.1	117.6
Change	−.001%	−.01%	+4.4%	+2.0%	+1.1%

Source: OECD National Accounts, vol. 1, 1951–80, p. 80.

As will be seen, contrary to the usual perceptions and statements, it appears that the balancing of a government budget, low levels of taxation, or lower levels of government expenditures (as a percentage of total economic output) are not keys to a better economic performance of a nation. Other forces seem to be at work. What are these other forces, and how do they translate into policy implications?

Other Fantasies—Part II

Why has the United States not been able to achieve the higher levels of economic performance of Japan and West Germany? Unemployment levels of close to 10 percent, very low levels of economic growth, almost zero rates of productivity gain since 1978, and interest rates that almost guarantee continued low levels of investment confront us. What is to be done? Is this situation characteristic of an advanced industrial economy? Probably not. Other major industrial economies have been doing far better than we. Then they must have balanced budgets, or spend less for social expenditures, or have lower tax rates. Not really. Perhaps it would be helpful to get rid of some of these old crutches for explaining away the reasons for our poor economic performance.

Table 1.7. Rates of Change in Consumer Price Levels, 1976–81

	United States	United Kingdom	Japan	West Germany	France
1976–81 average	9.8%	13.4%	5.7%	4.4%	11.2%
December 80–81	8.9%	12.0%	4.3%	6.3%	14.0%

Source: OECD Observer, no. 115, March 1982.

Table 1.8. Taxes and Social Security Contributions as Percentage of Gross Domestic Product

	1975	1976	1977	1978	1979	1980
United States	30.18	29.29	30.30	30.19	31.32	30.72
Canada	32.93	32.51	31.81	31.48	31.41	32.88
United Kingdom	39.91	35.56	35.24	33.78	33.51	36.14
Denmark	41.35	41.55	41.99	43.43	44.65	45.67
Belgium	41.82	42.38	43.77	45.04	45.62	44.74
Netherlands	45.80	45.43	43.97	44.58	45.07	46.19
Germany	35.68	36.68	37.91	37.73	37.47	37.37
France	37.44	39.36	39.42	39.50	41.08	42.59
Australia	29.14	29.68	29.67	28.78	29.70	30.87
Sweden	44.10	48.54	50.88	51.40	49.98	49.63
Switzerland	29.61	31.30	31.63	31.58	31.08	30.79

Source: 1975–79: *Revenue Statistics of OECD Member Countries 1965–1981,* 1982, p. 68, Table 3.

First, let's look at tax rates. Many have been concerned over high levels of taxes, which were supposed to be crippling our motivation and willingness to work long hours. The so-called Laffer curve was proof positive that we had gone beyond the point where you could expect a really productive effort since the tax burden was now excessive. No numbers or real evi-

Table 1.9. Total General Government Outlays as Percentage of Gross National Product

	United States	Japan	Germany	France
1980	33.1	30.1	—	45.1
1979	31.2	29.5	44.7	44.3
1978	30.7	29.1	45.1	44.1
1977	31.4	27.7	45.1	43.2
1976	32.2	26.8	45.4	43.1
1975	33.3	26.4	46.4	42.6
1974	30.9	24.8	42.7	39.1
1973	29.4	22.0	40.0	38.0
1972	30.4	22.1	39.3	37.7
1971	30.6	21.0	38.2	—
1970	30.4	19.4	36.6	—

Note: General government includes central, state, or local as well as activities under the control or affiliated with any government agencies.

Sources: 1979–80, United States—*Economic Report of the President* (Washington, D.C., January 1982). 1970–80, all countries except the United States: *National Accounts of OECD Countries 1963–1980,* vol. II, 1982.

dence was provided to support this contention, but never mind, it seemed right.

In Table 1.8 we see the total amounts of all taxes and social security payments going to all government units as a percentage of gross domestic product. Of the countries shown, only Australia has usually been below the United States. What must be surprising to most readers is that the very model of a free enterprise, industrious, aggressive, and recession-proof country like Switzerland has almost the same percentage level of payments to government as the profligate United States. It is like discovering that the leader of the temperance movement is an alcoholic.

Well, what about all of the expenditures of government as a percentage of gross national product? Our defense burden is higher by far than that of any other country, except the USSR, so we must certainly be at a disadvantage. It must have an impact on interest rates. Table 1.9 is very revealing. Both Germany and France have a higher percentage than we do, and Japan is not that much lower.

Finally, what about the problem of an unbalanced budget? Government expenditures as a percentage of receipts cannot be above 100 percent for more than a couple of years without serious problems it would seem. Table 1.10 does indeed show that we are in a deficit position more frequently than our chief industrial competitors. But, surprisingly, Japan has been in a deficit position since 1975, and in 1977 to 79 exceeded the United States in the average of expenditures over receipts. At best, the deficit as a source of trouble is questionable.

Table 1.10. Central Government Expenditures as Percentage of Receipts

	United States	Japan	Germany	France
1980	113	115	97	96
1979	106	117	96	99
1978	110	111	96	102
1977	115	118	94	98
1976	120	114	99	93
1975	130	111	105	101
1974	111	89	88	89
1973	112	77	85	88
1972	115	83	90	88
1971	118	84	80	88
1970	114	79	80	87

Sources: 1970–79, 1980, except United States: *National Accounts of OECD Countries 1962–1980*, vol. II, 1981. 1980, United States: *International Financial Statistics* (Washington, D.C.: International Monetary Fund, January 1982).

It would appear that the nostrums of the conservative economists, presidents, members of Congress, and industrialists are not helpful in explaining the poor economic performance of the United States and the good performance of its industrial competitors. Nor have the so-called liberal economists, presidents, members of Congress, and industrialists been able to keep the United States in the economic lead when they held political power. The answer can only emerge when we achieve a better understanding about a major change in economic philosophy that has taken place since the 1950s and how this change has led to the emerging economic leadership of other countries.

Notes

1. Adam Smith, *An Inquiry Into the Nature and Causes of the Wealth of Nations* (New York: Modern Library, 1937), pp. 736–37.

2. *New York Times,* August 1, 1982, p. E20.

3. G.D.N. Worswick, "Is Progress in Economic Science Possible?" *Economic Journal* 82 (March 1972): 78–79.

4. Joan Robinson, "The Second Crisis of Economic Theory," *American Economic Review* 62, no. 2 (May 1972): 4.

5. E. H. Phelps Brown, "The Underdevelopment of Economics," *Economic Journal* 82 (March 1972): 3.

6. Ibid., p. 7.

7. W. Leontief, "Academic Economics," *Science,* July 9, 1982, pp. 104–07.

8. George Katona, *Psychological Economics* (New York: Elsevier, 1975), p. 3.

9. John Maynard Keynes, *The General Theory of Employment, Interest and Money* (New York: Harcourt, Brace, 1936), p. viii.

10. Ibid.

11. *Washington Post,* July 4, 1982, p. A16.

12. Milton and Rose Friedman, *Free to Choose* (New York: Avon, 1979).

13. Ibid., p. 48.

14. *Washington Post,* May 24, 1982, p. A17.

15. *American and Foreign Attitudes on Productivity,* Hearing before the Committee on the Budget, U.S. Senate, 97th Congress, First Session, June 3, 1981 (Washington, D.C.: Government Printing Office, 1981), p. 7.

How Did We Ever Get to This Point?
════════2════════

Adam Smith's Contribution

Many of the dogmas haunting economics today can be traced to the eighteenth-century origins of modern economics. The central figure is Adam Smith, whose classic work, *An Inquiry Into the Nature and Causes of the Wealth of Nations,* was written in the flush of Enlightenment optimism in 1776.

Smith's contribution consisted in refuting the approach to economics he called "mercantilism": the philosophy, viewed in the age of Smith, as essentially conservative, vesting in the monarch or the sovereign the duty to subject the economy to central regulation and control. Control by a central authority was viewed as conservative because it preserved (or it seemed to preserve) order and to ward off chaos.

Smith's approach, laissez-faire and the free market, is viewed as "conservative" today, but in the eighteenth century, it seemed to be essentially liberal, a major reform. With the weakening of feudal class structure, the release of innovative energies and new inventions, and the ever increasing specialization of labor, it seemed to Smith that the motivation of the individual, and not the power of the sovereign, led to the maximization of wealth for the whole society. And it was beautifully self-regulating: Freedom was a higher order. If a price rose because of individual greed, this would only serve to induce more production and selling of that particular commodity, driving the price back down. Too many producers or sellers would produce too low a price for all to remain in business; enough would be driven out of business or shift to more lucrative endeavors, to ensure a somewhat higher price. The "invisible hand" of the market would harness individual greed to the social good.

But Smith began his inquiry because of, and was guided by, another "invisible hand." This "hand" was that which resulted from a completely different set of intellectual interests. The imagination and curiosity of humanity is a garment not only without seams, but constructed of threads that bring together all sorts of (apparently) separate ideas and fields.

Adam Smith's great work did not just happen to occur because of mere economic forces. It was part of Enlightenment culture. The Enlightenment stretched from the end of the seventeenth century into the mideighteenth century, when Western Europe and England moved away from what might be called the theological basis for understanding the world toward a scientific base (at least in pretension). Just imagine the age when such giants as Newton, Descartes, Pascal, and Voltaire were thinking and writing. Imagine the excitement surrounding the thinking person as Smith grew to maturity: major breakthroughs in discerning natural causation, theological assumptions giving way to reasoning, observation, and experiment. To discover the hidden hand of natural causality, the logic of why was the basis for worthwhile endeavor and achievement.

Voltaire was the great public relations man of this age, and his followers included individuals from every walk of life, from emperors to mathematicians—and economists. Turgot and Quesnay, the two leading French economic thinkers of the early and mid-1700s were avid members of the Voltaire claque. During his travels in France, Adam Smith was intrigued by the thinking of these French economists, especially by their efforts to diagram a rational set of relationships depicting how an economy works. Based on the general stimulus of Enlightenment thinking, he converted economic thought into a rational series of market forces, the famed "invisible hand," directing personal interest to social benefit. Smith was of the Enlightenment as surely as were Newton, Pascal, Descartes, LaMettrie (who in 1748 wrote a book with the telling title *Man the Machine*), and Maupertius, the great mathematician.

But lurking in Enlightenment "science" was a great deal of cultural ephemera. Inspired by the physics of Newton and particularly the soothing vision of a universe in constant balance, intellectuals began to apply the Newtonian themes with an almost religious zeal. The Deists made popular the vision of a perfect "clockwork universe": its parts in such exquisite balance—for such was the skill of its infinitely perfect Maker—that it ran automatically and always in perfect "tune" without any necessity at all for divine intervention. Political theorists ventured to suggest that constitutions should be crafted to mirror the Newtonian heavens. And social observers, like the wit Bernard de Mandeville, suggested that social discord was really an illusion, for the jarring of interests in society was closely akin to the workings of the natural order, with actions triggering equal and opposite reactions. Hence, in his *Fable of the Bees*, Mandeville quipped in 1714:

> Though every part was full of Vice,
> Yet the whole Mass a Paradise,
> Such were the Blessings of that State,
> Their Crimes conspired to make them great . . .
> The worst of all the Multitude
> Did something for the Common Good.
> This was the State's Craft that maintained
> The Whole of which each part complain'd:
> This, as in Musick Harmony,
> Made jarrings in the main agree.

And Alexander Pope, in his famous *Essay on Man*, used the same idea as a universal plea for "submission" to the automatic providence of balance, wherein society was nothing but a cog in a larger machine:

> Each individual seeks a sev'ral goal,
> But Heav'n's great view is One, and that the Whole.
> That, counter-works each folly and caprice;
> That, disappoints th' effect of ev'ry vice.

And in line with the pious slogan of the *Essay on Man*—"Whatever is, is right"—Pope bade his readers look on with serenity as

> . . . jarring int'rests of themselves create
> Th' according music of a well-mix'd State . . .

> in which

> . . . God and Nature link'd the gen'ral frame.
> And bade Self-love and Social be the same.

The examples of this eighteenth-century thought could be compounded in the manner of the great historian of ideas, Arthur Lovejoy. But the essential point is clear: As the old theological forms gave way to Enlightenment "science," the providence of God was replaced in the minds of men like Smith with the surrogate providence of social balance: the best of all possible worlds indeed, with individuals free to pursue their interest in complete assurance that nothing could ever "go wrong" in the free market system where, in effect, "Whatever is, is right."

There were those, however, who looked upon the Smithian system with great foreboding, and the irony is that these early critics of the pure

free market were preeminent conservative minds. Such are the perils of
the current equation of conservative philosophy and laissez-faire economics, doctrines that, as the following examples will show, are by no
means eternally equivalent. As Smith's political economy was applied by
Jeremy Bentham and his followers—the Utilitarians of early nineteenth-
century liberal thought—men like Samuel Taylor Coleridge and Thomas
Carlyle reacted with profound disgust and alarm. With exquisite Tory dis-
dain, Carlyle rejected "the pig philosophy" of every man for himself. "I,
for my share, declare the world to be no machine!" he exclaimed, and as
Roland Stromberg elaborates:

> The contrast must be noted, for American students: British and Euro-
> pean conservatism has been an enemy of laissez-faire. Coleridge be-
> lieved in government regulation of manufacturers, government aid to
> education, the duty of the state to enhance the moral and intellectual ca-
> pabilities of its citizens. . . . British utilitarianism and Political Economy
> postulated the free, self-reliant individual, the "mainspring of social
> progress" because his energies were released by the knowledge that
> what he gained would be his own, capable of enriching himself, and
> thereby also enriching the nation. . . . But an accompaniment of this far
> from unworthy idea was the loss of a social sense. The market was an
> impersonal force . . . impersonal and selfish. Society became only a col-
> lection of individuals, and thus something necessary to man was lost. . . .
> The conservatives whatever their sins in other respects surely per-
> formed a valuable service to modern Europe in defending the commu-
> nity against atomization.[1]

To these examples could be added the French conservatives Joseph
DeMaistre and Vicomte DeBonald. In America, one might also add John
Quincy Adams, Henry Clay, and the early founders of the modern Republican party, who, opposed to the laissez-faire economics of Jacksonian Democracy, supported a program of public works, land-grant colleges, and
federal economic responsibility. One might also add the conservatism
preached by Theodore Roosevelt early in the twentieth century and even,
to a certain extent, the ideas of the late Senator Robert Taft.

Through a long and complicated process of cultural transition, conservative and liberal values began to interchange in American society. By the
1920s under Harding and Coolidge and under the New Deal of F.D.R.,
conservative philosophy was seen to be equivalent with laissez-faire and
the "welfare state" as a liberal innovation. As we have seen, however, this
is hardly an eternal correlation. "Conservative" and "liberal" are relative
and fluid terms, and by the same token that conservative values can liber-
ate, so can "liberal" values conserve, depending on time, place, and circumstance. Laissez-faire, as bequeathed to the modern economic world

by Adam Smith, is a doctrine whose pertinence today in a world of advanced technology, of postindustrial and multinational economic life, must be carefully assessed without reference to "true," pristine conservative and liberal creeds (which do not exist) or the myths of economic "science."

We must free ourselves from the dogmas that, however daring in the eighteenth century, are stale economics today. We must dare to confront the economic world with open minds, for the liberal, conservative, and "scientific" nostrums of America today are in desperate need of revision. Men of good will, whether liberal, conservative, or radical, must be made aware of a sea change in economic life that is emerging from Japan and from Western Europe. It is not the "free market"; neither is it truly socialist. What it is—and how we can adapt it—this book attempts to show.

Science and Dogma: From Smith to the World of Keynes

Not until the mid-nineteenth century was there a debate over the direction in which economics was heading. In the great arguments that had Malthus and Mill opposing David Ricardo, with the latter supporting the science-based approach to economics, the outcome moved economics in the direction it still maintains. Ricardo held that the laws of production and distribution were equally natural laws and hence part of a science. Malthus and Mill maintained that though this might be the case for production, it was not so for distribution. Decisions ruling distribution could be subject to the controls of the society, reflecting its cultural values. Unfortunately, I believe, Ricardo was by far the better debater. His position won the day, and economics moved along the path of what was early viewed as a science, albeit a dismal one.

The significance of this to our contemporary problem is that, at least in America and Britain, the training of economists centers on quantitative, theoretical models. Emphasis in graduate education is not multidisciplinary but on the more abstract models and theories that are perceived as solely economic in character. This is not the case in Europe, or at least not to the same degree.[2]

In returning to the historical survey, we encounter another major thinker in the history of economic thought, Karl Marx. Lost in the competition for power between the communist world and the noncommunist world, between the USSR and the Western democracies, is the fact that among the original thinkers concerned with explaining how and why economics "works" is Marx. Marx was concerned, as were Adam Smith, David Ricardo, John Stuart Mill, the Reverend Malthus, and the other classical economists, with discovering the "laws" of economics.

By the time Karl Marx had grown to adulthood, the pace of industrial change in England and Western Europe had altered the world of Adam Smith, as a world of complex production, distribution, exchange, and consumption systems took its place. Capitalism by the mid-1800s, had emerged as a full-blown system of capital equipment acquisition, labor exploitation, industrial conflict, and the existence of a government largely insensitive to the conditions and pleas of the working class. The sweet social harmony supposed to result from the economic forces of the market as perceived by Adam Smith was, according to Marx, fantasy. Rather, Marx contended, the real world was one of conflict—increasing misery, decreasing government concern, and eventual crisis all of which would lead to a dictatorship of the proletariat. According to Marx, this had to happen. Marx, too, was caught up in the notion that he was a scientist discovering great, permanent laws of economic behavior.

There is no doubt that Marx moved our understanding of economic forces farther along. Marx's perception of the role of conflict in the marketplace, the growth of large industrial firms and monopolies, and the presence of business cycles were all new to the body of economic knowledge. But Marx's predictions on how and under what types of economic conditions a revolution would have to take place were quite wrong. His complete attachment to economics as the vortex of motivation, his assumption that government could only support the capital-owning class to the detriment of the workers, now appear to be highly dogmatic, if not simplistic.

Marx performed a major service in providing significant insights that have helped to understand the economic dangers of the nineteenth and early twentieth centuries. But when he sought to provide a model with long-range predictive power, he failed. The significance of nationalism, adaptability of government and social institutions, and the stake of organized labor in a form of society never envisioned by Marx made a shambles of the Marxist model. A government that could legislate a Sherman Antitrust Act curbing monopoly and a Wagner Act encouraging workers to organize and unionize in order to bargain more effectively with management was inconceivable to Marx. In the mid-1930s the National Labor Relations Act declared that "employees shall have the right to self-organization, to form, join, or assist labor organizations, to bargain collectively through representatives of their own choosing, and to engage in concerted activities, for the purpose of collective bargaining or other mutual aid or protection." This act was a major repudiation of the philosophy which had, until its passage, been reflected in court cases that held that such actions by workers were illegal constraints and a form of monopoly.

For a government to provide such support for labor to offset the power of the capitalists was inconceivable in the milieu of the mid-1800s, but not in the 1930s as social and cultural values changed. What was economic certitude to Marx, in short, was eroded and erased with the passage of time and circumstance.

In the Federal Republic of Germany, the home country of Marx, we have an instance of workers brought into the management structure of private companies by virtue of a series of laws dating back to the years of the First World War. The culmination of the right of workers to participate in corporate decisions affecting their wages, conditions of work, and even employment came in 1951. It was in that year that the first Co-determination Act provided for ". . . co-determination of workers in the supervisory and management boards of undertakings in the mining industry and the iron and steel production industry."[3] The Co-determination Act of 1976, which followed a series of expansions of the Act of 1951, enlarged co-determination to include all but the smaller firms in Germany. Representatives of workers share equally in number with management on the supervisory boards of companies.

Is Keynes Passé, Too?

While it would seem logical that the theories developed by Adam Smith and Karl Marx in the eighteenth and nineteenth centuries might, by the mid-1900s, appear to be somewhat outdated, why should this also be the case for so recent an economic thinker as John Maynard Keynes? Were the problems to which Keynes addressed his major work, *The General Theory of Employment, Interest and Money,* in the 1930s so different from those now confronting us? Was the society, the economy, the value system so different as to render his general theory less useful today than in 1935 when it first appeared? I believe so.

It is not the intent of this book to discuss in detail the technical aspects of Keynes's general theory. But it is amusing to note the degree to which the name Keynes is associated with consumption expenditures and a profligate government budget.

Keynes saw the depression of the 1930s as a case of the private sector, for various reasons, in a condition of underinvestment and underconsumption. The levels of underinvestment and underconsumption were such that, without a helping hand from government, depressed economic conditions might well continue for a long time—so long a time, indeed, that the private enterprise system might well be displaced by a truly radical system. The major rethinking implicit in Keynes's *General Theory* was that government was a balancing force, a force that had to come into play during those periods when the market forces were inadequate to maintain healthy rates of economic growth, stable prices, and high employment. Government was seen as a player trotting on and off the playing field only when needed, and not as a constant member of the team.

Due to hesitant government policy—F.D.R. was never fully convinced by Keynes—America's economy did not emerge from depression until 1939, when the level of investment and consumption expenditures by both the public and private sectors, in an economy bolstered by war orders, produced a sufficient amount of economic activity. Though the theory of the need for government to operate as a balance wheel was accepted, the levels of investment and consumption needed to rescue the economy were greater than were viewed as acceptable. The crises of World War II quickly overcame this political timidity and customary thinking on how big a partner government should be in our economy.

After the end of World War II, the enactment of the Employment Act of 1946 set the stage for a mandated application of Keynesian theory to our economy. The psychology of the war years had caused an imperceptible but nonetheless major shift in the mind of the average American with regard to government and its role in the economy. Government was no longer seen as a part-time partner but as a full-time partner, using interest rates, growth of money supplies, and tax policy to help guarantee high levels of employment, high rates of economic growth, and stable prices.

Based upon the economic experience since the end of World War II until the late 1960s, the Keynesian approach seemed to result in the achievement of the three goals of a successful national economy. With the exception of the immediate post–World War II conversion years and the Korean War years, low unemployment, stable prices, and high rates of economic growth were ours. From the late 1950s to the late 1960s, America was graced with a golden economic age.

The tarnish began to set in with the early 1970s. No small part was played by the economics of Vietnam, in both Democratic and Republican administrations. But during the 1970s what emerged as never before in public debate was the growing support for the economic policies set forth by Milton Friedman of the University of Chicago. The economics of Friedman is not some new body of thought as was the case of Smith, Marx, or Keynes. The presence of Friedman on the scene of debate over economic policy derives from his skill in presenting the positions of Adam Smith and the classical school of economics in the setting of the twentieth century.

The World of Milton Friedman

Within and beneath the refinements of Milton Friedman's "monetarism"[4] is the theory of Adam Smith, applied with debater's agility. The Friedmanesque view of reality is one in which "Whatever is, is right" within the principles of laissez-faire. Messy discordant phenomena vanish into thin air, or are quickly blamed upon the interfering power of government. There is nothing in the Friedmanesque world that doesn't "fit"—at least on paper.

But the agile debater must eventually slip into severe contortions when his powers are exerted on behalf of an underlying dogma. Reality, ever shifting into new and more complicated patterns, refuses to conform to a frozen theory, however "classical." Hence, to study Friedman is to ponder the disheartening spectacle of forceful argumentation in the service of wishful and delusive reasoning.

To supply an example at random: in *Free to Choose* Friedman states: "In the Far East, Malaysia, Singapore, Korea, Taiwan, Hong Kong, and Japan—all relying extensively on private markets—are thriving. Their people are full of hope."[5] But in *Capitalism and Freedom,* Friedman observes: "Historical evidence speaks with a single voice on the relation between political freedom and a free market."[6] A few sentences earlier he states: "The kind of economic organization that provides economic freedom directly, namely, competitive capitalism, also promotes political freedom because it separates economic power from political power and in this way enables the one to offset the other." It is interesting to note that when this statement was written in the early 1960s, Korea was controlled by a strong political dictatorship. The capitalist system in other countries, such as Argentina and Chile, exists without promoting the political freedom that Friedman supposes. Such are the risks of economic "science" and the messier facts of our political and social world.

We must, of course, favor the maximum amount of economic, social, and political freedom consistent with our personal safety, national security, and economic goals. And yet readers of Friedman must wonder at times about the world in which he, Friedman, sees himself living. For example, when I told a chief executive officer of a major corporation that we really should eliminate the licensing and certification of medical doctors and dentists by state medical boards, he looked at me and said that if I was really serious, I was completely lacking in judgment. I said that *I* was not, but possibly Friedman is. While I was jesting, Friedman is not jesting. The CEO refused to believe that his "economic god" would ever be quite so dogmatic. It was easy enough to refer him to the passage in question.[7] Of course, Friedman has a rationale for eliminating licensing of physicians, lawyers, and dentists: "It has reduced the opportunities available to people who would like to be physicians, forcing them to pursue occupations they regard as less attractive."[8] Friedman feels that legal penalties for malpractice and the fact that hospitals, and medical partnerships, would be self-policing are all that is necessary to deal with the incompetent or fraudulent physician.

In all fairness to Friedman, I questioned a number of physicians about self-policing by hospitals, group practice situations, and other organizations Friedman saw as likely sources of such quality control. All physicians I spoke with are personal friends and were, I believe, frank. The unanimous reply was that it would not work, any more than such peer control has worked in university faculties, the courts, or teacher associations. Not the least complication in the medical field is the legal problem of proving incompetence and defending yourself in a suit should you take steps to deprive a physician of his or her livelihood.

In addition, a key point that Friedman makes about licensing by state authorities is that a license granted "twenty or thirty years earlier is hardly assurance of quality now."[9] That is true. But what is also true is that common practice is for states to require continuing education by physicians in order to ensure that at a minimum physicians keep up with new developments in their fields of specialization.

The reason for this rather lengthy reference to Friedman is that he and his adherents are purveyors of social chaos. Unless we understand their philosophy, in all of its destructive power, it is highly unlikely that the United States will be able to deal with the problems of low productivity, low economic growth, high rates of unemployment, and loss of foreign and domestic markets.

Whether or not we have national parks does not depend upon the presence of a sufficient number of people willing to pay tolls to drive through or camp in the park. Yet Friedman holds that "If the public wants this kind of an activity [Yellowstone Park] enough to pay for it, private enterprises will have every incentive to provide such parks."[10]

There are several problems with this sort of reasoning, from the strictly business point of view, I might add. To begin with, although there may indeed be a sufficient market for a Yellowstone Park (let us say for the sake of the argument by 1960) so that it would pay to develop it, unless the park had been set aside for the public use (as it was, in 1872), what guarantee would there be that such an area would not have been used for some other commercial purpose well before 1960? It is all well and good to see a success after the fact, but the real challenge is to see the potential before the fact. Even Milton Friedman is not that clairvoyant! A second point is that even if National Parks were not sufficiently profitable for private development, are there not other factors involved that would lead most of us to see them as a national asset, to be set aside, supported by government funds, for present and future generations to enjoy? Are there not social, cultural, and historical factors in this equation? Of course there are, and most citizens understand this well. Indeed, by understanding this we often create the basis for economic success.

A case in point is the fact that Japanese industry started its revolution of a new approach to production with the commitment to quality. Prior to World War II, Japanese products were known for shoddiness and lack of quality. In the early 1950s in a reversal of philosophy, Japanese producers determined that a hallmark of Japanese products had to be quality and reliability. They correctly assumed that though resultant prices might be higher, if they were still within a reasonable range, consumers would be willing to pay for quality. The goal then became quality and predictability of performance. This was the reverse of the economic goals of most Western producers. The results are well-known to most of us. Pride of workmanship, pride in company, pride in product were key factors in producing Nikon cameras, Sony televisions, Toyota automobiles, and Seiko watches which have so plagued Western competitors. Pride is not a term one finds listed as a factor in economics. But it certainly does have an impact on the success of a company.

Achieving pride in product and affiliation is not a Japanese innovation. In the United States some companies and organizations have long histories of a sense of common purpose, pride, and loyalty by employees and managers. Yet, by and large, ours is an adversarial kind of society. What most typifies our relationship is the sense of conflict: government versus business, management versus labor, big business versus small business. The word "versus" appears as frequently here as does "harmony" in Japan. In a country like West Germany, the term "social partners" is used to describe relationships among management, trade unions, and government. But in the United States, and countries like Great Britain, Canada, and Australia, there is little of this sense of commonality and mutual sense of purpose. Rather, the prophets of either-or are looked to in order to "get government off our back" or, in government, "control the crooks in business."

In brief, we have placed ourselves in an impossible situation. We envision a world of either-or, in which economic models are restricted to purely economic values. But the world is not like this at all. The countries that excel in economic performance have recognized this already. We in the United States are just beginning to understand it, and not a moment too soon.

The Emerging Model

What has happened to such countries as Japan and West Germany is that since the end of World War II, their economies have developed along paths that fit no simple mold or form. They cannot be labeled free enterprise or socialist. They have, since the early 1950s, developed models of governance and economics that fit no simple description, and relationships have evolved among government, industry, and labor that have provided the basis for economies far more productive than America's since the late 1960s. Only the British can claim with us the burden of resistance to the new economic realities.

Both the United States and Great Britain adhere to a system of philosophy based on stale, outmoded assumptions. Both claim to believe in the free market system, which, in its simplest form, is based on the willingness to wait long enough for long-term changes to occur. Hence, in 1981 and 1982 it was held that high interest rates would eventually come down if the level of unemployment is high enough for a long enough period of time and if government budgets are reduced. After the rates of inflation and interest had leveled off, through natural forces, and inventories of goods had been sold off sufficiently, an economic recovery would take place—it was thought by many.

While this may be true in terms of some long-term economic model, this sort of solution is not acceptable in most modern societies—not only to individuals but to industry as well. The values of most modern societies have changed dramatically since the early 1900s when such visions of the natural economy were still viewed as "pure" economics. Much has changed in our thinking since then, mostly as a result of the previously unparalleled experience of the Great Depression of the 1930s. Very few people emerged from that experience really committed to waiting patiently for long-run changes—including businesspeople!

Another factor that has eliminated an economic philosophy based on a long-term equilibrating of natural forces is that since the 1950s the pace of industrial and economic change has increased far beyond what had previously existed. The more rapid development of new products, new production techniques, the more rapid rise of new international competitors, the increasing pace of obsolescence of skills, an exponential increase in the availability and use of information have all resulted in the obsolescence of economic models that assume a "long run."

We are now confronted with the economics of change. Unless we understand this, and develop new policies reflecting this fact of life, America's economy will not recover its former preeminence. Basic to such new policies are new industrial relationships based on nonadversarial, mutually arrived-at goals among government, industry, and labor. Completely new concepts of human resource investment, public budgeting, public-private joint investment strategies, and management of change in order to meet socioeconomic goals will have to be designed.

This point was made very effectively in an article by Robert B. Reich:

> The economic choice facing the United States over the next decade is between protection of the national economy from the international market or rapid adjustment to the new realities of international competition. Either way, government will be actively involved. Many Americans cling to the idea that the Federal Government should refrain from interfering with the market. The tenacity with which the free-market ideal is maintained illustrates the power of ideology over political reality. The vast array of tariffs, quotas, export agreements, Federal loans and loan guarantees that now protect America's declining industries are viewed as isolated exceptions to the preferred Government role of neutrality, while our defense-related contracts, targeted tax breaks, and assorted subsidies for other industries are regarded as somehow unrelated to industrial development or to market dynamics.[11]

In Italy, prolonged economic problems have triggered consideration of completely new forms of joint ventures and concepts of public versus private. In early 1982, the Italian government took steps to bring Fiat, the private auto manufacturer (Italy's largest), into a new set of cooperative relationships with state-owned companies in the auto, steel, and telecommunications sectors. Montedison, the state-controlled chemicals group, is cooperating with private chemical companies, such as the Occidental Petroleum Corporation. With regard to the future types of economic relationships and concepts, Alberto Mucci, chief economist, Banca Nazionale del Lovoro, Italy's largest commercial bank, said of their institutional relationships: "We must find new forms."[12] In Italy, where state-dominated industry has been the pattern, the change being urged is "privatization." But more significant than this is the growing recognition that a philosophy of either-or—the "purity" a senior German economist referred to as a hallmark of American thinking in economics—is unworkable. Commenting on this, Vittorio Barattieri of the Ministry for Industry observed that "ten years ago, public was good, and private was bad. The attitude has changed."[13]

Economies such as those in Japan and West Germany, which are based on institutional relationships geared to the reality of change, are far more successful than the economies geared to a static, unchanging ideology. One must manage change or the increasing frequency of change will produce an economy of constant crisis. Shifts in technology, social values, and international trade have, since the late 1960s, created a new set of economic imperatives. To ignore this is to guarantee a continuation of economic crisis. Unless we accept the fact that the economic world is different from that envisioned in the economic models we think we follow—unless we accept the fact that there is no unchanging and immutable set of economic principles arising from economic "science"—our problems will worsen.

Confronted as we are with a decade or more of economic decline, as compared with our foreign competitors, what answers are provided from the body of economic thought as developed between 1776 and 1982? Very little of use, insofar as we define economic thought in America. And that applies to Great Britain as well. The terrible complexities of economic, social, cultural, political, legal, psychological, and historical relationships in achieving a prosperous economy belie the alternatives of either-or: the unfettered free market versus government. The energies expended on this simplistic debate would be comic were it not for the fact that the results produced have so often been foolishly tragic. Economic life, like all other forms of relationships, is neither all white nor black. Most of us, including politicians, know this well. But because of ideology, we fix our hopes upon policies that, in the cause of "unchaining" the economy, stifle its growth. Without this economic growth, we cannot achieve the other goals of our society. Employment security, the security of a stable price level, the security of producing the means for an increasing standard of living for each new generation cannot be achieved unless we gear our economic policies to the only basis for economic well-being. What is this basis?

The answer is deceptively simple in a way. It can be found in Table 1.5, which compares rates of gain in productivity. Public and private sector policies and practices designed to increase productivity also tend to produce healthy economies. And, fascinatingly, this was the nature of Adam Smith's original question. His concern, and title of his monumental study, was that of *An Inquiry into the Nature and Causes of the Wealth of Nations*. Smith, very early in his study, pointed to the key importance of increasing output per worker as the source of national wealth. He was talking about productivity gain! Given the background of mercantilism, both in England and on the Continent, he correctly saw government as it was then conceived as the key obstacle in the economy. So long as the sovereign and parliament conspired against the market system, the economy could not grow as much as its potential offered.

But this was the society of more than 200 years ago—literally everything is different. The corporate form of government, the mode of transportation, the family, what we eat, and what we wear: the list is interminable. But uppermost our values and expectations have changed. That is the key. The countries that have done best in their economies have recognized this. Their policies and institutions reflect it.

West Germany and Japan are very different, in just about everything. Japan has no resources other than its people. It has no coal, petroleum, iron ore, copper, tin, zinc, lumber, or large-scale agriculture. Though it has about half the population of America, its size is only about that of the state of Montana, with far less usable land than Montana since its topography is more mountainous. Japan seems to be as much up and down as it is level.

West Germany is a country more replete with such resources as coal, iron ore, and lumber and with a terrain more conducive to an agricultural base. In addition, the culture and value system of Germany are far closer to those of America than of Japan.

However, West Germany and Japan, though very different in all outward respects, have a fundamental set of social and economic characteristics that are quite similar. Fundamentally, both countries have developed economic policies based on a body of economic thought that has changed to reflect the real values of the society. As the social values changed after World War II, so did the economic philosophy and policy guidelines, both public and private, reflecting those values. Economics was not perceived as an independent, freestanding discipline reflecting eternal verities. It was seen as a body of knowledge that could help to achieve the goals of the society. As John Stuart Mill correctly sensed in the mid-nineteenth century, society and not immutable economic laws determine how the product of its economic endeavors could and should be used to achieve the goals of the society.

Let us now look at how, and why, the economies of the two countries that have done best, West Germany and Japan, were able to achieve high levels of economic performance.

Notes

1. Roland Stromberg, *European Intellectual History Since 1789* (Englewood Cliffs, N.J.: Prentice-Hall, 1975), pp. 54, 58–59.
2. What is also intriguing is that the theoretical nature of graduate economic study in America and Britain is sharply in contrast to the study of business. Indeed, one of the best kept secrets of graduate economic education is that the overwhelming majority of graduates with master's and doctoral degrees in economics

have never taken a business course. Accounting, organizational theory, business finance, marketing, management, and international business are rarely found in the curricula of graduate studies in economics. This is comparable to training physicians without letting them see or deal with real patients until after they have received the M.D. degree.

3. *Co-determination in the Federal Republic of Germany* (Bonn: Federal Minister of Labour and Social Affairs, 1976), p. 10.

4. See the Appendix for a brief description of the quantity theory of money and its usefulness and limitations.

5. Milton and Rose Friedman, *Free to Choose* (New York: Avon, 1979), p. 48.

6. Milton Friedman, *Capitalism and Freedom* (Chicago: University of Chicago, 1962), p. 9.

7. Ibid., pp. 157–59.

8. Ibid., p. 158.

9. Ibid.

10. Ibid., p. 31.

11. Robert B. Reich, "Adjust to Compete," *New York Times*, April 8, 1982, p. A23.

12. "Italy's New Industrial Strategy," *New York Times*, February 11, 1982, p. D1.

13. Ibid.

The Fall
and
Rise of Germany
3

The economy of the Federal Republic of Germany (FRG) in 1982 was the product of the most amazing internal and external factors. Foremost among the external factors that come to mind is the unique intelligence and insight that combined in 1947 to deal with defeated Germany as a key to the restoration of the European economy. It is easy to forget, 36 years later, that many leaders in industry and politics were urging that Germany be dealt with as a vanquished enemy, deserving to be dismembered economically and converted into a dependent, primarily agricultural nation. Happily, Secretary of State George C. Marshall heeded other advice and urged a far different approach. Former President Herbert Hoover had been appointed by President Harry Truman as honorary chairman of Truman's Famine Emergency Committee in 1946. In 1947, Hoover undertook, at Truman's behest, an analysis of economic conditions in Germany and Austria. In his report, based upon his detailed study in Europe and his unique experience as an engineer, businessman, statesman, and former U.S. president, Hoover concluded:

> There is only one path to recovery in Europe. That is production. The whole economy of Europe is interlinked with the German economy through the exchange of raw materials and manufactured goods. The productivity of Europe cannot be restored without the restoration of Germany as a contributor to that productivity.[1]

Within the U.S. State Department, a small staff, headed by George Kennan, began to develop the department's position on a strategy for economic aid to Western Europe. In a May 6, 1947, statement Kennan not only summed up the philosophy relating German rehabilitation to that of Western Europe; he also made an observation that has gone largely unheeded by lesser men of stature who have followed men like Marshall, Truman, and Kennan.

> . . . It may be fairly stated, as a working rule for dealing with the Russians, that only those people are able to get along with them who have proven their ability to get along without them. . . . Today, we find ourselves before the recognition that the economic rehabilitation of Western Europe is of urgent and primary importance. The restoration of German productivity, if only in part of Germany, is essential to that rehabilitation. We cannot wait for Russian agreement to achieve that restoration.[2]

We did not permit Russian delaying tactics to prevent the start of a massive program to help Germany get back on its feet as the key to the recovery of Western Europe's economy. Interestingly, both Kennan and Hoover used the term "productivity," not just "production." This was no slip of language or simply using one term synonymously with the other. Productivity was indeed seen as key to economic recovery and continued growth, as we shall see.

Though this is no effort to retrace the enormity of the recovery task, a few statistics would help the reader, especially those who did not live through the post–World War II years as adults, to comprehend more fully the task at hand. By the end of World War II, 10 million homes in Germany had been destroyed. Large industrial centers like Nuremberg, Stuttgart, Hanover, Dusseldorf, Duren, and Julich were almost totally destroyed, and other major cities like Hamburg, Darmstadt, Cologne, Frankfurt, Essen, and Dresden were largely in ruins. Ninety-five percent of Berlin was in ruins. In the streets of Berlin alone there was more than 400 million cubic meters of rubble. One estimate concluded that if 10 trains a day with 50 cars each were used to remove it, the clearing process would take 16 years.[3] In western Germany, out of 958 major bridges, 740 could not be used, 50 percent of all the railroad locomotives were not in working order, only 40 percent of all railroad cars were operable in northwest Germany, and in southern Germany, 90 percent of its factories and 85 percent of its industrial plants were out of action. Total industrial output in this area was operating at 5 percent of capacity.[4]

But these statistics are symptomatic of what existed in Europe in general. How could it have been otherwise when one understands that in monetary terms, World War II had cost all of the nations involved more than the combined costs of all of the European wars since the Middle Ages.[5] Knowing this, it is difficult to credit the revival of Germany, or of the other European nations that had similarly been affected, solely on the basis of the external help they received, almost entirely from the United States.

Also of major importance were the internal factors. Though the United States moved ahead, in spite of the obstacles interposed by Russia to the Marshall Plan, it could only succeed in its rehabilitation efforts if the European people, especially Western Europeans, were sufficiently motivated and energetic enough to cooperate. And of course no small part of the problem of rebuilding was that it had to be done with a large percentage of able-bodied men, most of whom were no longer available. In Germany, more than 3.5 million military were dead or missing, with 24 percent of all Germans born in 1924 either dead or missing. An additional 31 percent were severely mutilated. As a result, at the end of World War II, with a population of about 70 million people, in Germany there were now more than 7 million more women than men.[6] (All of these figures concerning the dead are exclusive of the huge number of civilian deaths.)

However, the rebuilding process did take place, and by the end of the 1950s, Western Europe had recovered from most of the destructive economic effects of the war. Though the dead could never be restored and the maimed returned to former health, by a decade after the end of hostilities, the Federal Republic of Germany was competing effectively on the world scene. The miracle of Germany had taken place.

As is evident from Tables 1.1 to 1.3, by 1970, West Germany had moved past the United States in rates of economic growth and productivity gain. In addition, the rate of unemployment was well below that of the United States, and it has remained so. In any explanation of how this was achieved, there are at least three areas of what might be called overt economic policy: human capital investment policy, monetary policy, and fiscal policy. These policies reflect a basic philosophy, and it is this philosophy that has permeated the West German economy, reflecting values in the society. Contrary to the belief of many who have looked at the West German economy since the 1960s, many of these values existed before World War II and were already embodied in economic policies before the advent of Adolf Hitler. It is the same sort of enigma as how a nation that produced and honored a Mendelssohn, a Schiller, a Beethoven, a Mann, and an Einstein could select and follow a Hitler.

Human Capital Investment Policy

In 1969, the government of West Germany passed the Employment Promotion Act. This act established the right of every worker, employed or unemployed, to take up to two years of retraining, with all costs paid, with an income stipend of up to 95 percent of the last previous wage. This act is also extended to most of the "guest workers" who came to West

Germany from other European countries. In 1982, despite claims by U.S. economists that all guest workers were sent home in order to alleviate the unemployment problem in West Germany, almost 10 percent of the West German labor force is still composed of the guest workers. The 1969 act was not evidence of a new concern by Germans over the need to invest in the labor force. This act was based upon earlier acts concerned with upgrading the labor force.[7]

Before 1918, local communities established labor exchanges in an effort to match unemployed workers with job vacancies. But it was during the post–World War I period that the central government, in cooperation with trade unions and employers, established national labor exchanges. It was also in 1918 that a national unemployment relief program was established, about 18 years before the United States started its unemployment insurance program. By 1924, Germany had established an unemployment relief program based upon insurance principles. A national health insurance program had been instituted well before this period. In 1927, the National Institution for Placement and Unemployment was established, combining in one federal agency the responsibility for placement, job vacancy information, and payment of unemployment benefits.[8]

During the National Socialist (Nazi) regime, most of the existing functions concerning employment, placement, and a democratic distribution of benefits were suspended. Immediately after the end of World War II, steps were taken to reinstitute all of the employment, placement, and insurance programs. On March 10, 1952, the Federal Institution for Placement and Unemployment Insurance stipulated equal representation of the "social partners" and the public corporations. This term, "social partners," became the key phrase in a broad series of efforts to bring government, labor, and employees together to develop an effective manpower policy. It was this policy that established the basis for the development, on a continuing basis, of a highly skilled labor force available in sufficient numbers with the necessary skills to support the anticipated dynamic needs of a modern, industrial economy.

The legislation of 1952 was built on a long history of a philosophy of social investment. It is difficult for an American to accept that what was first considered only in recent decades in the United States as a necessary function of government to deal with the problems of our most critical resource, people, Germany had accepted before the twentieth century. Germany introduced a health insurance program in 1883, industrial accident insurance in 1884, and old-age, survivor, and disability pensions in 1889. The basic philosophy concerning its human resources was best stated in the February 1978 issue of *Labor News and Social Policy*:

Although—in 1977—Germany spent almost 32 percent of its gross national product on social services (more than any other nation in the world), the Federal Republic does not regard itself as a welfare state. Unlike the United States, Germany has relatively few natural resources. Its area—96,500 square miles—is just about the size of Oregon. One third of its food and most of the raw materials for its industries have to be imported and paid for mainly by exports. The major resource on which the Federal Republic relies is its 61 million people, among them 13 million refugees from Central and Eastern Europe and 2 million foreign workers and their families from all over the world. What makes the German economy work is, above all, sound industrial relations and the skills of its people which are encouraged by massive social investments. In Germany today human skills and mobility are regarded as the most important facts in economic growth, more important even than capital.[9]

This last sentence is in startling contrast to the position taken by most economists, political leaders, and industrialists in the United States. In all of the debates about economic policy in the United States, during all of the discussions in Congress, at the White House, and by powerful groups representing the private sector, emphasis is solely on fiscal and monetary policy. As distinct from West Germany and, as we will see, Japan, the United States does not view manpower policy as a key ingredient in the effort to deal with problems of low productivity, economic growth, or inflation. More about the U.S. philosophy on social investment at a later point. Suffice it to point out that our current philosophy on unemployment, placement, and retraining is reminiscent of the following statement, which refers to Germany:

Before the year 1914 the idea was still prevalent that anybody who could not find work had only himself to blame and the thought that this could have anything to do with the state of the labour market appeared absurd in those days.[10]

Mere reference to the German retraining program enacted in 1969 does little justice to its coverage and impact. When, in 1970, the author was in Germany doing research on manpower programs, it was disheartening, to say the least, to learn that the act of 1969 was consciously based on the U.S. World War II GI Bill, which provided for full-time training or education, plus a stipend sufficient to cover normal rent and partial food costs for all eligible veterans. The German retraining program is briefly described below:

Keeping people in permanent productive employment and enabling them to earn a decent living is a cardinal aim of social policy. Paying people unemployment benefits and assistance is regarded as a last resort—to be used only when all other means of safeguarding and promoting employment have failed. The other means employed include:

- Occupational and labor counseling;
- Placing people into other jobs;
- Industrial training, further training, retraining and rehabilitation combined with the creation of new jobs;
- Benefits for the maintenance and creation of employment, in particular financial assistance for those on reduced shifts, and assistance in taking up employment;
- Wage supplements and employer grants to ensure year-round employment in the building industry ("bad weather money").

All these measures to prevent unemployment take precedence over payment of actual unemployment benefits. In order to encourage workers to take up further training or retraining instead of drawing unemployment benefits, the Federal Employment Agency offers incentives for training which are higher than the unemployment benefits they would receive.

Under the Employment Promotion Act (1969) every worker in Germany *(including nationals from Common Market countries)* has a statutory right to paid training, further training, retraining or rehabilitation, and he or she can claim this right from the Federal Employment Agency. Since 1977 prisoners in penitentiaries are also included in the scheme. Full-time instruction for adults may be granted for up to three years (though normally it should not exceed two). During this time the trainee receives an allowance of 80 percent of his former net income.

Those who for one reason or another cannot or do not take a course of training, receive either unemployment benefits or unemployment assistance.

Unemployment benefits are paid from the first day of unemployment for a maximum period of 52 weeks. The basic rate for both single and married persons is 68 percent of previous net earnings. Married workers receive, in addition, the usual family allowances, payable for every child as follows: $24 a month for the first child, $38 for the second, $70 for the third and each additional child.

Unemployment benefits are not payable if a worker is temporarily unemployed as a result of taking part in a strike. Benefits can be suspended if a worker refuses a reasonable offer of employment or a course of training.

Those unemployed who have exhausted their claim to unemployment benefits may draw unemployment assistance, but this is normally at a lower rate (58 per cent) and is subject to a means test.[11]

As of January 1, 1982, these provisions were modified somewhat, but not drastically.

In 1976, what one might regard as the ultimate step in a social partnership philosophy was taken. The Co-determination Act of 1976 was passed. What it basically does is mandate that for all public corporations and limited partnerships with more than 2,000 employees, the supervisory board will share equally in representation from management and employee representatives. The 1976 act built on earlier co-determination acts of 1951 and 1956, which applied only in the coal and iron and steel industries. Under the Works Constitution Act of 1952, there is a one-third representation of employees in supervisory boards of companies with fewer than 2,000 employees. In order to understand the significance of board membership, it is necessary to distinguish between the supervisory board and the management board in a German firm.[12]

The supervisory board's major tasks and responsibilities are the appointment and dismissal of the management board as well as the supervision of the management of the firm. Moreover, the bylaws of the company, or the supervisory board itself, may provide that certain matters require the consent of the supervisory board. It is quite usual that investments above a certain financial volume, credits and loans above a certain limit, as well as the recruitment and dismissal of managerial staff, require the consent of the supervisory board.

The management board conducts the day-to-day business of the firm on its own responsibility. It has not only entrepreneurial functions in the narrow sense of the word, but also functions as employer of the employees of the company.

Thus, what we have in Germany is the control of a corporation at the very highest level in the hands of a board in which the employees' representatives share governance rights and responsibilities with the representatives of the shareholders or owners of the firm.

The history of co-determination is not one that grew out of a voluntary act on the part of the stockholders to share decision making with the employees. It began with legislation before World War II.

> During the First World War, the "Act on Civilian War-Work Service" was passed. The setting up of workers' and salaried employees' committees was prescribed by law for establishments which were vital for the war effort and for supply and which employed over 50 persons. Yet there was no co-determination in the sense of participation in the decision-making process.
>
> After 1918 the statutory basis was enlarged. The 1920 Works Councils Act prescribed works councils for all establishments with at least 20 workers.

These workers' representatives were now granted above all the right of full participation in the elaboration of work regulations. Participation rights existed to a certain degree in the field of personnel and finance. The Act on the Representation of Works Council Members in the Supervisory Board introduced the representation of workers in the supervisory boards, this meant that at least one works council member had to be represented on the board.

The Nazi regime brought this development to a sudden stand-still. The trade unions were dissolved. The Act to regulate national work repealed the Works Council Act.

After 1945, works councils were re-established at first along the lines of the 1920 Works Council Act. The Allied Control Council Act No. 22 of 1946, authorized the setting up of works councils. It was followed by legislation passed by the Länder (State).

After co-determination at the board level had been practised since 1946 without statutory basis in the iron and steel industry of the British Zone of Occupation, a decisive step was taken in 1951. At the insistence of the workers and their trade unions and after violent disputes and quarrels in and outside Parliament, the Act on the co-determination of workers in the supervisory and management boards of undertakings in the mining industry and the iron and steel production industry was passed. In 1956, it was followed by a supplementary Act which governs co-determination in combines in the coal, iron and steel industry.

The Works Constitution Act of 1952 (for the private sector) and the Federal Staff Representation Act of 1965 as well as the Länder Staff Representation Acts (for the public sector) governed the field of co-determination at the level of the establishment. The Works Constitution Act provided for a one-third representation of workers in the supervisory boards of large and medium-sized undertakings.

Co-determination at the level of the establishment was considerably expanded by the new Works Constitution Act of 1972. It repealed the Works Constitution Act of 1952 apart from its provisions on the one-third representation in the supervisory boards. The 1974 Federal Staff Representation Act and several Länder Acts constitute a considerable step forward in the co-determination at the level of the establishment in the public sector.

Länder Acts constitute a considerable step forward in the co-determination at the level of the establishment in the public sector.

On 20 February 1974 the Federal Government adopted a bill on workers' co-determination.

On 18 March 1976, the Bundestag passed the Act on Workers' Co-determination.

The Bundesrat approved the Co-determination Act on 9 April 1976. It was published in the Bundesgesetzblatt No. 51 of 8 May 1976, page 1153 and entered into force on 1 July 1976.[13]

Though one might conclude that the highly vaunted reputation and record of German workers grows out of the co-determination principle, significant as it must be, there is another very important feature of worker participation in the day-to-day operation of the firm. This feature is the works council.

Under the provisions of the Works Constitution Act of 1972, the worker in a German firm was placed in the position of being able to have a direct effect on policies concerning the organization of work, employment, and dismissal of employees, as well as various rights and obligations under the employment relationship.[14]

Works councils are elected for a term of office of three years in any establishment of private industry with at least five employees with voting rights. Employers and managerial employees are not represented on the works council.

Duties of the Works Council

The works council safeguards the interests of the employees in dealings with the employer. The works council and the employer shall work together in a spirit of mutual trust and in co-operation with the trade unions and employers' associations for the good of the employees and of the establishment. It has a genuine right of co-determination in a series of matters such as:

- Working hours, e.g., the introduction of short-time work,
- The introduction and use of technical devices designed to monitor the behavior or performance of the employees,
- The assignment and notice to vacate company-owned accommodation,
- The fixing of job and bonus rates and comparable performance related remuneration.

Works councils have a far-reaching right of participation and co-determination in matters concerning the structuring, organisation and design of jobs, operations and the working environment, manpower planning and personnel management as well as in-plant training.

In the case of engagements, gradings, re-gradings and transfers the employer must obtain the consent of the works council. If the works council refuses its consent it can be substituted only by a decision in lieu of consent by a state court (Labour Court).

Dismissals are effective only if the works council was consulted in advance. The works council may oppose a routine dismissal with the effect that the employer must keep the employee in his employment until a final court decision is given on the case at issue.

The works council has the right to be informed on a large number of matters. Moreover, the finance committee, which is to be established in undertakings with more than 200 employees, and whose members are all appointed by the works council, has a substantial right to be informed and to be heard in financial matters.

In the case of alterations, such as the reduction of operations, the close-down or transfer of an establishment, the works council may require the conclusion of a social compensation plan in order to compensate for any financial prejudices sustained by the employees.

Organisation

The number of works council members depends on the number of employees of the establishment. Where the works council consists of at least 3 members, wage earners and salaried employees must be represented according to their relative numerical strength in the establishment.

The Works Constitution Act contains a series of provisions in order to protect and facilitate elections to the works council. Thus, works council elections take place during working hours and their costs are borne by the employer. Dismissals of members of the election board, election candidates and members of the works council are not permitted. Works council members are to be released from their work duties without loss of pay in order to be able to discharge their functions; furthermore the Act provides that in any establishment with more than 300 employees a certain number of works council members, depending on the size of the establishment, are to be permanently released from their work duties.

Considering the various and often complex functions of the works council the Act makes special provision to enable works council members to obtain the knowledge required. To this end works council members may attend training courses without any loss of pay and, under certain conditions, at the expense of the employer.

Taking account of the special interests both of young employees, who usually have not yet completed their training, and of the disabled the Act provides for youth delegations and representatives of the disabled to look after the interest of these categories of employees in close co-operation with the works councils.

Under the legislation, a careful definition of who is an employee makes the intent of the law quite clear.

Employees

(1) In this Act, the term "employee" comprises wage earners and salaried employees including persons employed for the purpose of their vocational training.

(2) The following shall not be considered as employees for the purposes of this Act:

1. In establishments belonging to a corporation, the members of the organs that are legally empowered to represent the corporation;

2. Partners in an ordinary commercial partnership or members of another association of persons, in the establishment belonging to the partnership or association, in so far as they are empowered by law, its own by-laws or the articles of association to represent the association or to exercise management functions;

3. Persons whose employment is not primarily for the purpose of earning their livelihood but is chiefly inspired by charitable or religious motives;

4. Persons whose employment is not primarily for the purpose of earning their livelihood but principally for the cure or recovery, rehabilitation, moral improvement or education;

5. The spouse as well as the relative by blood or marriage of the first degree living with the employer.

(3) Unless this Act expressly provides to the contrary it shall not apply to executive staff who, by their status and under their contract of employment—

1. Are entitled on their own responsibility to engage and dismiss employees on behalf of the establishment or one of its departments; or

2. Are endowed with general authority (power of procuration) or full power of representation or power to sign ("Prokura"); or

3. Essentially carry out duties on their own responsibility which are normally assigned to them because of their particular experience and knowledge in view of the importance of the said duties for the existence and development of the establishment.

The law also provides that minorities and young people (those employees under 18 years of age) be represented. Further,

(1) The works council should be composed as far as possible of employees of the various departments and non-autonomous ancillary establishments. At the same time the works council should as far as possible comprise representatives of the various employment categories to which the employees of the establishment belong.

(2) The sexes should be represented according to their relative numerical strength.

The question is how effective are works councils in ameliorating employee-management disputes, encouraging rather than opposing innovations and permitting the displacement of workers as a result of loss of markets or introduction of new processes or technology. In 1976, a major study was undertaken in an effort to answer these questions, under the auspices of the Anglo-German Foundation for the study of Industrial Society.[15] The study examined a sample of enterprises in both countries to determine how large companies dealt with major changes affecting employee-employer relations. The coal, steel, automotive, retail, paper, and insurance industries were included. Research followed the case study approach.

Given that since the oil crises of 1974 there has been a marked shift in Germany away from the "expansive" phase of industrial innovation to "intensive" innovation, which introduced more technology of a labor-displacing effect, the results have special significance. Jobs decreased in numbers and German workers were called upon to develop new skills for very different types of production processes. Workers, under works councils and co-determination, were confronted with management proposals to dismiss fellow workers.[16]

The study applied an interesting term to the industrial relations approach in West Germany: "cooperative conflict resolution." Without a lengthy report on the research, for the purposes of this book the following sums up what was found to be most significant.

> In Britain, industrial affairs are carried out against a background cacophony of press headlines, sombre television coverage and a publicity glare that sometimes almost blinds the participants; while by contrast Germany conveys the impression of a well-ordered smooth-running, almost trouble-free system which, when it occasionally erupts into confrontation over pay or technical change or the further extension of worker participation, surprises observers. Our investigations suggest that these impressions contain a good deal of significance. . . . In Germany, the prevailing style is essentially cooperative while in Britain it takes an adversary form.[17]

If one were to replace the word Britain with the words United States, the description would be equally applicable. The study makes it quite clear that in general the German approach produces a far better result. In the next chapter, on Japan, the parallel in the German and Japanese approaches in industrial relations is uncanny.

Monetary Policy

Nowhere does the continuing search for an either-or answer to a complex economic problem show up better than in debates over monetary policy, at least in the United States. Though his reference is to fiscal policy, West Germany's former chancellor, Helmut Schmidt, recently observed about the economic policies of the Reagan administration: "There is no such thing as an economic panacea—it is misleading to construe a super-Keynesian, deficit-spending fiscal policy as supply-side economics."[18] In the same statement Schmidt cautioned, with Europe's economy in the throes of a major recession: "Every national economic policy of the United States is at the same time a world policy—This is not the time for the faithful application of new theories or ideologies." Perhaps a less polite admonition to an obviously failed set of U.S. economic policies during the first half of the Reagan administration would be to remind ourselves of one definition of a fanatic—one who when proven wrong, redoubles his efforts.

Since the last year of the Carter administration, monetary policy in the United States has dedicated itself to the proposition that price stability, eventually low interest rates, and economic growth can best be achieved if the money supply is constrained to a long-term growth rate of roughly between 3.5 and 5.5 percent per year. There are two problems with this. The first is that economists can rarely agree on what is meant by money. If they can, then the problem is which form of money, M-1, M-2, M-3, or some combination.[19] The second problem is that countries like Japan and West Germany seem to hold that the goals of price stability, low inflation, high rates of economic growth, and low unemployment levels can only be achieved if monetary policy is seen as being in tandem at all times with fiscal and manpower policies.

The German consensus that has spanned all economic sectors from the private bankers to the trade unions is reinforced by the formal and informal arrangements that characterize the German system. Although the edges of this agreement were increasingly tattered as the 1980–82 recession went on, the consensus is still there, and at the center of it stands the Deutsche Bundesbank. Since its creation in 1957, the bank has carved out a reputation for intelligent planning and forceful implementation that keep all other sectors of the economy reacting to its moves. That is exactly the way the Bundesbank wishes it to be.

The Central Bank's policy decisions are, by and large, taken with respect to the overall economic conditions of the country, and not with overriding attention to any particular policy priority, or special interest, or to please any particular academic sect. Furthermore, the bank has been aware that its success depends upon the cooperation and understanding of all sectors of the economy. For these reasons, the bank has been in constant touch with all major interests in the country, including both private and public sector representatives.

The West German economy dealt successfully with a series of shocks through the first half of 1980 that left most Western European countries in some economic trouble. Germany's monetary policy, administered by the independent Central Bank, and the capacity for industrial adjustment of the German private sector have been key elements of this success. In both areas, the overriding concern of all participants, public and private, has been the same: economic stability.

Economic stability does not mean simply low inflation rates, although they are an important element of any stabilization program. The range of concerns that motivate German economic planning are set forth in the 1967 Act to Promote Economic Stability and Growth. They include stable prices, appropriate growth, high employment, and balanced trade. There is general agreement that all of the policies are important, and that the successful implementation of any one of them requires stability in the other areas.[20]

But what is of perhaps even more interest is that the Bundesbank, though obviously an economic institution, makes many of its decisions only when "the political, psychological and historical aspects of Germany's national life" are seen as being "crucial" to the success of its economy.[21] That this is known and commented upon in congressional studies seems to have no impact upon those who design U.S. policies. The following excerpts from a major congressional report makes this point, as well as impressing one with the effectiveness of the German approach.[22]

> From 1945 through 1948, unemployment continued to grow, while production and housing remained at minimal levels. The people, many of whom had suffered social and economic chaos twice in their lives, came to value security above all else. The consensus that grew out of this shared deprivation has continued to dominate Germany to this day.
>
> The first postwar leaders, Adenauer in politics and Erhard in economics, knew very well that security was uppermost in citizens' minds, and that any form of government or economic arrangement which failed to provide such security would not survive.
>
> The first order of business was to reconstruct the country's steadily deteriorating production and supply capabilities. By early 1948, Lucky Strikes cigarettes had replaced the disgraced Reichsmark as Germany's accepted currency. With the previous hyperinflation of 1922–23 burning in their minds, officials recognized that a stable and hard currency was necessary for further progress. With this in mind, on June 20, 1948, the American government unleashed Operation Bird Dog. The 10 billion newly minted Deutsche marks. It was announced that each German citizen could exchange 400 Reichsmarks for 40 Deutsche marks. Two months later, citizens were allowed to exchange 200 more Reichsmarks for 30 more Deutsche marks. That was it. The government estimates that 93 percent of all paper wealth was wiped out by this conversion.
>
> Its effect was immediate, astonishing, and positive. As Henry Wallich has noted: "It transformed the German scene from one day to the next. On June 21, 1948, goods reappeared in the stores, money resumed

its normal functions, and the black and gray markets reverted to a minor role."

"But the longer term performance was even more impressive than the immediate impact. In the 22 months after introduction of the Deutsche mark, industrial production rose by 83 percent."

The overwhelming importance attributed to maintaining the strength of this currency can be seen in the government's fierce determination to keep the mark stable and prices down. The pride with which Germans came to view the Deutsche mark is illustrated by the festivities of June, 1968, to commemorate the 20th anniversary of its introduction. The other side of this pride, however, are the dark fears of losing the security this currency brings to their lives. These fears are reflected in Heinrich Böll's words:

"The ownership of land, of real estate . . . has remained the sole stable factor; and a currency, a mark that has already reached 28 years (after two other marks had melted away within 25 years), has likewise become a stable factor, and anyone interfering with either of these factors has little chance of obtaining votes."

The obsession with security that dominates economic discussions is evident in the campaigns between the conservative Christian Democrats and the more progressive Social Democrats. The differences in the few major economic issues separating the two parties begin to melt away when the talk turns to details of economic programs for the country. The two parties often find themselves in the position of a Christian Democratic gubernatorial candidate who had to admit that he "didn't know what his party would do differently for the economy if it were elected."

It was the Christian Democrat Ludwig Erhard who epitomized the German approach to economic reconstruction, combining a free-market orientation with social welfare concerns to arrive at what he termed sozialemarktwirtschaft or the social market economy. As the most noted German voice in postwar economic planning, Erhard implemented a hybrid approach which sought to assure that all sectors of the economy benefit from any general economic improvements. This led to an extensive social welfare system, strict labor laws, a form of industrial democracy, and three decades of relative labor-management peace.

Crucial to the industrial recovery was the system of German banking, which had developed during the century before the war, and which the allied forces did their best to destroy after the war. The Occupation forces broke the big three banks into 30 successor banks, with each of the three having one new bank created in every state (Land) of Germany and in Berlin. The demands of history and reconstruction were too much, however, and these banks slowly recombined into the original Big Three so they could afford the massive loans necessary to finance postwar recovery. The existence of very large banks, with the attendant capital facilities and investment expertise, are a part of German history that could not be purged successfully by foreign intervention. The banks and business have traditionally worked hand-in-hand in ways that violate most received ideas about sound banking in Anglo-Saxon countries.

While there are reasons to wonder about the medium-term future of the German economy, there is no denying the successes of the post-war period and most particularly of the 1970s, when most other industrialized nations were suffering prolonged doldrums. The past is part of the explanation for the country's success, but institutional arrangements within the public and private sectors are also important to the economic "miracle" of modern Germany.

The Central Bank

The German Central Bank (Deutsche Bundesbank) was created in 1957 by merging the state (Länder) banks and the Bank Deutsche Länder. Its primary goal is to assure the continued high performance of the Deutsche mark. It is charged secondarily with assisting the federal government's economic policy, but in the case of conflict between the two goals, it must choose to assure the mark's stability. This ordering of goals is evident in the DBB reply to questions from the U.K. House of Commons Treasury and Civil Service Committee in June 1980:

"The accepted interpretation of the relevant sections of the Bundesbank Act, which has never been disputed by the government, is that in the event of a conflict with the objectives of the government's general economic policy the Bundesbank has to give priority to its primary task, namely, safeguarding monetary stability."[23]

The few outbreaks of conflict between the Central Bank and the federal authorities illustrate that this is a true state of affairs and not merely public relations.

One of the most interesting tests of DBB autonomy came in March 1970. At this time, the stability of the mark was threatened from many sides. First, there were foreign exchange pressures. The mark had been upvalued by over 9 percent only 6 months before in the wake of its emergence as the second major reserve currency in the world, after the United States (roughly one-eighth the size), the reserve currency status left the DBB faced with profound difficulties in its attempts to control the domestic money supply. Compounding this was the Bundesbank's pledge to support the dollar, if not within the old Bretton Woods parity range, then at least within moderate parameters. Finally, the DBB had to note a surging inflation rate that officials believed was in danger of destabilizing the entire economy. The coincidence of all these circumstances was thought sufficient to spawn the widespread inflationary psychology the Bank was determined to avoid.

Following the federal government's failure to invoke the strong inflationary program proposed by then—Economics Minister Schiller, the DBB raised the rates at which it loans to banks to their highest level since

World War II. It took this action against the advice of labor, management, banks, and the government itself. Coupled with this was a 30-percent increase in the reserves which banks had to hold on deposit with the Bundesbank against nonresident liabilities. This double-barreled action was intended both to slow credit expansion and to decrease the huge foreign capital inflow resulting from speculation about new upvaluations of the mark.

This did not end the DBB action to slow the economy. It continued to pressure the federal government for strong fiscal measures to dampen inflationary pressures in the economy. Political pressure from business and labor to avoid such "restraining policies" caused the newly elected SPD coalition to reject the bank's pressure. Finally, after 4 months of behind-the-scenes lobbying with no results, the Bundesbank took a step it had never taken. It announced an intent to raise the banks' reserve requirements by 10 to 20 percent. While the effects of such a squeeze would be severe, the DBB chose this announcement of intent as the most dramatic signal it could give of its seriousness to follow whatever course necessary to smother the rising inflation rate.

Only 4 years earlier, the Bank had generated a recession sufficient to oust the Chancellor when it was forced to use its rather broad-stroke instruments in the face of fiscal impotence by the government. Since that time, the 1967 Act to Promote Stability had been ratified, offering the government a broad range of countercyclical weapons that stood less chance of overcompensating for the liquidity glut than did the additional weapons at the disposal of the DBB. The Cabinet met shortly after this announcement to reconsider anti-inflationary measures it had shelved in March, but no action was taken.

After seeing that no governmental action was forthcoming on July 1 the Bundesbank raised the reserve requirements by 15 percent, hitting the middle of its threatened range. It believed no more increases in its lending rate were possible, since higher rates would attract more speculative capital from abroad, thus compounding the liquidity glut. The continued pressure of the Bank and its clear determination to blunt the economic upsurge finally outweighed private sector pressures, and the Parliament ratified a government plan to increase personal and corporate taxes and to suspend capital depreciation provisions. On the same day that this measure passed the upper house of Parliament, the DBB reduced the rate at which it lent to banks to guard against more speculative capital inflows.

It is exactly the DBB's willingness to press its case against strong political opinion, along with the undeniable intelligence it has brought to its goal of monetary stability, that makes the Bank a major force in determining the course of the German economy. The Bank is fully aware that public perception of its determination, and a thorough understanding of its instruments and goals, are crucial to its task. It does not operate in a vacuum guided only by neo-Keynesian or monetarist theory but recognizes the importance of presentation, persistence and consensus for the success of its policies."[24]

The lesson? Monetary policies *must* be geared to the real world, not an academician's perception of what the world would, and should, look like.

Fiscal Policy

Fiscal policy in West Germany is, as in the United States, utilized to achieve the multiple goals of maintaining a growth economy, obtaining sufficient tax revenues for expenditures resulting from government policies, providing impetus for innovation of new products and technologies to deal with inflationary and deflationary forces, and generally relating to national objectives. In doing this, there is a constant concern with a budget that subsequently is in sufficient balance so that government does not become an engine of either inflation or deflation. In Germany, the concern over inflation at times almost borders on morbid fear. This is understandable, as West Germany is almost alone as a major industrial state which has really experienced hyperinflation. The post–World War I and II experiences transmit intergenerational shock waves. And yet, from what we have seen in their human investment programs, they seem to start from a different premise than we do. They not only "seem"; they do! Though the history of Germany has vagrant aberrations, such as the Nazis, it also has a pattern of consistency. On a commitment to human investment Germany is consistent, as it also is concerning community facilities. German towns, villages, and cities are replete with charming parks, bridges, walking areas, and "restored" medieval streets and houses. The German railway system, state owned, is an absolute joy to both experience and behold. Few champions of the free enterprise system seem to object to the efficiency, cleanliness, speed, and predictability of their rides on the German railway. The most often heard critical remark is, "Why can't we do this in the United States?" For anyone who has traveled by the Amtrak "People Cocktail Shaker" between Washington, D.C., and New York City, the comparison is a physically painful one.

Although Germans are by no means perfect, they do design fiscal policy from a rather different perspective than we in the United States. Generally, they start by taking very seriously what they say they mean to do. After they are really certain about the objective, they then tend to be willing to make the sacrifice, that is, to pay money, to achieve the end desired. We in the United States tend to be very lyrical about things like full employment, the right of everyone to have a skill, or to be able to read and write at the sixth- or seventh-grade level. But when it comes to putting up the tax money, we have second thoughts.

The Germans, or for that matter most Europeans and the Japanese, simply cannot understand how the United States can have so high a level of functional illiteracy. Often-announced "Right to Read" programs seldom get off the ground because of inadequate funds provided by Congress or local communities. Functional illiterates in Germany and Japan make up no more than 1 to 3 percent of the population. Estimates for the United States vary from 20 to 30 percent. For some groups in the United States it is much higher. More will be said about this problem at a later point.

Germany's fiscal policy is more geared to its national and social objectives than is that in the United States. No clearer or simple statement reflecting the German position exists than that made by Chancellor Schmidt. In a *New York Times* article, written by John Vinocur, Vinocur said:

> I heard Schmidt talk in Ludwigshafen and Ludwigsburg during the campaign, and I heard him say something I thought honorable and fine. The Germans had to do something about integrating their 4.65 million foreign workers, especially the Turks, he said. Their welfare in a country that had a history of intolerance was a moral priority.
>
> Dead air in the audience. Nothing. He looked around. "On the other hand," Schmidt said, "Four million is enough." Cheers.[25]

In the midst of recent debates about providing free education for the children of migrant Mexican workers, or even for our own itinerant workers, who are citizens, the willingness of Germans to pay taxes for education, training, counseling, and housing for foreigners is a real shocker. Just think of the budgetary implications for a country of 60 million. Schmidt's statement is interesting for another, not quite unrelated reason. Very often in lectures I have given on the subject of manpower policies in Germany, people (often economists, business leaders, and politicians) will stridently tell me that German unemployment rates are low because they export their guest workers as soon as jobs become scarce. Apparently, they know something about the German economy Chancellor Schmidt does not know.

The guest worker population increased from 80,000 in 1955 to more than 2 million in 1981. In some years, the government urged some workers to return to their countries as output declined. But the percentage that left was small. In 1973, 100,000 returned out of 2.5 million in Germany. Because of severe criticism of this policy, after five years of working in Germany, the guest worker now is entitled to an unlimited residence permit. Guest workers make up between 8 and 10 percent of the German labor force. The larger number of foreigners referred to by Schmidt include the family members.

As can be seen from Table 1.10, government expenditures are generally balanced by tax revenues. Deficits occur, but not as frequently as in the United States. But this is less because of cutting the suit to the availability of the cloth than the willingness to raise revenues to pay for the desired goals.

Not only is monetary policy well articulated with fiscal policy, but fiscal policy is seen as an instrument that must be flexible. There is no sense of ideological commitment, other than the ideology that a policy must be related to reality and workable. The extent of manipulation authorities use to control the economy in order to achieve the goals of price stability, low unemployment and inflation, and economic growth can be seen by the government activities during the oil crisis in 1973. This crisis came at a particularly bad time for West Germany because the government and the Bundesbank officials were in the latter stages of attempting to cut back on overheating the economy and controlling capital inflows that had plagued the economy during 1968–73. The government had revalued the Deutsche mark upward by a trade-weighted average of 9.4 percent in 1973, while the Bundesbank continued to raise interest rates and bank reserve requirements. But when the oil crisis called for a new set of fiscal measures, the result was nine budget freezes or releases, three bond floats, fourteen tax changes, three discount rate raises, and six reserve borrowing authorization moves. Most of these changes were small and were coupled with announcements of expiration dates. The object was to send signals without unduly jarring the underlying fiscal and monetary structures.

Once again, the Joint Economic Committee Report is quoted at length:

> By mid-1973, the combined efforts of monetary and fiscal braking had managed to stall the domestic economy. Foreign demand for German products, however, continued unabated with the largest increase in trade surpluses of the postwar period being registered during the year. It was this surge of export demand that laid the groundwork for the Federal Republic's recovery after the shock.
>
> By late December, the authorities were presented with a major dilemma. On the one hand, they were not sure that the inflationary pressure had been squeezed out of the economy. There were signs that the wage-price spiral was still working through the system. Prices rose at an unacceptable rate in December, hitting the highest year-on-year inflation rate of the decade—8 percent. On top of this, wage negotiations had resulted in a larger-than-expected average increase for the year of 11 percent.

On the other hand, Germany had to face the oil shock and its expected effect on export demand. Domestic demand had slumped sharply in response to the government's midyear economic stabilization plan. Particularly hard hit were car sales, which dropped 46 percent in November. Unemployment in November, although only 1.5 percent of the work force, was nearly double that of July, and short-time workers were up 600 percent over 1972.

This was a perfect test of the German commitment to price stability. If the authorities were predominantly committed to price stability, they could be expected to maintain restrictive policies at the expense of further souring the economy.

In the event, the authorities followed a dual strategy, trying to knock the wind out of both inflation and recession at the same time.

On the 19th of December, the federal government relaxed nearly all of the fiscal measures it had put into effect during the February and May tightenings. Particularly important were reintroduction of depreciation tax credits, and the abolition of investment taxes. Meanwhile, the Bundesbank announced that it would continue to pursue its restrictive monetary policies in full force.

The authorities were able to turn around in December on economic policies created less than 6 months before, and to do this without losing credibility. By leaving the Central Bank to guard monetary expansion, the federal government was able to smooth out the recessionary impacts of the 1973 oil shocks.

The effect of this dual-fronted policy was to create a shallow 2-year trough with recovery picking up a great deal of steam in the first quarter of 1976. Only in 1975 was there negative growth in real GNP (-1.8 percent), and peak unemployment was 4.7 percent with just over 1 million workers unemployed.

The Bundesbank was clear that the oil cost push would not be translated directly into prices, and that a profits squeeze would have to be tolerated by business. There was a short-lived attempt to moderate wage demands in 1974, but it failed and settlements averaged 13.7 percent. This made DBB's success at convincing business not to pass on the full amount of its increased costs the more remarkable. While the need to maintain market shares in a slumping world economy bears some responsibility for business' price moderation, Bundesbank pressure was still an important factor in the final analysis. As a result, 1974 was an extremely rough year for profits. While gross wage and salary income rose 10 percent for the year, profit and entrepreneurial income rose only one-tenth of 1 percent. The increase in income to the two sectors from 1972–75 is shown in Table [3.1].

One startling result of this price restraint was that the Federal Republic's trade surplus spurted ahead to record levels in 1974, at a time when most other countries were moving toward large deficits.

Table [3.1].   Wages and Profits Change in Percent, Year-to-Year

Wages and Profits	1972	1973	1974	1975
Gross wage and salary income	9.9	13.0	10.0	4.1
Gross property and entrepreneurial income	7.6	7.5	.1	5.4

Source: OECD.

The recovery from 1974 picked up steam in a way that displays the ability of various sectors to work together with some degree of trust. Largely because of the trust between labor and capital in Germany, government and business were able to present a convincing case to workers that the 13 percent wage increases in 1974 could not be repeated. Since neither the Central Bank nor the world export market would allow businessmen to pass through increased labor costs, many medium-sized companies would have tottered toward bankruptcy if the 1975 round of wage negotiations had not resulted in more moderate wage hikes. When the case was presented to labor, there was a significant drop in wage demands, as the 1975 round of bargaining ended in agreements that just about kept pace with the 7-percent inflation rate.

Labor's cooperation was not entirely altruistic. The facts of the economy convinced workers that the businesses were not hiding behind a facade of phony financial trouble. Firms could not afford to invest in capital if the 1974 experience were repeated and as they folded, jobs would be lost. Furthermore, in the crucial export markets producers had swallowed a 9-percent increase in the value of the Deutsche Mark over the 1972–73 rate. It was clear that they could not pass through much in the way of labor cost increases if their market share was to remain healthy. Finally, the labor market itself was barely avoiding a collapse. While unemployment was around 5 percent, short-time workers had jumped from an average of 44,000 during 1973 to 900,000 in February of 1975. Unless wage demands were lowered, many companies would be forced to follow Volkswagen's example when it agreed to a 13-percent pay raise and immediately put 33 percent of the work force on short time.

The result of cooperation and moderation on nearly all fronts by the various actors in Germany's economy was that, after a mild 2-year slump, there was a rise in real GNP of 5.3 percent for 1976, and a rise in real fixed capital formation of 4.7 percent, after 2 years of decreases. The recession was moderate by most standards and the recovery was complete, continuing to pick up steam through 1978 and 1979.[26]

The Current Situation

During the last couple of years, the high level of performance of the German economy has lagged. Unemployment in mid-1982 was 7.5

percent, very high by German standards. In July 1982, the federal government forecast an $11.43 billion deficit in 1983, based on an inflation-
adjusted 3 percent growth in total output of goods and services. That
projection was estimated, however, on an expected output increase of 1.5
percent in 1982. On the plus side, during the first five months of 1982,
exports totaled $7.92 billion, up from $1.85 billion a year earlier. This nar-
rowed the deficit in current account to $240.7 million, well down from the
previous year's level of $4.61 billion.[27] All of this is to say that Germany is
no exception to the world of problems.

Some of these problems flow out of those confronting the United
States. The capital outflow from Germany to the United States is a result
of the high interest rates prevailing in the United States. A part of the trade
deficit grows out of the major change in the relationship of the Deutsche
mark to the dollar. But the question at hand is not if the German economy
can have problems. Of course it can. No economy is problem-proof. The
question we are dealing with is in what way is the German society, and its
economy, structured so it can deal with its problems more effectively than
the United States can?

The answer is that since World War II, West Germany has evolved a
set of relationships that has as its cultural cement the concept of a social
partnership. Adversarial relationships are minimized. Government, business, and labor look to each other as necessary team members, all of
whom must play a continuous, though changing, role in achieving the nation's economic and social goals.

During the summer of 1982, in the series of interviews I conducted
with senior officials in the West German government, labor leaders, and
business executives, the importance of this cooperative relationship to
gains in productivity, economic growth, and price stability was
highlighted. In a discussion with an official in the Ministry of Research
and Technology as we talked about research and development programs, I
was struck with a feeling of a lack of clarity about how the government
relates to industry. A question I finally felt compelled to ask was, "How is
science policy formulated; what role does government play?" The answer
was that policy grows out of in-depth, informal discussions among industry, professional consultants, government officials, and at times representatives of the unions. For example, the federal government's programs
supporting research in the field of robotics grew out of such discussions.
"Only in this way," the official said, "could we understand what industry
was doing, where they needed help in research areas, or help in funding
tests. Only in this way could we get some sense of the problems which
would grow out of an increasing use of robots for workers." One result
was that the unions became involved in social science and economic research as they tried to determine likely retraining needs growing out of

job displacement resulting from increasing use of robots. Given an "inside seat" on the likely pace of robotic development, industry, labor, and government could deal with what the Germans call "rationalization." This is the German phrase for nearly all types of production changes designed to increase efficiency or reduce labor costs.

As the official continued to talk, I still could not envision the role government played. He appeared to be saying that government is a catalyzer not a leader. It was only later, in discussions with one of the most senior officials in the Ministry of Economics that the picture became truly clear to me. He contended that the perceived role of government, especially during a crisis situation, is not to lead but to bring the key players together to determine jointly the role to be played by each. When I asked him what he meant by the word "determine," he quickly amplified this to mean "define more clearly what each would choose to do and what they all felt the implications for the economy might be." He volunteered an interesting observation. In his experience, he liked to get in contact with those below the highest level of union leadership. The reason, he stated, was that leaders are often less flexible than their membership.

In a discussion with a labor leader, I asked about what most affected West Germany in the drive to emphasize productivity. His answer: "The American aid program after World War II." It was the U.S. aid programs that forced each country receiving aid after the war to establish productivity centers and involve workers in management decision making. It was, he contended, the U.S. trade union people who insisted on a tripartite (labor, government, and industry) operation of the productivity centers in Europe. The countries followed this advice in setting up the productivity centers because, unless they did, there would be no counterpart funds available from the United States. So, he said, the crisis of recovery and the U.S. dollars were the source of real motivation. The alternative, he reminded me, was the general concern throughout Germany of a real possibility of violence and revolution. U.S. dollars and U.S. occupation troops were seen as the only way to achieve a secure rebuilding of the economy. In brief, a crisis drove Germany to what resulted in the social partnership. But, he was quick to remind me, well before World War II, the spirit of social concern and investment in people existed. It existed in the long history of the social security programs initiated, not by Karl Marx, but by Chancellor Bismarck. "Bismarck pulled communism's teeth by taking from the dunghill of Marx the few diamonds that existed," he said.

The German government has targeted growth industries in such a way that small and medium-sized companies have responded in large numbers to expand output and innovate rapidly. For example, the Ministry of Research and Technology designed a three-year program to accelerate the application of new technology in the microelectronics industry. In order to stimulate productivity and growth in this critical area, as of January 1, 1982, 40 percent of all development costs are subsidized if the output is based on new, hitherto unutilized processes or technologies. Three hundred million Deutsche marks were appropriated each year, over a three-year period. By June 1, 1982, this subsidy fund was oversubscribed. Less than 10 percent went to large companies. Of the remaining companies, 20 percent were established during the last four years, most of them in the computer-assisted design and computer-assisted manufacturing areas. In explaining how this happened, the official describing the process stated that Germany still has not developed the efficiency of Japan's Ministry of International Trade and Industry in being able to "bring together all the pieces for a long-term, overall plan."

When I discussed the idea of an "overall plan" with a senior official of an employers' association, his reaction was to differentiate the social partnership approach from that of central planning. He made the point that the social partnership philosophy in Germany results because of a sense of need to coordinate and plan together in such a way as to maintain independence but arrive at achievable goals, goals of significance to the partners as well as the nation. Only a healthy society and a healthy economy, pursued by the social partners, could keep the partners healthy. He agreed that the crisis of the late 1940s and early 1950s was a major force in developing an effective social partnership. But he referred to that crisis as a crisis of hope as differentiated from what he feels is now emerging as a different sort of spirit in Germany. Now, he said, the younger generation of Germans seems to be in a crisis of fear of the future. Other Germans with whom I met also seemed to sense a different perspective by the younger people. Perhaps this will change the approach that has brought Germany from the crippled economy of 1946 to being one of the most productive and stable economies in the world since the late 1950s.

As of the middle of 1982, West Germany too is a part of a worldwide recession. But its unemployment level is a third lower than that of the United States, and its economic and productivity growth rates are higher. Thus far, the social partnership has produced an economy that weathers recessions better than that of the United States, recovers more quickly, and has been able to maintain overall higher levels of performance during the intervals between economic downturns. Its model, most Germans seem to agree, is neither the classic form of socialism nor unfettered, laissez-faire private enterprise.

A final observation may be of interest. One German labor leader commented, "The English-speaking countries do not believe in their governments. On the continent of Europe, they tend to believe in their governments, but do not think they are perfect. Thus, we can work together as partners." In thinking about this, as one looks at Great Britain, the United States, Canada, and Australia, the remark certainly seems to apply. With infrequent exceptions, these countries all share the same economic heritage, the philosophy of an economic doctrine that, in 1776, saw government and the private sector as adversaries—each, by natural law, in conflict with the other. On the European continent, this has not been so. Neither has it been so in Japan, to which we now turn.

Notes

1. Herbert Hoover, cited in Richard Mayne, *The Recovery of Europe* (New York: Harper & Row, 1970), p. 98.
2. Ibid., p. 99.
3. Ibid., p. 30.
4. Ibid., p. 32.
5. Ibid.
6. Ibid., p. 34.
7. H. E. Striner, *Continuing Education as a National Capital Investment* (Kalamazoo, Mich.: W. E. Upjohn Institute for Employment Research, 1971), p. 42.
8. *Federal Employment Institution* (Nuremberg, West Germany, 1971–72), p. 10.
9. *Labor News and Social Policy* (Washington, D.C.: Embassy of the Federal Republic of Germany, February 1978), pp. 1–2.
10. Ibid., p. 9.
11. Ibid., p. 2.
12. *Co-determination in the Federal Republic of Germany,* Federal Minister of Labor and Social Affairs. English Translation, International Labour Organization, Geneva, 1976, p. 12.
13. Ibid., pp. 9–11.
14. Ibid., p. 99.
15. Eric Jacobs, Stanley Orwell, Peter Paterson, and Friedrich Weltz, *The Approach to Industrial Change in Britain and Germany,* The Anglo-German Foundation for the Study of Industrial Society (Guildford, London, and Worcester: Billing & Sons, 1978).
16. Ibid., p. 85.
17. Ibid., pp. 115–16.
18. *Washington Post,* August 9, 1982, p. A13.
19. M-1 is the sum of currency, demand deposits, travelers checks, and other checkable deposits. M-2 is M-1 plus savings, Eurodollars, repurchase agreements, and so on. M-3 is M-2 plus, for example, large time deposits.
20. *Monetary Policy, Selective Credit Policy, and Industrial Policy in France, Britain, West Germany, and Sweden,* Staff Study, Joint Economic Committee of the Congress of the United States, June 26, 1981, p. 92.

21. Ibid., p. 93.

22. Ibid., pp. 95–102.

23. Memorandum by the Deutsche Bundesbank, Memoranda on Monetary Policy, Treasury and Civil Service Committee, House of Commons, Session 1979–80, vol. 2, p. 11.

24. Ibid., pp. 95, 96, 97, 100, 101, 102.

25. *New York Times Magazine*, August 8, 1982, p. 25.

26. Joint Economic Committee, *Monetary Policy*, pp. 131–33.

27. *Wall Street Journal*, July 7, 1982, p. 25.

Japan—
The Ever-Rising Sun?
4

The Origin of the Miracle

By now, hundreds of books and articles have been written about the miraculous Japanese worker and manager. This chapter will have little to say about either. My object is to describe how government and business in Japan have worked together to achieve mutual goals and by so doing have gained the highest levels of productivity and lowest levels of unemployment of any major nation.

The matter of culture is of major significance. The sense of harmony that exists between manager and worker also exists between the businessman and government official. But this cultural attribute is not too dissimilar from the concept of social partnership in West Germany. Without getting into the question of what are or are not uniquely Japanese cultural assets, the visitor in Japan is often reminded that most of what has been accomplished in the matter of business organization and industrial engineering is based upon Western, mostly American, thinking. The Japanese, like the West Germans, since World War II have evolved a new form of capitalism that does indeed work. Japan—about the size of Montana, with half the population of the United States, no coal, no petroleum, no iron ore, no copper, no lead, no timber, very little arable land, and no history of industrialization until the end of the nineteenth century—is now one of the major industrial nations in the world.

As one might expect, there are ample explanations of how this came about, especially since World War II. Most of these explanations are wrong. Some do not even refer to critical areas. By the time the reader gets to the end of this chapter, it will be hard to believe that a scholarly book, published by a great research institute, with the title *How Japan's Economy Grew So Fast,*[1] does not even list the Ministry of International Trade and

Table 4.1.   Exports of Goods as Percentage of Gross National Product

	1960	1970	1977	1978	1980
Belgium	33	45	47	44.6	53.3
Netherlands	36	37	41	38.2	44.0
Switzerland	22	24	28	27.6	29.2
Sweden	18	21	26	24.9	25.2
United Kingdom	15	16	24	23.2	22.0
Germany	16	19	23	22.2	23.4
Japan	9	9	12	10.0	12.5
United States	4	4	6	6.8	8.5

Source: OECD Trade Statistics, Series A and B, 1960, 1970, 1977; OECD Observer, 1978 and 1980.

Industry in the index; nor does it refer to government as a major factor. The outstanding performance of Japan's industry cannot be understood without a comprehension of its relationship to the government agencies and their policies that are designed to work with industry. At the other end of the spectrum are those who assume that a "Japan Incorporated" exists, a Japan where every industrial whim or desire by industry results in an immediate, favorable response from government. As will be shown, this has been far from true.

Other myths about Japan abound. One of the most widely accepted ones is that Japan's exports account for a major share of its economy. Much has been made of the alleged fact that because Japan is a major exporter, Japan's industrial base depends upon its overseas markets. Table 4.1 reflects a far different picture.

Japan has a population of more than 100 million, a large domestic market. The history of Japanese industry has been that of basing its early growth of markets on home consumption, not exports. The strategy has been to have long production runs to get unit costs down by virtue of very substantial domestic markets. Only at this point do export markets assume a significant role in overall production. And the long-run goals of an increasing market share is seen as being more significant than the short-run goal of a profit. Profits follow market share, not the reverse.

To understand what has brought Japan to its position of preeminence as a great industrial nation is to understand not only what is but what is not. All Japanese business is not successful nor competitive. Indeed, U.S. firms like Caterpillar, Coca-Cola, Dow, DuPont, Eastman Kodak, IBM, McDonalds, Proctor & Gamble, and Texas Instruments, as well as whole industries such as synthetic fibers, have more than met Japanese competition in the United States. In many of these cases, they have competed well against their Japanese competitors in Japanese markets. Because of the sudden rise of Japanese competition in industrial areas, always considered to be the special preserve of the United States—steel, autos, home appliances, and television sets—we have looked for simple answers, and ones that somehow implied the presence of unfair tactics or strategies, such as subsidies, low wage rates, using our technology, and of course no unions—all of which are obviously "un-American." But very few U.S. firms, or whole industries, receiving U.S. government subsidies would choose to give up their subsidies in exchange for a similar sacrifice by Japanese firms. And the U.S. auto industry, which used to boast in the 1950s and 1960s that it had the highest paid workers in the world, but because of high productivity could compete with any foreign auto producer, seems to have forgotten that boast in 1983. Now it complains of low-paid Japanese auto workers. But that really is not the problem, as we shall see. What are we confronted with in the case of Japan?

We are confronted with a nation that has an overwhelming commitment to an economic ideology only as long as it works! We are confronted with a nation that views the key actors in its economy, industry, workers, and government, as a team. Each of these actors is seen as having a major role in helping each other to develop an economy that has low unemployment, stable prices, and high productivity. Finally, we are confronted by a people who are tenacious in their dedication to sensing where the future lies and developing their policies and using their resources in order to achieve specific goals. In short, they are not committed to an ideology that does not produce for them; they are patient; they are nonadversarial; and, despite their smiles, they are deadly in their cooperative efforts to win the war of competing economies. They are also, usually, ready to sacrifice for these goals. These are the underpinnings of Japan's industrial policy.

Once again, to understand a problem in economics we have to spend a few moments with the history of the country. The industrial Japan that is competing with us today had its origins during the so-called Meiji era, named for the emperor who, in 1868, took Japan out of its feudal history. Well after the end of the American Civil War, Japan was still under the control of clans led by feudal lords. After a brief civil war, the shogun surrendered power to the emperor who, however, did not have clear sailing until after the Satsuma Rebellion in 1877. It was only in 1889 that the imperial government, led by reform groups favoring Westernization, was able to have a constitution adopted that provided the political base for a modern Japan. This constitution was adopted 101 years after that of the United States.

Of much more significance is the fact that the Meiji Restoration and industrialization in the late 1800s and early 1900s took place without benefit of the great debates concerning laissez-faire, government regulation, and Adam Smith's central thesis of the adversarial role critical to a non-mercantilist economy. In addition, the overwhelming Western concern with Marx and communism was of little interest in Meiji Japan. Japan moved into the modern era without an overriding concern for those philosophical issues that the West, especially Great Britain and the United States, thought were of central importance for modern, industrial capitalism. In Japan, there was no concern for labeling itself as laissez-faire or socialist. There was also no concept of a delineation of the private sector from the public sector. There was only one concern—doing what was necessary to become a modern, industrial nation. This newly emergent Japan developed an industrial, capitalist base capable of militarily defeating the Russian Empire in 1905, only 16 years after its beginnings as a constitutional nation. And it did this with a political and economic system that defies easy application of the labels we in the West so like to apply to everything.

This is not to say, however, that there have not in the past existed differing Japanese philosophies over the proper roles or relationships between business and government. Before World War II, the prevailing philosophy was that typified by Yataro Iwasaki, the founder of Mitsubishi. His was a view that very closely coincided with what we would regard as rugged individualism, but within the confines or perspective of the harmony of the larger family of Japanese institutions. It was only after the economic tragedy of World War II and the monumental task of recovery facing Japan that a different attitude prevailed. It was the philosophy that had long been urged by Eiichi Shibusawa, an entrepreneur and business philosopher of the nineteenth century, that business leaders take responsibility for larger social objectives and meld private goals to the larger national interest.

One of the best insights into this system that brings together the private and public sectors to achieve a highly effective use of its resources to meet its objectives can be found in a recent discussion conducted under a very unlikely aegis. In 1980, the U.S. General Accounting Office convened a one-day round table discussion comparing Japanese and U.S. management approaches to quality control and productivity.[2] At this discussion, a question was posed about how the Japanese government and industry work together. How do they plan and set goals together? The chairman inquired:

> I would like to ask Dr. Tsurumi, who is very familiar with the Japanese system, to describe for us his impression of how the indicative economic planning process works, and then we want dialogue as to what portions of that system, that process, may be implantable within our U.S. system, if any Dr. Tsurumi?

Dr. Tsurumi: Now, how does the government indicative economic system fit this picture? The indicative economic system clearly emerged after World War II when the government was put into the subtle role, I would say, of allocating the scarce resources, technology, capital, among diverse private firms for industrial activities.

At the outset, it was just a trial and error method, and out of that something had emerged. When you talk about the indicative economic planning system of corporate growth, you're discussing some kind of corporate visions which the economic planners of the government or business or labor share. The only vision they share is that somehow the world is in a state of flux. This is nothing but common sense observation of reality. Therefore, they have to live in the world of uncertainty. But they want growth, and growth meant a betterment of living standards.

Then, what government can do is to provide some kind of framework for the industrial allocations of the crucial resources, in particular scarce resources, like technology. Technology was clearly identified from the outset as an independent policy variable by the Japanese government. From the very outset, technology as much as capital or financial investment, has been recognized as an independent and necessary policy variable by the government and by private industry.

The government role is more like giving the first draft of their future vision of the world, like the economic situation 20 years from now. And right after the World War, it was easy for Japan to come up with that kind of vision because the only thing Japan needed to do was to look at the United States or the industry of leading nations and study their industrial structure and all the other things and then say, well, what did it take for them to do all these things? Where are we right now and what will it take for us to move from here to there? And we know that, unlike the United States, Japan doesn't have ample resources to spare. So from the outset, for both government and businesses, the planning concept as we teach it in business school was how to manage growth under scarcity and shortage. The growth target was very easily drawn at the outset by looking at the United States structure.

What government did was to propagate this general notion about the desired target for Japan. To be very efficiently drawn by the government in close consultation with industry and labor, each industry must reconcile different views. Otherwise, diversity of views emerge, and diversity may bring about all kinds of conflicts of interests and jockeying for their own interests. In terms of drawing up a national vision as to, say, the makeup of the economic situation or the desired industrial structure of Japan say 20 years from now or ten years from now, which will again be adjusted as they go on, both government and industry cooperated and tried to come up with some kind of shared understanding of what it's like to be living in the years ahead and what it takes to get there.

The indicative planning was, as the Callahan paper pointed out, nothing but an indicative system.

The word "indicative" is as opposed to a planned "coercive" measure. The government was to indicate what was the desired goal and what were the necessary technologies for private industries to acquire in order to attain their particular goals. The government, then, used foreign exchange allocation and capital allocation processes to simply favor the successful firms which came out of the survival of the fittest to prove that they can produce efficiently and competitively.

Similar Approaches by Other Countries

Now, the indicative economic system, as we understand it, is not unique to Japan. France implemented, rather successfully in my opinion, the indicative economic planning after World War II because that country also faced the problem of managing growth under scarcity and catching up with Germany and the United States.

But the contrast between Japan and France might be interesting. I don't think this is a superficial contrast. In order to implement the goals of the indicative economic system in France, I don't think the government was able to count on informal but effective cooperation from private sectors. Accordingly, in order to implement the targeted goals, they needed to own the three major commercial banks and use capital rationing processes so that the funds would be channelled into the targeted industries. Also, they came to own some key parts of manufacturing industries, the automobile industry in particular, as well as others.

Why Indicative Planning Works in Japan

The indicative economic planning system was not unique to Japan, but the way they went about implementing it might be somewhat characteristic of Japan. This was because there existed in the main, the cooperative mode of interaction between business and government, between especially business elites and government elites. They went to the same school and all kinds of things and they've been doing things together for about half a century now, and after World War II they wanted to do things together.

Therefore, once some kind of shared goal emerged as to the future makeup of the Japanese industrial structure, it was easier for the government to communicate the key targeted industry to the private industries and leave mainly the rest of the implementation to private industry.

The way the government uses the industrial policy is through administered competition. All governments try to administer market competition, but what it does in Japan is to promote the philosophy of "survival of the fittest." You're trying to develop new industries. You don't know which companies are going to succeed. You cannot simply select from the outset the winner and simply get the whole thing done. All you can do is simply call for the candidate entrants into that industry and see which ones will succeed. At the same time, you cannot let too many guys into the play from the outset because the domestic market will be too small to permit any economy of scale.

The government tried to regulate the first of three entrants or four entrants as the domestic market size increased, rather than simply letting the initial entrants cover the increase in growth; let's try to bring in a few more competitors and go through a whole shakedown process. Eventually, they tried to reward the survival of the fittest, and meanwhile, always mindful of allocating the resources out of the declining industry into the future growth potential.

This may be changing in Japan today, but still, I believe that's the Japanese government industrial policy. And this is shared by private industry and is characterized by the survival of the fittest. It's not a conglomerate or a conspiratorial sort of group cooperation.

Mr. Fritts: There are exceptions, in other words. Honda, for example, was an exception to indicative planning because they were not one of the preferred or early winners in the game.

Dr. Tsurumi: That's right. It's not a rigid system. It leaves enough leeway for entrepreneurial things. And obviously, the key industry like steel got much more leeway than others, and the government directed the protection of, say, consumer electronics and others. There's enough industry difference.

But the only point I wanted to make here about the indicative economic system is that the government's role has emerged as the kind of conveyor of the future vision of the industry, so that they can signal business opportunities for any private firms to exploit. As a result, the government has emerged as the allocator, the key allocator, of the scarce resources to targeted industries and let the private industries sort of bid for them. Again, I come back to the point of technology, and especially production process technology. When you talk about technology, let's start classifying it. I classify it into the product feature-oriented technology and the production process technology—how to make this particular product once you design it. Then, all these technologies are considered as an independent policy variable. Private firms have internally absorbed that concept and have built their export growth strategy as well on the notion that the quality is the key factor of their success in sales and growth, and sales only follow the reliability of product.

While referring to this conference, one additional insight from Tsurumi is of interest concerning quality in Japanese products. Earlier, in Chapter 2, reference was made to the post–World War II decision to adopt high quality as a centerpiece of Japan's new industrial strategy. On this point, Tsurumi said:

Product Quality as Integral Part of Business Strategy

Personally, I have traced the evolution of product quality as an integral part of the Japanese business strategy. This means that you do not go for pricing or cheap products, et cetera, but certainly for product quality as the distinct competitive strength of firms. Therefore, the firms have endeavored to produce the managerial systems which do not create a physical notion of productivity—how many units per hour, et cetera—as a tradeoff against the quality. If you can characterize the Japanese firms, they might be seen as an entity which treats the physical notion of absolute product quality—how many units you can produce—and the scale economy of large scale production as their overriding strategic weapons. Anybody can produce lots of things if they're allowed to produce shoddy things. By doing anything that everybody can do, you do not obtain any competitive edge.

Therefore, a competitive edge in the worldwide export of domestic products can only come from the system which can produce many products, and therefore milk the economy of scale or learning curve effects, and also improve the product quality at the same time.[3]

Tsurumi was describing the fundamental basis for Japan's industrial policy. This policy became a formal reality when, in 1925, the Ministry of International Trade and Industry (MITI) was created. But other agencies, such as the Ministry of Finance (MOF), are also a part of the rather tangled web of public and private relationships and policies that make up Japan's industrial policy.

What is important is that neither the highly touted successful Japanese management system nor the very effective government agencies, as we shall see, could be effective without the joining of industrial strategy with a national industrial policy. For example, if the average large firm manager in the United States were to attempt to guarantee workers lifelong employment or ignore the concerns of stockholders for decisions guaranteeing continued short-term profits for dividend purposes, this manager would be bucking major obstacles without U.S. government counterparts of MITI and MOF policies available to his firm. To achieve these objectives, a firm must have tax and credit policies to alleviate the problems of slack markets and economic downturns. Interest and credit policies must guarantee the availability of a lending source, with long-term objectives, for firms that are seen as essential to national objectives. These types of commitments are a part of Japan's industrial policy. The United States does not have an industrial policy.

Industrial Policy in Japan

Much of what we see as impressive Japanese industrial policy is fairly recent in its development. Although the basic Japanese philosophy, and culture, have been supportive of industry, and there has been a long tradition of harmonious rather than adversarial relations, national industrial policies were not readily accepted until after World War II.

Shortly after the creation of the early version of MITI in 1925, there was a severe financial panic and economic downturn in 1927. No real recovery took place before the military adventures and military fascism that began in 1931 with the invasion of Manchuria and war with China, in 1937–41, culminating in the war with the United States in 1941. It was only after World War II that an industrial policy was joined to a new form of Japanese management. This latter is also a surprise to most who think that the harmonious, participatory, quality-oriented approach by Japanese managers has existed over a long period of time. This is not so. At least it is not so in terms of large-scale existence in the system. For example, take lifelong employment. Though only about 30 to 35 percent of the labor force in Japan enjoys this sort of informal guarantee, when one looks at such major companies as Matsushita, Nippon Steel, Nissan, Sony, and Toyota, the proportions can range from 50 to 80 percent.

This practice had an early history when the large proportion of the industrial labor force in the early 1900s was coming from the rural farm economy and was dependent on the new employer for security and paternalistic help. Additionally, after World War I, lifelong employment became necessary for large companies to hold a valued, trained labor force. But aided by various aspects of industrial policy, as well as with the growth of major trading companies and large industrial enterprises, since World War II it has become of even greater significance.

The acceptance of, and the friendliness of the Meiji government toward this very sophisticated type of commercial organization was based on its preexistence in the preceding Edo, or Tokugawa, period (1603–1868). The great Mitsui Trading Company has its founding in an ancient enterprise, which was, at least implicitly, a joint-stock company, with control by the descendants of the original founder. The tradition of responsibility and education of leaders has its source in the traditions of the samurai. Some of the commitments of the Meiji period were instrumental in the rejuvenation of the industrial economy after World War II.

No commitment to a philosophy of broad-based education at the post–high school level ever paid off better than it did in the late 1940s. Had it not been for such a base of human resources, the purge for wartime activities of 2,210 officers from 632 zaibatsu corporations and 2,500 high-ranking officers and major stockholders of other large companies would have been far more crippling than proved to be the case.[4] Their replacements were not only well educated enough but, in the tradition of Japanese education on the job, were well versed in all functions of the firm and highly skilled entrepreneurs.

But, as earlier stated, we are not going to repeat here what is already so plentifully available in the literature, both popular and scholarly, about the Japanese management system. Our interests lie in ways in which the government and the business firm have come together in building a far more effective force for economic growth in a democratic society than has been the case in the United States. Nowhere is this better illustrated than in two of the key government agencies already referred to—MITI and MOF.

MITI—Its Role

At the outset it is important to understand that the policies and responsibilities of the Ministry of International Trade and Industry have not been applied across the board to all Japanese industries. Nor have they even applied to all of the major Japanese firms. The power of MITI exists only where it is viewed as being critical to the stated goals of economic growth or foreign trade. Its effectiveness in achieving its goals is high but not universal. In part, this grows out of the fact that it is not always correct in assessing the future, in part because the companies or industries it is trying to affect do not always agree with MITI, and finally because MITI has to compete, at times, with differing views and policies of other powerful government agencies. Having said this, however, MITI is very powerful and very effective, indeed.

The modern MITI was formed in 1949 by combining the Ministry of Commerce and Industry with the Board of Trade. All but a few of the major industries are within its scope of responsibility. Its charter includes broad policy formulation, regulation, ad hoc problem solving, and mediation of regional policy problems. Its legislative authority is stronger in some areas than in others. For certain industries its impact and authority are diluted by other more directly related ministries. Such is the case with telecommunications equipment, shipping, pharmaceuticals, and railroad equipment. But in almost all other areas, MITI is key to the formulation of industrial policy and responsible for:

- Providing guidelines for the effective development of industries, including production, distribution, and strategic marketing aspects.
- Guiding foreign trade and commercial relationships.
- Guaranteeing an adequate supply of raw materials and energy necessary for economic growth and industrial health.
- Managing specific areas of activity, such as patent policy, technology, small business, and cooperative ventures.

- Providing the vision of the long-run structure of Japanese industry.
- Developing the means for alleviating the perturbations and dislocations flowing out of industry transitions.

MITI deals with the overall "system," which includes capacity and price controls, tax policies, monopoly and antitrust, loans, import-export measures, purchasing and procurement, subsidies, raw material availability, and regional growth policies. Depending on the industry and problem, some or all of these factors will influence the nature of MITI's policy developments and involvements. MITI itself is subject to many constraints, in terms of both policy and funding. Its budgets are subject to Ministry of Finance scrutiny and reaction, and its activities impinging upon likely antitrust situations are limited to a degree by the Fair Trade Commission (FTC). Conflict between MITI and the FTC has been frequent, and sometimes bitter. MITI has usually had the upper hand, however.

In 1966, in a joint memorandum of understanding, MITI agreed to avoid undermining the Antimonopoly Law, obtaining in return from the FTC agreement that it would be more permissive toward mergers and forms of joint action within and between industries where national goals were at stake. MITI has also clashed with other government agencies and industries when their views were at odds. MITI had a major dispute with Japan Telephone and Telegraph over the use of telephone lines for time-sharing systems. In the case of the auto industry, MITI attempted to convince the industry in its early post–World War II development period that it should consolidate all firms around Toyota and Nissan to achieve greater economies of scale, R&D, and marketing. The MOF as well as the stronger medium-sized firms were in disagreement, and MITI's efforts were doomed to failure.

MITI, as well as other ministries and agencies, operate not only through regulations and laws but also operate to achieve objectives by the widespread use of "administrative guidance." This can be a euphemism for arm twisting or sanctions. Both the carrot and the stick are applied. For example, if MITI believes it essential for a joint venture in R&D to develop a new technology that is basic to an industry, it will meet informally to discuss this need and its recommendation. Should the industry representatives not be convinced, MITI may utilize a subsidy approach or withholding of capital, the "stock" counterpart, in order to achieve "cooperation." Usually, MITI requests are honored, not necessarily because of the carrot or stick, but also because MITI has achieved an excellent track record for long-term visions that have indeed benefited the individual companies as well as achieving the larger social objectives the companies feel to be in the interest of the nation. Such efforts were referred to by Douglas D. Danforth, vice-chairman and chief operating officer of Westinghouse Electric Corporation:

> For example, Japan's Ministry of International Trade and Industry (MITI), in cooperation with major Japanese companies, is helping to fund a 60-million-dollar Flexible Machining System complex.
>
> This system will use high energy lasers to manufacture diverse machined parts. This technology could revolutionize machining of small batches of diverse parts by combining the efficiencies and economies of a fully automated production line with the capability of manufacturing small-batch quantities as low as one.
>
> The U.S. has no comparable effort under way.
>
> MITI also is funding a 140-million-dollar effort to advance the manufacture of high-quality integrated circuits, and a 150-million-dollar program to develop a "super-computer" that will be 66 times faster than anything on the market today.
>
> By far, the most ambitious and exciting project under way in Japan, also with MITI sponsorship, is a "5th Generation Computer" for the post-1990 period.
>
> This computer, according to MITI, would have artificial intelligence and the ability to solve problems with no direct software instruction— much the way a human brain solves problems. It will incorporate voice and pattern recognition instead of using keyboard inputs.
>
> There are no other known computer R&D projects of such far-reaching nature anywhere else in the world.[5]

The fifth generation computer project referred to by Danforth is typical of a MITI "vision" of what should be done, with MITI as the catalyzer and partial funder, in order to gain a major advantage for Japanese industry. If it succeeds, it could well displace the United States as a leader in computer hardware and software by the end of the 1980s or early 1990s. Basically, MITI currently has allocated $300 million on a ten-year plan that has now been set in motion. Most of the MITI funding will be in the form of 100 percent grants to industry.

In addition to MITI acting as the catalyzer bringing the major Japanese computer manufacturers together in order to articulate their plans, reduce unwanted duplication, and provide grants tied to specific types of performance, MITI also has played a key role in allocation of scientists. This has been done on the task to develop the gallium-arsenide devices needed for computing with light pulses rather than electric signals. Under MITI guidance, some 30 government scientists and researchers plus two scientists or researchers from each of the nine Japanese firms involved started work in October 1981 in a laboratory loaned to the project by Fujitsu.[6]

An insight into the enormity of what is contemplated by MITI is well put by an *Economist* article in its Science and Technology section:

Computers that work directly with light will be indispensable once optical-fibre links start replacing conventional telephone cables wholesale. Japan's national telecommunications agency, NTT, recently demonstrated a special sort of optical device (continuous-wave-distributed feedback laser) that proves it is now possible to get most of the bits needed to make an optical microprocessor onto a single chip.

What the supercomputer and the optical computer are expected to do for Japan's semiconductor and computer hardware skills, its fifth-generation computer programme is likely to do for the country's software know-how. A fifth-generation machine of the 1990s will have the ability to "infer." Instead of merely manipulating data or words, it will process knowledge—writing its own programmes, deciding for itself which steps to take to solve a given problem, automatically retrieving information from a library, extracting rules on its own from sets of facts, and then applying its new findings to solve problems of which humans may be unaware.

Above all, a fifth-generation computer will be more tolerant of people, accepting their ill-defined problems (in the form of spoken language or free-hand sketches), and presenting the answers in a manner humans can easily understand.

Such a superfast knowledge processor will have to have an architecture (relating its hardware and software) vastly different from that of today's computers. Until now, computers have been based on a piece of hardware (a central processor) that can execute only so-called floating-point arithmetic (i.e., data expressed in two parts—say, the "a" and "b" of the number $a.2^b$). The machines can make only a few, very simple logical decisions—e.g., they can say "and" (i.e., add) and they can say "or" (i.e., make a choice). Each instruction can be applied only to one bit of data at a time in a step-by-step procedure.

Fifth-generation machines will be quite different. Their architecture will be arranged so that all the parts of the computer can work in parallel, allowing every scrap of data to be operated on by every instruction at the same time.

If Japan's computer scientists succeed, what will a knowledge processor do? For one thing, it will allow anybody to use a computer without any training. For another, it will provide really good machine translation of foreign languages. Fifth-generation technology will also provide vast data bases that can be interrogated (by telephone) from an armchair at home. Above all, it will spin off into industry to provide fully integrated design, development and manufacturing facilities—enabling products to move from concept to customer's shelf almost untouched by human hand.

And what if Japan's computer scientists should fail? MITI will not be overly disappointed. Behind Japan's plan is the hidden objective of trying to correct the country's natural propensity to concentrate more on making excellent hardware, while leaving the software side underdeveloped. If it costs $300m to make Japanese programmers as ingenious as American and European ones, MITI will consider the money well spent.

Although news of this major venture to capture the lead in computer technology had been discussed in magazines and newspapers in the United States, response by U.S. government officials was late in appearance. On October 28, 1982, in a major story in the business section of the *New York Times*, warning of Japan's "push" to surpass America's computer companies in the production of large, high-speed computers, this effort was seen as a major threat to national security industries. Kent K. Curtis, head of the computer science section of the National Science Foundation's division of mathematical and computer sciences, quite properly saw that "in the absence of a coordinated Government effort, the Japanese will repeat in computer systems, what they did in semiconductors." He was referring to the success of Japan's electronics industry in winning more than half of the computer memory chip market, which is expected to grow to more than $1 billion in annual sales in a few years.

The concern over Japanese inroads in supercomputers originated in early 1982, when U.S. scientists from atomic laboratories visited Japanese computer centers. In their trip reports, these scientists stated the fear that the Japanese could surpass U.S. companies, and the labs that design nuclear weapons would have to rely on computers purchased in Japan. Political factors could then play a role in the availability of Japanese computers vital to the U.S. defense effort. An interesting precedent for just such a possibility occurred in the late 1960s. The U.S. government barred IBM and Control Data from selling to France large computers for nuclear weapon development.

There was little of a sense of urgency, however, in the central administration. N. Douglas Pewitt, assistant director for general science in the White House's Office of Science and Technology Policy, said: "I have not seen any basis for justifying a massive Federal effort. . . . The reaction that we have to counter the Japanese plan by becoming Japanese ourselves is not going to wash. That's not going to find much support in this administration." If, by 1990, the U.S. computer industry has been displaced as the world's leader, with all of the attendant employment and trade consequences, this White House reaction will be seen in an interesting light, to say the least.

This most recent major Japanese effort had an earlier precedent, in the very same industry. In the 1960s, MITI recognized the need to develop the technology for very large scale integrated circuits (VLSI). The VLSI technology was a basic building block for the next computer generation and vitally needed if the Japanese computer industry was to remain competitive with the United States. Before 1966, MITI subsidies to the computer industry had not exceeded $1 million per year. During the period 1976–80, MITI subsidized a $350 million effort to develop a competitive VLSI system or technology. It brought together the major Japanese computer firms—Hitachi, Fujitsu, Mitsubishi Electric, Toshiba, and Nippon Electric—in a consortium effort. Staff were loaned by the companies, facilities were provided on a loan basis, and the research effort was completed on time.

Although MITI's share in this effort was around $145 million, its key role was to bring the major computer firms together in a format that increased substantially the probability of Japan having a much needed technology for a key industry, computers. The industry was not only viewed as key in and of itself but also key to the development of other industries such as automotive and robotics. MITI not only helped to fund the effort. It also worked out the basis for sharing the results of the research among the members of the consortium as well as with other Japanese firms. MITI guidance affected the filing and ownership of patents, licensing of patents granted to each company, and sharing of patents with government.

MITI's presence is felt in many areas of Japanese industry and many parts of the world. On the editorial page of the New York Times (p. 26) on March 20, 1982, the headline was "The IRT, Made in Japan." The reference was to the recent purchase by the New York Transit Authority of 325 subway cars from Kawasaki Heavy Industries for the IRT subway system in New York City. In commenting on the purchase and the fact that all of the competitors for the contract were capable of producing equally good cars, the final decision came down to Kawasaki, a Japanese firm, and the Budd Company, a wholly owned subsidiary of the West German Thyssen Company, the article stated. But Kawasaki won because "Kawasaki was the faster, promising a 10-car test train by December 1983 and complete delivery by June 1985. To nail down its bid, the Japanese company also offered a bargain 12¼ percent loan on half of the $250 million order, with the backing of Japan's Export-Import Bank." This is one of MITI's functions in support of its export industries.

MITI is also heavily involved in subsidizing by loans or grants, promoting interfirm cooperation, and providing vast amounts of information on new markets to Japanese firms in such diverse areas as the factory of the future, laser technology, medium-range commercial aircraft, solar energy, and biotechnology.

In biotechnology, for example, MITI is allocating developmental funds for the first time. MITI has picked 14 companies to undertake research. Although only about $3 million was allocated for initial funding in 1982, it is contemplated that during the next ten years, $113 million will be spent by the government. MITI funds will be used for two purposes, research and investment. The latter includes funds for investment in foreign firms to obtain process and production information. Recently, a group of Japanese investment firms and academic institutions spent $4.5 million for a 2 percent interest in an American firm that has been leading in biotechnology, Genentech. Other U.S. firms that have been approached in various ways by the Japanese for information-sharing arrangements are Abbott Laboratories, Centers Corporation, Genex Corporation, Warner-Lambert, and National Patent Development Corporation.[7]

MITI's efforts even extend into the field of "image enhancement." Sensitive to the increasing concern by foreign governments to the difficulties of penetrating Japanese markets, MITI has been developing new activities to deal with this. In an article in the April 3, 1982, issue of *The Economist*, notice is taken of a MITI meeting with Britain's Department of Industry to promote hi-tech commercial projects between British and Japanese companies. MITI is also conducting similar talks with other European countries.

An international cooperative approach to the fifth generation computer project is under consideration. Executives from France's C11-Honeywell Bull and from Burroughs Corporation have already discussed details of the project with MITI. In an article in *Business Week*, on this development (April 13, 1981, p. 124) the observation was made that in these efforts at international cooperation, "The resource being developed in these MITI-subsidized programs is experienced people. . . . The Japanese companies may try to hide their secrets from one another, but, as a result of MITI's role, they will each come away with vast knowledge without having to invest much." The basic resource is always seen as people.

Long-Term Investments by the Japanese Government

Articles about Japanese companies make special references to the long-term nature of management decisions. We have seen something of this on the government side as well. Planning for the new technology in VLSI and the fifth generation computer project involve periods of six to ten years. But these only begin to approach the long-term decision-making process that must have been involved in Tsukuba Science City. Here we have an entire city dedicated to research and technology. There is no better way to describe what is involved than to provide a direct quote from a lengthy article on this endeavor written by Toru Namiki, director, Technology Research and Information Division, Agency of Industrial Science and Technology, MITI.

General Outline

Tsukuba Science City is a modern academic community systematically planned and constructed by the Japanese Government. Centered around Tsukuba University and other public research institutes either newly established or relocated from the Tokyo area, the city comprises private research and educational organs, as well, and forms a complete academic community. Given this favorable research environment, Tsukuba contributes in an important way to the improvement of Japanese higher education and to research and development in science and other disciplines which constitute the foundation for a more technologically-advanced Japan.

At present, there are forty-five research and educational institutes located in Tsukuba where about 5,000 government researchers (roughly-half the national total) and 2,000 university and private researchers carry out their studies. Through close cooperation and frequent joint research efforts, Tsukuba's various institutions and individual researchers combine to form an integrated research body.

As of fiscal 1980, roughly ¥ 1.1 trillion had been invested in Tsukuba's research and educational facilities. Tsukuba is a highly livable city. After almost 20 years of diligent effort, the core facilities envisioned in the 1963 Cabinet plan for Tsukuba have been finished and most of the remaining public research and educational facilities are virtually complete. Present plans call for further projects to provide a high level of overall services to the city and region as a whole so that Tsukuba will combine big city amenities with its peaceful rural setting.

Outline of the City

Surrounding Region

Tsukuba Science City covers some 28,500 hectares of gently rolling land at a level of twenty to thirty meters above sea level. The city encompasses the towns of Tsukuba, Oho, Toyosato, Yatabe, Sakuramura, and Kukizakimura, but an area of about 2,700 hectares, roughly six kilometers from east to west and eighteen kilometers from north to south, is designated as the Central Research Area, in which the research, commercial, cultural, administrative, and main living facilities as well as the University are located. The area surrounding the Central Research Area is designed as the Regional Development Area, and efforts are being taken to raise this area to the same level of development as the Central Research Area.

Population

As of January 1982, there were 133,000 people in Tsukuba, of whom 30,000 were research and education personnel, their families and students living within the Central Research Area. Currently, the Govern-

ment is upgrading the overall living facilities of Tsukuba to meet the goal
of having 100,000 people in each of the two areas in the future.

Highway Transportation and Water Supply

Tsukuba presently has 56 kilometers of trunk roads, a water system
capable of supplying 100,000 tons of water per day and modern sewage
and storm sewer systems.

Parks and Public Plazas

Within the Central Research Area of Tsukuba are ninety-four parks
and plazas comprising about 100 hectares of land. One of the best known
public areas is Horamine Park. Its twenty hectares contain a memorial
hall and a pool and gymnasium complex heated by a solar energy system
with the largest energy-absorbing surface areas of any such system in the
world. For the safety and convenience of pedestrians, the residential and
commercial areas, schools, and parks are linked by 48 kilometer pedes-
trian walkway.

Educational Facilities

Located in the three residential areas of Tsukuba are five kindergar-
tens (a total of 12 planned), four elementary schools (12), three junior
high schools (six), and two high schools (four), all newly built in accordance with the overall development plan.

Other Facilities

In addition to the daycare centers, children's amusement hall, medical facilities, public auditoriums, shopping malls, and other amenities already completed in Tsukuba, construction is proceeding on a cable
television system and a vacuum dust removing system to be installed
citywide.

Also, in the fall of 1982, the Gakuen Center Building is scheduled to
open in downtown Tsukuba. This building will contain a hotel, department store, theater, and an information center, among other things.

The International Exposition, Tsukuba, Japan, 1985

Beginning on March 17, 1985 and lasting for six months, an international science and technology exposition will be held in Tsukuba Science
City. Preparations for the exposition are already well underway.

The aim of the exposition is to increase public awareness of the contribution that science and technology can make to the improvement of
the human condition. Such awareness must begin with a deeper understanding of science and technology's relationship to man and the environment. This relationship, in fact, is the theme of the exposition.

Twenty million people are expected to attend the exposition, in
which over 3,000 companies and groups, one hundred and sixty-one
countries, and fifty-four international organizations have been invited to
participate.

It is earnestly hoped that the exposition will serve as a forum for international communication whereby all countries can deepen their awareness and understanding of one another and cooperation. Further, the exposition should provide an opportunity for Tsukuba Science City to develop as world center for science and technology in the 21st Century, and, as such, as a valuable asset to all of mankind.[8]

Before closing this section on MITI, a few observations are in order. MITI is in the business of stopping things as well as starting them. The VLSI was started by MITI not only for the immediate technology but also because it knew that there would be long-term ramifications in the electronics, computer, telephonic, automotive, robotic, and other industries. An article in *Science* (November 14, 1980, p. 751) referred to the major milestone of Japan's development of the 64,000-bit random access memory chip as being a product of the MITI-sponsored VLSI project. With the completion of that project, MITI stepped aside. It was now up to the private sector to build successful commercial and industrial ventures on this mutual public-private investment in Japan's future.

But what about declining industries? Does MITI have an obligation to shore them up? Not if MITI's analysts and industry advisers feel that the industry in question has little future based upon true market competition. The Japanese shipping and steel industries are good examples. Though these industries had been helped by MITI policies to achieve positions of preeminence on the world scene, when events brought these major industries to their declining phases, no MITI help was available to save them or subsidize them. They are on their own. MITI shifted its promotional efforts to steel mills abroad where there are better comparative advantages. In the case of shipping, it has ceased any support or efforts to encourage investment elsewhere.

What about the future? What does MITI see as its emerging visions for development? MITI is fairly open about its reading of the future concerning its policies to enhance Japanese economic growth, productivity, and investment in human resources. One can see this in Appendix B, from portions of the "Statement of the Ministry of International Trade and Industry on the Vision of MITI Policies in the 1980s." When one compares what MITI intends to do in the 1980s, and remembers the success of its past programs, with what little planning is being done in the United States for the next decade, it makes for grim reading.

The Financial System

An interesting parallel between the U.S. approach to economic growth and the Japanese approach is that of judo and boxing. In the latter sport, brute strength, albeit skillfully applied, is used to achieve success, the knockout. In judo, use of leverage, the opponent's energy, and a quick, precise application of thrust are used to floor the victim. Nowhere is this analogy more applicable than in the use the Ministry of Finance makes of its powers. Its philosophy is based upon the assumption that the government can and should apply just the right amount of force, at just the precise moment, to exploit the drive of the private sector. In the United States, we not only feel committed to large-scale, massively applicable approaches, but we also often seek approaches that tend to eliminate completely government action in order to "free up" the forces of the marketplace. We try to be neutral in a very unneutral world.

An excellent insight into this perspective appeared in congressional hearings on industrial growth and productivity problems in the United States in 1981. Senator Lawton M. Chiles, of Florida, was conducting a dialogue with an outstanding fiscal and monetary economist, Henry C. Wallich, a member of the Board of Governors, Federal Reserve System.

> SENATOR CHILES: Dr. Wallich, the arguments are strong that we should not get the Federal Government into the game of favoring one industry over another with our tax policy. I wonder if there is any such thing as a neutral tax policy.
>
> Last year, we asked the Congressional Budget Office to look at the various tax proposals to increase capital investment, and it found that each proposal favored a different set of industries.
>
> Now, how do you see us getting a truly neutral investment policy when our industries have arranged their financial practices in relation to a hodge-podge of tax codes that we have built up over a number of years? Would there not be total chaos if we just cleared out all the special provisions and went to a simple rate of tax on personal and corporate income with no exceptions at all?
>
> DR. WALLICH: There are various plans, as you know, and they have these effects of favoring either long-lived equipment or short-lived equipment or structures. I would think that one could devise plans that would reduce these biases. For instance, the 10-5-3 seems to have the effect of particularly favoring long-lived equipment and doing little for short. The Senate plan seems to eliminate that and come closer to neutrality; I do not know whether it comes anywhere near perfect neutrality.[9]

In these same hearings, an industry representative seemed to be somewhat more appreciative of the non-neutral tax policies pursued by nations whose firms were scoring impressive gains. E. Floyd Kvamme, vice president, National Semiconductor Corporation, addressing Senator Chiles, had this view.

There is not equality in terms of market access, there is not equality in terms of access to capital and cost of capital. If the United States Government is not equal to the challenge, then we will lose something that is very important indeed and that is what I am here to tell you about today.

If we are to maintain our technological lead, an American response is needed to offset the advantages offered our major competitors abroad by their Governments and their economic systems.

The semiconductor industry advocates the following tax incentives to increase industry rate of return and thereby ameliorate the effect of the structural disadvantage of having a higher cost of capital than Japanese and other foreign competitors. The following measures will not solve the problem, but they are positive steps that can be taken in the immediate future to begin to respond to the challenge we face as a nation.[10]

Kvamme then followed with a series of recommendations concerning various changes in tax policy calculated to help alleviate problems of capital availability.

Contrary to the usual impression of the role of tax policy in Japan, it is not reserved exclusively for helping "targeted industries" or industries whose futures are seen as desirable, not only because of a good potential competitive position, but also because of a critical relationship to other important Japanese industries. Tax policy is also used aggressively to support socially desirable changes. For example, 27 percent initial depreciation on capital is provided for plant and equipment used for prevention of air and seawater pollution, smoke disposal, and noise abatement. This was used as an incentive because of Japan's decision to follow a much tougher policy of pollution control than the United States. This statement would appear to be at such variance with the usual view that U.S. regulatory policies impose a handicap unmatched by such competitor nations as Japan or West Germany that welcome support comes from a surprising source.

In his testimony before the Subcommittee on Trade, Productivity, and Economic Growth, of the Joint Economic Committee, Charles B. Breecher, adviser on tax policy, Republican National Committee, responded to a query from Senator William V. Roth, Jr. that related to an earlier statement by Congressman Frederick W. Richmond. Congressman Richmond had stated that Japan and West Germany have "very strong environmental laws" so that the United States couldn't blame U.S. regulatory laws for "our inability to compete with Germany and Japan."[11]

Breecher's comment on this statement was "He [Congressman Richmond] said that regulation was as strict or stricter in Germany and Japan than in the United States. That's basically true."[12] Breecher then went on to make the point that it was not the regulations which caused the problem, but the long judicial processes that followed when industry is confronted with lawsuits and so on. It is hard to know how to comment on this rather novel response. Industry in Germany and Japan do tend to respond, with less litigation involved, to regulations concerning health and safety. But of course, the legislative process involves them in a proceeding that has very little of the adversarial aspects we are so familiar with. And yet, as Breecher acknowledges, the regulations in these other countries are at least as strict as ours.

The miracle of Japan is the result of many things—a superb management system, an excellent, nonadversarial, complementary relationship between the public and private sectors, and a well-educated and trained labor force. But there is one other ingredient that receives too little attention in most analyses: the effective policies emanating from the Ministry of Finance. The wheels of the highly vaunted Japanese industrial economy are lubricated by just the necessary amounts of capital, in just the right places, at just the right times. The meat-ax approach of U.S. financial policy is in sharp contrast with the venture capital scalpel used in Japan.

Before discussing the role of the MOF in the use of monetary and tax policies to enhance economic growth and the competitiveness of Japanese firms, it is important to approach the subject honestly. Terms like "financial intermediation" are often used in contrast to "government control." There really is no difference, save in degree. And, of course, a matter of degree is, like beauty, in the eye of the beholder. "Control" means an act that can clearly be seen to have had an important effect on an outcome. The financial "intermediation," via loans, of the U.S. government in such cases as Chrysler or Lockheed was a form of "control," whether we like it or not. These loans controlled the fact that these two major companies did not go out of business. The U.S. government's preferential tax and quota treatment of the beet sugar industry "controls" the continued existence of U.S. sugar beet farmers, at the cost of all U.S. sugar consumers paying a higher price for sugar. Not exactly a sweet idea to the free market, laissez-faire enthusiasts—but applauded by "laissez-faire" sugar beet farmers.

The right to rise above principle is one of humanity's most treasured possessions. When it serves our purposes, we believe in government control, Democrats and Republicans alike. To test this theory, just suggest elimination of government "help" (read "control") for the tobacco industry, or more aggressive federal-mandated labeling of cigarettes warning smokers of the cancer peril. You will see some odd, schizophrenic behavior on the part of arch conservative senators and congressmen from the home districts of tobacco farmers. The key questions, however, in this whole matter of control are its pervasiveness, length of time, openness of debate over control policies, ease of change, and source of initiation of such policies.

The financial system in Japan starts with the Ministry of Finance, which controls the Bank of Japan, the nation's central bank. This is as though the U.S. Treasury Department controlled the Federal Reserve System. The Bank of Japan effectively controls the commercial banks, including interest rates and the availability of venture capital. Hence, those industries or firms viewed as essential to the economic well-being of the country enjoy the prospect of having access to the entire lending power of the government of Japan. No small asset! Interest rates are managed and bear little resemblance to those that react to more normal market forces, as is the case in the United States and most of Europe. Thus, when in mid-1982 the prime rate was about 15 percent in the United States, its equivalent in Japan was about 8 percent.

What most intrigues us about Japan's financial situation is a savings rate that is approximately 20 percent, three to four times that of the United States. What is most significant though about Japan's high rate of savings is not the amount, but how it is selectively channelled into a vast array of key markets for triggering economic performance and growth. A keystone in this financial arch is the Japanese government's Postal Savings System. A major component in the long-term loan arrangement between government and industry is generated by this savings system. In fiscal 1981, this system produced $42.4 billion, or 8.9 trillion yen, per year. These funds were then distributed via a government trust fund into industrial development, public corporations, and local governments. Most of the development money was used for business loans. The Japan Development Bank and Export-Import Bank of Japan also share in the use of this fund for economic growth and stimulation of industry.

The Postal Savings System is attractive to Japanese savers for many reasons. To begin with, the rate of interest is the same as the rate for time deposits in commercial banks. But the saver in the Postal Savings System can set up accounts in different names, his own, his relatives, his children, to obtain the maximum amount of tax-free interest. Also, it is said that the Ministry of Postal and Telecommunications enforces tax code regulations very liberally in the Postal Savings System, while the MOF enforces the tax code strictly for time deposits in commercial banks.

A key role in financial intermediation is played by the Japan Development Bank (JDB). The JDB was established in 1951 and since then has been effective in the reconstruction of the postwar economy as well as promoting the development of successful industries and companies. JDB initially used loan funds to rejuvenate the electrical, shipping, and coal-mining industries in the early 1950s. Emphasis in the 1960s shifted to heavy industries and chemicals. In the 1970s its resources were used to stimulate the energy resource and technology industries targeted by MITI. For example, the JDB financed the highly successful commercialization of Sony's Trinitron tube for color television sets.

The JDB obtains 70 percent of its investment funds from the Postal Savings System. It raises the remaining 30 percent mostly by selling its own bonds, in foreign markets. The rate of interest the JDB exacts from its lenders will vary with the priority of the need. Loans made for technology projects by MITI call for no interest. In order to stimulate the use of computers, in 1980 the JDB loaned the computer industry $263 million. Most of this went to the Japan Electronic Computer Company, which buys computers from suppliers and leases them to users. As industries generate higher cash flows, the JDB accordingly pulls back on its loans. Thus, the electronics industry received $46 million in 1982, down from $68 million in 1981. Japanese high-technology companies were well fixed for cash in 1982. The Industrial Bank of Japan estimates that the 95 electrical companies it surveyed are generating 84 percent of their capital investment needs, $3.45 billion, internally this year, raising 11 percent by selling bonds and stock and borrowing about 5 percent from banks. Much of the internal cash comes, of course, from the tax policies that provide high depreciation rates and favorable treatment of R&D expenses.

Most Japanese companies use double-declining digit depreciation, thus doubling the amount of depreciation resulting from the straight-line approach, the method used mostly by U.S. companies before the Economic Reform Act of 1981. In addition, Japanese companies can write off as much as one-third to one-half the cost of many investments in the first year.

Not only do the government-controlled banks provide the financial lubricants required by MITI targets for growth, private banks are also a part of this scenario. For example, the Long-Term Credit Bank (LTCB), a privately owned institution, makes loans for R&D and plant expansion. A banker with the LTCB said, "The government of Japan, to implement certain industrial developments, purchases debentures from the LTCB, which in turn channels these funds into areas of the economy specified by the government."[13]

The combination of MITI, the financial policies and institutions, and the superb management of leading Japanese firms is difficult to challenge. Currently, the growth of the robotics industry in Japan follows exactly the growth and development pattern of the Japanese electronics industry. It was MITI that, in the 1950s, founded the Research Committee on Computers, made up of prospective manufacturers, research scientists, and industrial leaders. It was this committee that provided a pattern of guidelines for MITI and the JDB. By the mid-1960s, this effort had begun to pay off and permitted a response to the IBM System 360 computer. By the early 1960s, the significance of the computer, and especially the growing lead of IBM computers, caused MITI and the JDB to effect a major allocation of development and R&D funds into such firms as the Japan Electronic Computer Corporation (to stimulate leasing for companies that could not buy), Japan Software Company (a joint venture of Fujitsu, Hitachi, and Nippon Electric), Toshiba, and Iki.

The same approach has also worked in the rapid development of the robotics industry. A plan by MITI, in close concert with industry, and the financial intermediation to guarantee venture capital are the key elements. MITI does not determine or provide a plan. It provides the institutional environment and vehicle for developing a plan that is realistic and involves all the key actors from the beginning. All of this is viewed as part of an all-embracing system. This system includes a major set of relationships between companies, companies and banks, and between banks. Insurance companies hold stock in banks and sit on bank boards. Banks tend to hold stock in other banks, as well as specialize in certain industries, holding stock and making loans to companies in these industries. A bank that has owner interests as well as a loan interest sees more than a quarterly or semiannual profit and loss statement as being significant. With interbank connections, it is also probably easier than in the United States, even with its corresponding bank relationships, to broaden the base of a loan or gain additional insights from professional staff. For example, Nippon Credit Bank stock is owned by Dai-Ichi Kangyo Bank (2.9 percent), Nippon Life Insurance (2.3 percent), Sumitomo Marine Life Insurance (2.0 percent), Asaki Marine Life Insurance (1.8 percent), Dai-Ichi Marine Life Insurance (1.8 percent), and Mitsubishi Bank (1.7 percent).

Because the banks, both public (such as the JDB) and private, see themselves as owners as well as creditors of companies, they can also serve as trusted third parties by two industries or companies in a supplier-consumer relationship. A bank lending to both a computer software firm and a robotics firm is in a unique position to perform a key function of melding both interests. The application of computer programming techniques for developing a flexible robotics manufacturing process would be a natural concern of the two involved companies. The bank that lends to both and is involved in consulting with both on long-term needs, growth strategies, and R&D is in a unique position to act as an intermediary for bringing these interests together. In this process, the bank also increases the probability of a long-term success in both of its fiduciary interests.

Returning to interest rate levels, I find that this question has received too little attention in the United States. The availability of low-interest loans has many effects, some obvious, some not so obvious, but all very significant. A low interest rate has an immediate impact on the borrower's costs of doing business. This in turn affects price, which in turn affects competitive effectiveness. The easy availability of low-interest loans also enhances innovation of new technology and new processes, as the costs of translating the results of R&D or technology transfer into new products or processes are lower.

In addition, with a lender like a bank involved in long-term planning or plant expansion, there are far fewer pressures to show quick profits. There is a big difference between a dividend-hungry stockholder and a sophisticated bank staff looking over a corporate shoulder. The latter is interested in a long-term payoff and is understanding about short-term setbacks. The stockholder is usually only interested in relatively short-term returns on an investment. Consequently, the financial system in Japan results in a debt to equity ratio for corporations of about 4 to 1. In the United States the ratio is closer to 1 to 2. Because it is common practice in Japan for the lending banks to own voting stock in client firms, there is a healthy continuing interest in the value of the equity as well. These sorts of loans can either be long or short term, though the preference seems to be for short-term loans that are rolled over for longer periods.

Other devices ensure an investment environment conducive to long-term planning and innovation. To begin with, interest payments are a pre-tax expense, whereas dividends are an after-tax deduction. On the savings side, a number of policies motivate high savings levels. Interest on savings deposits with any financial institution up to about $14,000 is exempt from income tax for individuals. In addition, interest on savings deposits up to $14,000 with the Postal Savings System is also exempt from personal income tax. A further exemption on interest for personal income tax purposes exists for any employer savings plans up to $24,000. Thus interest is tax free for deposits up to about $52,000. Also, there are usually no taxes imposed on capital gains.

The situation in the United States is in many ways the reverse. Not only do we not provide an incentive for people to save by exempting a certain level of savings from income tax on the interest, we reward purchases that are made based on borrowing. Since interest paid on loans is a tax-deductible item, we tend to subsidize borrowing. As we know from recent years of high inflation, we even have periods of negative interest, which really stimulates dis-saving.

The major difference between the ways in which the Japanese use their financial institutions in their economy and the way we do is this: In the United States we view our public financial institutions largely as market forces to be used sparingly in order to alleviate major perturbations in the system; in Japan, public financial institutions are used to reduce the exposure of individual economic efforts in risky projects with higher than average expected returns. Thus, Japanese public financial institutions serve to support risky, high-return projects since the net result is a higher GNP, more growth industries, and increasing share of markets abroad. They have a system of social risk sharing, based upon a priority of significant economic goals for the nation.

What is really clever about this is that while the savings rates are enhanced by broad, generally applicable incentives, for example, tax exemption on interest for all savings accounts up to a certain amount, there is a very limited, judicious use of such funds only where the social risk taking is justified by a high probability of major economic gains.

If one were to compare the interaction of the financial and nonfinancial institutions in Japan with those in the United States, four major critically significant characteristics of the Japanese situation emerge:

1. Until the late 1970s, the Japanese government has been more a financial intermediary than a regulator or borrower. The large volume of Postal Savings funds provided the basis for socializing the risk of intermediation support while permitting a balanced budget.
2. The financial debt of the nonfinancial sector increased continuously since the 1950s, even surpassing the U.S. level during this period. But government and personal debt levels have been far less than in the United States.
3. This deepening of debt was made possible by the high degree of financial intermediation by banks, thrift institutions, and public financial institutions. This also served to reduce transaction and information costs as well. This deepening of debt, which could only be achieved by virtue of the high levels of personal saving, is in part affected by special income tax treatment for savings accounts interest.
4. Sacrifices were made by the consuming public, with mortgages and consumer loans held to very low levels, far below those in the United States.

What we see, then, is the ability of industry simultaneously to increase investment while reducing financial costs. This all took place in a highly competitive financial community. Thrift institutions and post offices, especially, compete with commercial banks for loan business. And firms within the same industry compete aggressively with each other. "For very large loans, the system of loan consortia allowed the banking sector as a whole to assume risks which could not be borne by a small number of institutions. The system allowed the scope of investment to become both larger and more long-term, overcoming the sometimes myopic perspective of stockholders."[14]

In addition to the above, many risk-sharing arrangements exist to stimulate high priority activities conducive to the achievement of nonindustry specific goals. The goal of increasing exports is a case in point. There are specific tax exemptions for exports, some of which are the following:

- Deduction of a percentage of export profits from taxable income during the period of overseas market development.
- Deduction for foreign exchange losses on net long-term receivables.
- Special deductions for a portion of the proceeds of certain overseas transactions such as technology transfers and the rendering of technical services abroad.
- Between 1961 and 1972 accelerated depreciation for export sales in general.

Key in all of these financial policies, however, is flexibility and bending to emerging, new consensus of meeting different goals with different arrangements. Japan is an intriguing blend of the traditional and the pragmatic. Even within the confines of the concept of harmony, much dissension and conflict take place. New businesses emerge and old ones disappear, and this takes place only because of internal economic competition. One must keep in mind that there are important exceptions to every handy cliché people keep looking for in order to explain Japan. For example, an old saying has it that, in Japan, "The nail that stands up gets hammered down." That may be true for many mavericks, but the founders of such successful enterprises as Sony and Honda were outstanding "nails" in their industries, and they were not hammered down. Similarly, though the point has been made that a high debt to equity ratio has been a characteristic important factor in aiding the growth of industry, such giants as Sony and Matsushita are both high-risk firms with very low debt to equity ratios.[15] Almost every general rule about Japan has a significant exception.

The Intrafirm Environment

In many ways, it is unfortunate that the concern of this book is with what economists call the macro economic level. Not dealing with the individual industry or firm leaves out a significant dimension of the success story of Japan. Those who have read any of the literally thousands of articles or numerous books about the Japanese business firm know that the way in which these establishments and companies are managed is a major factor for success. Financial intermediation or MITI "consensus planning" are of no avail without the creativity, managerial competence, and innovative spirit of the Japanese manager and worker. And this effectiveness results in part from a sense of obligation that is culturally bound. But only in part.

In the area of human resource investment, Japanese public investment is grossly deficient. Retraining is almost entirely dealt with by the companies, the large companies. Very little is done by the government to equip or reequip workers with vocational skills needed in the economy. But what a magnificent job the large companies do. The only reason that the highly touted system of lifetime employment works is because of the commitment to retrain the worker when he or she is displaced by a new technology, process, or product line. In an interesting reference to this, by a "Friedman-type" Japanese economist, two points are made. Regarding this retraining investment:

> This involves an enormous investment on the part of employers—an immense investment in human capital. Under this circumstance, Japanese cannot fire their workers as easily as their American counterparts, for in doing so they would suffer a huge capital loss.[16]

Another perspective is provided by Chie Nakane:

> Here is demonstrated a radical divergence between Japan and America in management employment policy: A Japanese employer buys future potential labour and an American employer buys labour immediately required. According to the Japanese reasoning, any deficiencies in the current labour force will be compensated by the development of maximum power in the labour force of the future; the employer buys his labour material and shapes it until it best fits his production need. In America, management buys ready-made labour.[17]

In another area, that of savings, the high rate in Japan, more than 20 percent, as compared with that in the United States, currently around 5 percent, can be explained only to a degree by the incentive of partial tax exemption on interest. Another reason grows out of an extremely inadequate retirement and pension system. Unless you have been saving at a high rate while employed, the meager old-age benefits can leave you in a rather precarious situation. Savings, part-time employment, and family help are the sustaining forces. The U.S. old-age retirement plans, both public and private, are infinitely superior to those in Japan.

So there are many exceptions that must be taken into account as we try to obtain a comprehensive picture of what the social and economic institutional environments are like in Japan and how they have helped to produce what is viewed as an economic miracle. What is clear and consistent, though, is that in Japan we see a society that prides itself on individual initiative, with personal rewards as well as social, and a responsibility for harnessing personal goals to social objectives. This has been done with little rhetoric or cant about free enterprise versus socialism. Relationships have focused on how to achieve individual private goals within a framework of harmony. Conflict resolution, not adversarial confrontation, has been the guiding principle. It has worked.

As we have seen, it has also worked in another country whose culture, history, and politics are very different. West Germany and Japan have evolved a type of capitalist system radically different from that in the United States, the United Kingdom, Canada, and Australia. Do the Japanese and West Germans have a different model of capitalism from that in the major English-speaking countries, or is it only a variation? I believe it is a completely new model, not found in our economic literature or bearing a familiar label.

Notes

1. E. F. Denison and W. K. Chung, *How Japan's Economy Grew So Fast* (Washington, D.C.: Brookings Institution, 1976).
2. "Proceedings of a Round Table Discussion on Product Quality—Japan vs. the United States," Tuesday, August 19, 1980. Mimeographed, General Accounting Office, U.S. Government, Washington, D.C.
3. Ibid., p. 6–9.
4. R. E. Caves and M. Uekusa, *Industrial Organization in Japan* (Washington, D.C.: Brookings Institution), 1976, p. 9.
5. Hearings, Subcommittee on Science, Research and Technology, Committee on Science and Technology, U.S. House of Representatives, 97th Congress, 1st Session, Washington, D.C., July 14, 15, 16, 1981, pp. 134 and 135.
6. *The Economist,* March 6, 1982, p. 95.
7. *Wall Street Journal,* October 9, 1981, p. 29.
8. *Look Japan,* May 10, 1982, p. 18.
9. *Industrial Growth and Productivity,* Hearings, Subcommittee on Industrial Growth and Productivity, Committee on the Budget, U.S. Senate, 97th Congress, 1st Session, January 1981, p. 176.
10. Ibid., pp. 99, 103.
11. Joint Economic Committee, *Tax Policy and Productivity in the 1980s,* U.S. Congress, 97th Congress, 1st Session, June 17, 1981, p. 36.
12. Ibid., p. 41.
13. *Business Week,* December 14, 1981, p. 52.
14. *Program on U.S.-Japan Relations, Annual Report 1980–81* (Cambridge, Mass.: Center for International Affairs, Harvard University), 1982, p. 47.
15. Jack Baranson, *The Japanese Challenge to U.S. Industry* Lexington, Mass.: Lexington Books, 1981, p. 11.
16. Chiaki Nishiyama, "Small Government and Japan," *Look Japan,* July 10, 1981, p. 11.
17. Chie Nakane, *Japanese Society* (Middlesex, England: Penguin Books, 1973), pp. 18–20.

The
Shared-Capitalism
Model
════5════

Laissez-Faire Capitalism Is Dead

"Laissez-faire died awhile back."[1] This statement, made by Lee Iacocca, chief executive officer of the Chrysler Corporation, might seem to be self-serving in the circumstances, since the Chrysler Corporation was asking for help from the federal government. But, in reality, there have been too many situations where a Chrysler Corporation, Lockheed Corporation, or whole industries such as shipbuilding, steel, sugar, tobacco, textiles, shoes (you can almost list manufacturers at will) have looked to the government for help to survive or compete more effectively. More recently, much to the disgust of "The Vestal Virgins of the Radical Right,"[2] labeled thus not by a flaming liberal, but by a conservative economist, industries not wishing to be deregulated have been hard put to ward off a Reagan administration philosophy that follows the holy grail of laissez-faire. The ones who do not really seem to believe in this latter-day form of Adam Smith revelation are those who are actually in business and know what the marketplace really looks and smells like.

A fascinating case has been the efforts to deregulate the nation's alcoholic beverage industry. Without consulting the brewers, distillers, or vintners, in the fall of 1981, the Reagan administration offered the alcohol industry what every businessperson seemed to be calling for before the 1980 election—"Get the government off my back." True to its word to restore laissez-faire, the alcohol industry was about to be "restored" to no federal regulation. Federal laws regarding licensing, labeling, unfair trade practices, and advertising were to disappear. What was the industry's response? "We were dumbfounded" said Douglas Metz, executive vice president of the Wine and Spirits Wholesalers of America.[3] They were not dumbfounded because of joy, however. They simply did not wish to be free of "the dead hand of government," at least not the federal government.

The reason for this position does not grow out of any fondness for government regulation. It results from the realistic fact that if the federal government were to abandon its role, then the industry would be confronted by 50 individual state regulations. "If the Federal Government got out completely from dealing with the devil's brew, it would give the neo-Prohibitionists a great opportunity. . . . Most of Tennessee and Kentucky—bourbon country, for heaven's sake—are dry," Metz groaned.[4]

We find most novel warnings and accolades from industry about a government bureaucracy. "If the Administration does away with the Bureau of Alcohol, Tobacco and Firearms and stops enforcing the Act, we could see a return of the abuses that caused Prohibition," said Richard B. Thornburg, spokesman for the National Beer Wholesalers Association. Frederick Meister, president of the Distilled Spirits Council of the United States, a trade group of the major companies, offered the view that "The Bureau is a very lean, highly efficient organization staffed with very professional, highly competent people. The public is getting a very high return for its tax dollar in the functions performed by the Bureau."[5] It took businesspeople to remind the Reagan deregulators that if Prohibition were to return to various parts of the country, we would once again be confronted by the monopolies, criminals, unethical behavior, including mass bribery of enforcement officers, that existed during the last "Noble Experiment" during the 1920s.

John M. Walker, Jr., assistant secretary of the treasury, who planned for the demise, was disappointed. It would have saved the federal government $11.5 million annually.[6] No estimates were made of any increases in costs that would have accrued to the states, local municipalities, or individuals in the form of property damage, higher insurance costs, loss of life, or additional law enforcement, trial, and imprisonment needs.

On another front, little notice was taken in the media when the president of General Motors announced that U.S. auto producers were probably out of that part of the auto market that accounts for about 60 percent of the cars purchased in the United States. F. James McDonald indicated that U.S. automakers are at a competitive disadvantage in producing small cars and must rely on foreign manufacturers for supplies of small cars, particularly those with front-wheel drive. "Competitive economics at the lower end of product offerings" make it impossible for domestic manufacturers "to build small cars competitively in this country," he said.[7] From Harvey E. Heinbach, an analyst with Merrill, Lynch, Pierce, Fenner and Smith, came this observation on GM: "Current product plans suggest that management does not believe it has the ability to produce small cars competitively in the United States."[8]

GM has worked out arrangements with Toyota, Suzuki, and Isuzu to purchase small cars from Japan for its GM label or jointly to produce cars in the United States, utilizing Japanese know-how. We have already seen that much Japanese know-how is a joint product of the private and public sectors in Japan, with the automotive sector benefiting from well-targeted tax policy, high-quality electronics components and robots, to say nothing of a management style based on nonadversarial relations rather than a "shoot-out" approach with both labor and government. But, to halt his retreat in a manner more identifiable as good old U.S. industry pluck, Mc-Donald also said: "It's time to stop demeaning our own competence. . . . The American giant is awake and in full stride. The changes we are making are far-reaching, and when we are through, we will have restructured the entire auto-producing sector of our country." There seems to be little doubt about this "restructured" U.S. auto industry; the real question is whether it will be largely U.S. or largely Japanese!

A somewhat less disingenuous reflection on how we see ourselves and our economic philosophy comes from another chief executive officer, who might have been chatting with Lee Iaoccoca, namely, Cornell C. Maier, CEO of Kaiser Aluminum and Chemical Corporation. In a speech given on July 27, 1982, at Stanford University, he said, "The basic reason we are in big trouble in this country is that in far too many cases we are still trying to solve today's problems with yesterday's methods and yesterday's thinking. The fact of the matter is that the conventional wisdom is wrong. Much of the conventional wisdom that has for the past 20 years guided the actions of our major institutions with their constituencies is wrong. The 'don't-get-involved' theory of social responsibility is wrong." What Maier was directing his remarks to was the problem of getting business involved in a more effective relationship with "government, the media, and public opinion."

The United States is confronted by the fact that the economic philosophy to which we pay lip service, laissez-faire economics, is taken sufficiently seriously by enough business and political leaders to cripple our economy. Politics, attitudes, and relationships based upon a structure that no longer provides the basis for effective economic production or competition must be changed, of course. But of even greater importance is a recognition that the laissez-faire form of capitalism is dead.

Another form of capitalism has emerged since World War II, as best demonstrated in the cases of Japan and West Germany and now emerging in other countries like South Korea, Taiwan, Hong Kong, and Singapore. These countries have modeled their industrial and economic policies after those of Japan. Lee Kuan Yew, prime minister of Singapore, put it succinctly: "The Japanese have got it right."[9] Further support for this new challenge appeared in a *Fortune* article that commented on South Korea,

Singapore, Taiwan, and Hong Kong. The point is made: "The transformation of these once-poor states into formidable manufacturers in only two decades did not happen by accident, it was directed, or at least encouraged, by government policies."[10] The *New York Times* article details the key common features of the "political economies" of these four nations and Japan as follows:[11]

- Government policies that promote savings and investment, rather than consumption.
- Economic policy development in the hands of highly trained, professionally competent staff rather than ideological politicians.
- An emphasis on manpower and educational programs to guarantee a highly skilled labor force.
- A relatively equitable distribution of income among the population.
- Regulating yearly wage increases in order to curtail inflation.
- Control of some key sectors of the economy by large corporations or industrial groups that are unfettered by American-style antitrust laws.
- Political control by a single party, which provides political stability for long-term planning.

In addition, contrary to Milton Friedman's touting countries such as Taiwan and South Korea as bastions of democratic, liberal capitalism, the *New York Times* article quotes a banker who does business in these countries as saying, "And in countries such as Taiwan and South Korea political and social stability is maintained at the point of a gun."[12]

An immediate question is how applicable would these characteristics be to the United States. Some might be, others would not. But this is *not* the point. The point is that we have confused laissez-faire, or an adversarial relationship among government, industry, and labor, with capitalism. They need not be the same. Indeed, they have not been the same in reality since the mid-1800s, but only the British and Americans have failed to realize it. Until we inter this myth and move on to a new model of capitalism, as the more successful industrial countries have done, we will limp from one economic crisis to another.

The New Model of Capitalism—Shared Capitalism

Capitalism is based upon the accumulation of investment funds and their use in rationalizing the production process. The term "rationalization" is used in the German sense—that is, the continuous modernization of the economy so as to produce the most effective use of human and physical capital to satisfy the objectives and needs of the economy.

Unfortunately, the term "capitalism" has taken on a political context or terminology. One of the great disservices of Karl Marx was to draw a simplistic picture of capitalism, juxtaposing capitalism to the reverse side of the coin, socialism. But the use of economic factors to accumulate and use capital wisely is as crucial in a communist or socialist economy as in any other economy. The stereotypical communist countries such as the USSR and China are also capitalist countries in the economic sense, but irrational in their political behavior. Their political philosophy offsets their efforts to accumulate capital in order to achieve their avowed economic objectives. It grows out of the Marxist need to identify the capital accumulation process with market forces as they existed when Marx wrote and thought in the mid-nineteenth century. Not only was Marx frozen in this view of the real world, so also were the classical economists. So also are most of the contemporary economists in the United States. What has emerged in Japan and West Germany is a model that melds capitalism to the values of the society. What has emerged since World War II is the model of shared capitalism.

Capitalism need not be, by definition, wedded solely to the laissez-faire system. Indeed, in its pure form, capitalism existed only briefly in the early 1800s in England in the form envisioned by Adam Smith. Since then, it has continued to exist only in textbooks written by economists for classroom teaching. Businesspeople's jokes about theoretical economics versus the real world have their origins in legitimate perceptions. The problem is not theory, per se. The problem is with *fallacious* theory.

Capitalism can be market-oriented. But the values of our society, reflected in our political system, call for more than that. They call for a form of capitalism that can coexist within a larger context of values. Capitalism, contrary to Friedman, is not consistent *only* with democracy. It works in democratic as well as nondemocratic political environments. Capitalism is as neutral as water; it can be a solvent for many different kinds of political chemicals or combinations of public and private enterprise from the United States to South Korea.

The success of Japan and West Germany results from their blending of private and public goals in a model of shared capitalism that promotes an economic system capable of meeting both these goals. This is the model for the foreseeable future in the United States. It is a model that calls for many changes in our perception of ourselves.

This model will call for basic changes in how the public and private sectors relate to each other, how we invest in human resources and how labor and management must begin to function together. But more than anything else, we must be willing to jettison our deeply held conviction that the free market, laissez-faire philosophy is not only correct and inescapable for us but also, somehow, a "given" for a truly democratic society.

West Germany and Japan aside, we must recall that in the discussions in Chapters 1 and 2 of this work, the point was made that in the history of classical economic thought, in the England of the mid-nineteenth century, there were strong arguments by major thinkers that Smith and Ricardo were wrong in a major part of their laissez-faire model. Though costs of production were held to be subject to fairly rigorous laws of the marketplace, not so with regard to the distribution side. Hence, it was felt by some that in the use of the economic product, larger nonmarket factors could well reflect social needs. Such social needs would call for the use of our economic output to deal with many problems, including productivity, employment, and so on.

Nowhere was this point made more effectively than by one of the major thinkers of the period, John Stuart Mill. In his great work, *Principles of Political Economy,* Mill stated:

> . . . the laws and conditions of the Production of Wealth partake of the character of physical truths. There is nothing optional or arbitrary in them. [But,] . . . it is not so with the Distribution of Wealth. That is a matter of human institution solely. The things once there, mankind, individually or collectively, can do with them as they like. . . . In the social state . . . any disposal whatever of them can only take place by the consent of society. . . . The distribution of wealth, therefore, depends on the laws of custom or society.[13]

Mill considered custom along with the competing forces of the marketplace as the mechanisms by which the distribution of society's output can be used, for whatever objectives. This was a crucial contribution to economic thinking and was a major departure from the theories propounded by Smith and his followers. It is largely a forgotten departure, at least by most economists. The values of the Japanese society for lifelong employment is custom- or value-determined more than economic-determined. In economic principles classes in our universities we teach good Smithian and neoclassical economic theory that labor is a variable cost. Hence, as production goes up we hire more people, and as it is cut back we fire employees. With the large Japanese companies, labor is more nearly regarded as a fixed cost, in direct contradiction to the principles we teach in economics—Western economics, that is.

Once again, it reminds one of Mill: "Custom is the most powerful protector of the weak against the strong; their sole protection where there are no laws or government adequate to the purpose."[14] Recall that the capitalism that emerged at the time of Adam Smith was viewed as a mechanical, self-regulating mechanism, which, in spite of its cruelties, would quickly alleviate inequities because of self-interest, or so the theory held. By the early 1800s, sensitive observers in government and industry had begun to hold otherwise. But the aura of a natural system still pervaded political and economic thought. Where Smith felt that parsimony and saving in the case of individuals would most contribute to wealth, early critics like Lord Lauderdale held otherwise.[15] Lauderdale could see a society where public wealth and private wealth were not equated to each other. He was probably the first to understand that saving did not automatically mean investing, at least in the short run. More than that, he held that unless consumption was maintained, somehow, at an adequate level, capital could accumulate and be unused. Lauderdale had a very early insight into what was later called business cycle theory. He criticized Smith because he believed Smith's premises of the "economic man" and natural, equilibrating forces of the marketplace to be wrong. Lauderdale was a very pragmatic person, well aware of the nonmarket forces that had to play a role in maintaining a "full-employment" economy, devoid of the harsher aspects of laissez-faire. He felt Smith to be excessively theoretical.

Even on the North American continent, there was early and valid criticism. Among the first American economists, Daniel Raymond wrote about the problems of the American economy and took strong exception to Adam Smith's equating of the sum total of individual wealth to national interests. In a particularly poignant reflection on this point, he cited the slave trade as proof that individual interests might be "perpetually at variance with national interests."[16] In a discussion that might be useful in the usual comparison between individual budgets and national budgets, Raymond held that a nation could not be likened to an individual, but had to be seen as a "huge artificial being composed of millions of natural beings."[17]

In Smith's England, pragmatic businessmen were also highly critical of the basic assumptions of the laissez-faire model of capitalism. Walter Bagehot, a banker and writer on financial subjects, as well as editor of *The Economist* for many years, was highly critical of Smith. Bagehot felt that the doctrines of classical economics "rested upon assumptions which were not universally true but realizable only under narrow, specific conditions and therefore lacking in universal validity."[18] He felt that the economic condition could only be understood within the much larger context of the values of a society. Writing in the late 1800s, Bagehot had the benefit of observing the capitalist system as it actually worked rather than as a theoretical model, as Smith saw it.

The point is that, contrary to the impression held by many, that during the formative years of economic thinking economists spoke with one voice, that of Adam Smith, this is simply not true. Further, substantial criticism came from major thinkers and figures in business as well as government. How strange that only the English-speaking countries of the world still find themselves encapsulated in this peculiar form of economic time warp.

The time has come to move on to a model of capitalism that will best accommodate the needs of a modern society. What are these needs?

Our Modern Needs

Uppermost in most societies is the desire for the freedom to achieve objectives in a manner consistent with the values of the society. In some of the so-called developing nations, capitalism flourishes while civil rights do not. In the United States the first given is that of maintaining personal rights. Without our personal freedom, most of us in the United States would feel that little else can be of offsetting value. Hence, any of our economic institutions must coexist with a system based upon personal liberty.

Along with this right, however, is the need for a secure existence. Since the 1930s, unemployment, retirement, medicare, and other forms of welfare legislation have provided, not a guarantee of complete security, but a level of support that at least maintains a state of decency for most, but not all, Americans. Recent experiences in both reputedly liberal and conservative administrations appear to make it quite clear that there will be no return to a society reminiscent of Calvin Coolidge. Efforts to move in that pristine laissez-faire–oriented direction were foreclosed by both Democrats and Republicans during the 1980–82 period of rather conservative leadership in the White House.

With these constraints or givens, it would appear from the experience of Japan and West Germany that a form of capitalism that brings government, industry, and labor into a close, complementary partnership is absolutely vital and can work. Other less democratic countries are following this model, as well. But for our purposes, an economic model that juxtaposes private as well as public efforts to achieve economic goals must be done in a context of democratic freedom.

To do this, it would seem that the fulcrum for action would be that of a human investment commitment linked to a value system based upon productivity gains. Many firms in the United States have developed such linkages in the form of bonus plans related to productivity gains. Even in the case of so-called depressed industries, such as steel, the few profitable firms are those that do this. In the depressed steel industry, one of the rare, profitable firms is Nucor Steel, which has a highly effective pay and bonus system related to productivity gains. The overriding goal would be that of maintaining rates of productivity growth calculated to provide for an expanding economy, in real terms, and an ample base of capital creation.

Our new model of shared capitalism, a capitalistic system relevant to the period we are now in, would be characterized by the following:

- Investment in human resources
- An orientation to productivity gains and indicators of stable productivity growth rather than stable monetary growth
- Gradual curtailment of nationally based policies
- A nonadversarial relationship between the key economic and political institutions

Investment in Human Resources

An economy is part of a larger structure, the society. No society can exist, at least as a stable, democratic society, unless there is a shared sense that the future holds a good possibility for individual security and well-being. A society where pervasive, continuing high levels of unemployment exist for substantial numbers of people cannot be viewed, by any definition, as one that holds out the hope of a worthwhile future. This is not only the case for those who are unemployed; it is also the case for the majority, even the large majority, who have few anxieties over whether they personally will be employed.

An unemployment level of 6 or 7 percent can and does mask the existence of unemployment levels of 30 to 50 percent for specific segments of the population (teenagers, minorities, and older workers). Such a level exceeds the 20 to 25 percent unemployment that during the 1930s triggered large-scale economic and social changes in our system. These changes were brought about because a continuing level of 20 to 25 percent unemployment was seen as a force for instability and suffering that could literally trigger violence and social chaos. God-fearing, rock-ribbed Republican farmers in the Midwest in the 1930s stood, shotguns in hand, defying legitimate court orders held by sheriffs ordering them to take over property because of mortgage or loan defaults.

Today in the United States expenditures for unemployment insurance, larger police forces and jails, welfare, and property damage affect every taxpayer and every firm in search of capital. They also affect every business confronted by a shortage of skilled people in the labor force necessary for new technologies and new processes. Public school budgets, vocational training programs, and schools of engineering, as just a sample, cannot obtain sufficient funds to provide for the necessary levels of education and training in a modern society. The 20 to 30 percent level of illiteracy, including functional illiteracy, in the United States is hardly in the same ball park as the less than 1 percent illiteracy in Japan. This is not merely a matter of national pride: The substantial number of people in the United States who are not only unemployed but unemployable by virtue of a lack of education or skills are the people who must be supported as a result of social legislation; and these laws will not be changed, no matter how conservative an administration is in Washington.

We are confronted by a simple choice. We either see, and accept, the logic of investing sufficiently in human capital or we suffer the consequences. This problem will not go away; it will only increase as poorly educated individuals, unequipped for jobs or a constructive role in our society produce new progeny who reproduce failure with each new generation. When confronted with the need to spend large sums of money to upgrade the education and skills of those coming from low-income ghettos, we resort to token programs. We look at a few "high achievers" who, somehow, manage to overcome tremendous obstacles in those ghettos in order to succeed, and ask: "Why don't all the others follow their example?" We do not, however, set the same standard for those coming from more affluent backgrounds. The larger percentage of those from backgrounds with more adequate family resources can achieve because talent is sustained with adequate support systems not found in low-income ghettos. Without the ample family resources, the better schools, and the willingness to keep investing in our own children, how many could succeed solely on talent? Social investment is necessary if we are to convert people who are liabilities in the system to people who can be assets.

Contrary to popular notion, the United States has not only never had a manpower policy, the United States has not in recent history had a level of investment in retraining and training adequate to meet the needs of a modern industrial nation.

> The experience of the Germans, French and a few of the other industrial countries of Western Europe shows that between 1 and 2 percent of the labor force must be retrained each year in order to keep up with the needs of an advanced industrial society. And that 1 to 2 percent is above and beyond what industry normally retrains on its own. The (U.S.) Manpower and Development Program of the 1960's and the Comprehensive Employment and Training Programs of the 1970's had training "slots" that ranged between 1/10th of 1 percent and 1/2 of 1 percent of our labor force. A far cry from the European experience.[19]

The last major investment in human capital in the United States was the GI Bill after World War II. Most would agree that it was a wise economic investment. In the chapter on West Germany, the legislation guaranteeing retraining was discussed. The average costs of this German program, including tuition and income stipend, came to about $3,500 in 1978 prices.[20] The only deduction from the gross cost per trainee was the saving on unemployment benefits which did not have to be paid. No allowance was deducted for the undoubted productivity gains and higher income taxes that resulted for the West German economy. This low cost per trainee results from almost no overhead costs. As under the American GI Bill, all the German veteran needed was evidence of an honorable discharge and a Veterans Administration claim number. This evidence, presented to an educational institution, was all the veteran needed to justify an application for admission. The veteran was a "walking checkbook" and there was no middleman to take a cut.

There is another overwhelming necessity for a massive training program that must be available on a continuing, individual-initiative basis. In the next chapter we will be concerned with the crisis in the United States concerning the maintenance and rebuilding of our national plant, our cities, our roads, bridges, railways, our national infrastructure. As we shall see, contrary to our concern that the industrial future brings technological unemployment, our nation's future and our way of life in a civilized environment will call for the employment of every individual desirous of work. The near-term agenda of this nation is one that will include a major shortage of workers in the construction and related industries unless we launch an effective retraining and training program as quickly as possible.

Productivity Gains

Adam Smith was absolutely correct when he perceived more than 200 years ago that a nation's real wealth must be based upon the increased efficiency with which it utilizes its resources in the production of goods and services. Put another way, productivity gain is the only way in which a nation can produce a larger pie. Unless we can produce a larger pie, there is no way we can increase our standard of living, increase capital, or maintain a competitive position in our domestic and world markets. For a nation as well as an individual firm, productivity is the bottom line.

In the past, the rate of gain in productivity in the United States was around 2 to 3 percent. Since 1978, the rate of gain has hovered around zero. During the recession of 1980–82 in the United States, the rate was 0.5 percent for the business sector. At the end of 1982 the rate of gain in U.S. manufacturing was -1.0 percent. In manufacturing, the rates for the same point in time in West Germany and Japan were 1.7 percent and 1.0 respectively.[21]

For the United States to regain its position, our rate must move to at least 3 percent and remain between 3 and 4, which would be abnormally high, historically. In West Germany the new form of capitalism has brought government, labor, and industry together as a team. This coalition is capable of achieving and sustaining higher rates of productivity gain than can be achieved by a more market-oriented, laissez-faire form of capitalism.

If we but look at our own experience in one area where our rates of productivity gain have been the highest in the world, and have been sustained over an extended period of time, this should come as no surprise. Productivity gain in U.S. agriculture has been the envy of the world. It is an "industry" where government and the entrepreneur have worked together since the mid-1800s. Beginning with the land-grant legislation of the 1860s, which established the colleges of agriculture (probably our first true manpower policy) and expanded the base for trained, professional agriculturalists, until the present, with massive government-supported R&D as an ongoing effort to help the farmer, this industry has been a model of a joint private-public effort. Special relationships via the Farmers Home Administration, the Extension Service, the Rural Electrification Administration, the system of county agents to aid in the process of innovation, coupled with favorable natural resources and a hardworking farm population, produced a development system and level of productivity in which even the Japanese MITI would take great professional pride. When one speaks of an effective relationship between the private and public sectors in the United States, no better example exists than agriculture. Even with the exceptional situations of subsidies that have outlived their usefulness, which also occurs in Japan, most nations envy the record of productivity gain in U.S. agriculture.

If we are to deal effectively with the problem of productivity, it has to be understood that the major problem confronting the United States is not an economic one; rather, it is a behavioral one. To regain the lead in productivity gain we have to understand that there are a multiplicity of factors involved and we must be willing to change in many of our perceptions, values, and relationships.[22]

Of the 12 factors that are significant for achieving and sustaining high rates of productivity gain, two have already been discussed, the role of government and worker quality and skills (the necessity for a constantly upgraded, trained labor force). The other factors that we must understand and deal with are

- R&D
- Promotion of innovation
- Institutional relationships and values
- Business saving and investment
- Personal saving and investment
- Natural resources development and substitution

- Production techniques and systems
- Management philosophy and techniques
- Performance information
- Knowledge transfer

1. *Research and development.* During the last decade, R&D and scientific resources in the United States have fallen behind those of the Japanese and West Germans. Our ratio of R&D scientists and engineers to total labor force has dropped, while theirs has risen. Unless this trend is reversed, the United States will no longer be the preeminent technological nation in the world; the implications for the need to regain higher levels of productivity are obvious.

2. *Promotion of innovation.* Producing new knowledge and new products is only the beginning. Unless we are truly receptive to using these new ideas and new approaches, there will be no innovation. Most people and most organizations do not like upsetting apple carts, but that is what innovation is all about.

3. *Institutional relationships and values.* Ideas about monopoly, labor versus management, or government versus business have produced an adversarial society. To achieve our national productivity goals, we must move in another direction that brings together common interests. Other countries have imported U.S. management techniques and used them well. We now have to import from these countries. The "not-invented-here" syndrome must not stand in our way.

4. *Business savings and investment.* Business savings must be stimulated: it is a critical source for new capital, R&D, and training. An adversarial hangup in Congress and in our society in general regarding profits reflects an ignorance of the relationship among profits, investment, and productivity gains. Tax policy, as well as changes in social philosophy, must begin to reflect this.

5. *Personal saving and investment.* Unless we stimulate personal savings, there will continue to be an inadequate pool of funds in commercial banks for investment purposes. An increase in personal savings must be seen as a major source of investment funds for business. Government policies must be changed to stimulate higher savings rates rather than higher borrowing levels.

6. *Natural resource development and substitution.* Changing patterns of resource use have always been with us, and will remain so. The history of technology is the history of "running out of things" and substituting lower-cost alternatives and new technologies. Americans have to stop using resource "crunches" as a crutch. The Japanese and Germans have paid the same prices as the United States has for a barrel of oil, but their record on productivity and inflation has been better than ours. We have to

use more of the only infinite natural resource that humanity has—its imagination.

7. *Production techniques and systems.* Production techniques are always on their way to obsolescence. Therefore we must adopt a continuous stance of assuming there is a better, lower-cost way to produce services and products. There is no formula for doing this. Hence, we have to rethink our basic approaches to how good we believe we are. It is tough being "number one," but it is tougher when you drop to "number two." Staying in the lead means never being self-satisfied or smug.

8. *Management techniques and philosophy.* Short-term gains that obscure long-term losses, discounting the competition, using crutches like "the Japanese are different," "higher energy prices are killing us," or "the American worker is not comparable to the German or Japanese worker"—these are nothing more than camouflages. Sony in San Diego uses those American workers. So does Honda in Marysville, Ohio. The Germans pay as much as we do for oil. And the Japanese, with all their cultural differences, acknowledge that they imported their management techniques from us. The Japanese say that their management techniques are 95 percent like ours, but different in every *major* aspect.

Americans can compete effectively with the Japanese, but we have to leap ahead of them, not copy them. We must innovate. And we can. To do this, our management philosophy must return to a production focus. The end product of a business is a commodity or service, not a list of merger "scalps." Finance, marketing, and accounting are all there to help us improve on our selling or market-share position. Somewhere along the line we seem to have lost sight of this principle.

9. *Performance information.* We need to understand and use indexes of productivity. They tell us where we have been. But never confuse the thermometer with the treatment of the disease. Improving our indexes does not improve our productivity. We have used the problem of imperfect indexes as an excuse for not treating the disease. Remember, all countries use about the same index construction technique.

10. *Knowledge transfer.* Knowledge is all around us. But only the truly intelligent, wise people know how to use it or have a strategy for using it. Because the United States is lagging badly in R&D, we have a special need now for a strategy of utilizing and building on knowledge from other countries. In the same context one industry must learn to apply knowledge from other industries. The not-invented-here syndrome can be more debilitating than we may want to admit. We had better become more honest about this; the cost of not using whatever is available, from wherever it is available, is prohibitive.

Thus, productivity is at once concerned with the "thing" and with the spirit. Willingness to see and think differently, to accept change not as a traumatic, threatening experience but as a grand opportunity to grow in effectiveness is the real key to productivity.

In a most insightful article, Peter F. Drucker views productivity as the real basis for value and for a new "first principle" of economics. I believe he is correct. Drucker put it this way:

> The next economics may even attempt to be again both "humanity" and "science."
>
> An anecdote popular among the younger members of Keynes' Cambridge seminar had one of the disciples ask the Master why there was no theory of value in his General Theory. Keynes answered: "Because the only available theory of value is the labor theory and it is totally discredited." The next economics should again have a theory of value. It may base itself on the postulate that productivity—that is, knowledge applied to resources through human work—is the source of all economic value.
>
> Productivity as the source of value is both a priori and operational, and thus satisfies the specifications for a first principle. It would be both descriptive and normative, both analyze what is and why, and indicate what ought to be and why. Marx, the "Revisionists" of Socialism around 1900 argued, was never fully satisfied with the Labor Theory of Value but groped for a substitute. None of the great non-Marxist economists of the last hundred years, Alfred Marshall, Joseph Schumpeter, or John Maynard Keynes, was in turn comfortable with an economics that lacked a theory of value altogether. But, as the Keynes anecdote illustrated, they saw no alternative. Productivity as the source of all economic value would serve. It would explain. It would direct vision. It would give guidance to analysis, to policy, and to behavior. Productivity is both man and things; both structural and analytical. A productivity-based economics might thus become what all the great economists have striven for: both a "humanity," a "moral philosophy," a "Geisteswissenschaft" and rigorous "science." [23]

In the long history of the search for a theory of value, economists were either deluded or politically biased. Marx was certainly the latter; all value was the worker. The owner of capital was the exploiter and capital equipment was the means for exploitation. Adam Smith certainly felt that labor was the key factor. Indeed, it was he who said that the wealth of a nation depended on the productivity of labor and the amount of useful labor that is employed. But Smith was as limited in his view as was Marx. Labor without the insights, skills, availability of funds, and imagination of the manager could never alone be the source of productivity. And as we have seen from the Japanese example the manager who taps the intelligence, motivation, and insights of the production workers produces an overall result that is far superior to that of an autocratic, anxiety-producing form of management.

The source of economic value is to be found in the human intellect. Only it can conjure up the most amazing ways of increasing our output. The surest way to measure this phenomenon is productivity gain. As a result of increases, or decreases, in productivity, the costs (prices) of goods and services change. But the ratio of different prices (or costs) is not value, as some economists think. It is only an indicator of changes in relative productivities.

If productivity gain is a basis for a value theory, how does this translate into economic reality? For example, if between 1974 and 1981, we had been able to achieve an increase of 3.5 percent productivity gain each year, with the exception of 1976, how much additional GNP would have resulted by 1981? Table 5.1 indicates that the difference between what actually occurred and would have occurred at the higher level was $469 billion. This amount is equal to 90 percent of the total increase in the federal debt during this same period of eight years. In the calculations, the increase each year, with the exception of 1976, when the gain was above 3.5 percent, was based on the difference between the actual gain in productivity and the hypothetical increase of 3.5 percent.

Table 5.1. Gains in GNP (1974–81), Assuming An Annual Rate of Productivity Gain of 3.5 Percent

	A GNP ($ billions)	B Actual Productivity Gain, % (business sector)	C Difference Between B and 3.5%	D GNP at 3.5% Gain ($ billions)	
1974	1,434.2	−2.6	6.1		87.5
1975	1,592.2	2.2	1.3	(1,592.2 + 87.5) × 1.3% =	21.8
1976	1,718.0	6.4	—		—
1977	1,918.0	2.4	1.1	(1,918.0 + 0) × 1.1 =	21.0
1978	2,156.1	.6	2.9	(2,156.1 + 21.0) × 2.9 =	63.1
1979	2,413.9	−0.9	4.4	(2,413.9 + 63.1) × 4.4 =	109.0
1980	2,626.1	−0.7	4.2	(2,626.1 + 109.0) × 4.2 =	115.0
1981	2,922.2	1.8	1.7	(2,922.2 + 115.0) × 1.8 =	51.6
					469.0

Table 5.1 is helpful in understanding the implications of our poor rate of gain in productivity. But once in a while, a really good "one-liner" catches even more of the substance of a problem. On the problem of our lagging productivity and what it means for the future of the United States, one of the best one-liners was spoken by Lloyd Dobyns, star NBC commentator. On June 24, 1980, at the end of the nationally televised NBC White Paper on Productivity, "If Japan Can, Why Can't We?" Dobyns observed: "Unless we solve the problem of productivity, our children will be the first generation in the history of the United States to live worse than their parents." That just about says it all.

Curtailment of Nationally Based Policies

All experience shows that even smaller technological changes than those now in the cards profoundly transform political and social relationships.[24]

These words, uttered in 1955 by the great scientist and social thinker John von Neumann, are even more applicable now than ever before. All visible signs point in the direction that economic policies oriented to national goals alone are often counterproductive to the national goals themselves. The beggar-your-neighbor proposals that blossom when home industries are endangered, if adopted, only tend to exacerbate the original problem. The decision in the early part of the Reagan administration to minister to the needs of the U.S. auto industry by exerting pressure on Japan to impose a "voluntary" quota of cars exported to the United States had little impact on the competitive ability of GM, Ford, or Chrysler. Indeed, the Japanese auto exporters could afford to raise car prices, given the restriction on supply forced upon them by the United States. If the U.S. producers do not increase their productivity and competitive abilities, they will continue to lose sales or develop new ventures with the Japanese. The earlier alluded-to statement by the president of General Motors makes it quite clear that the future will see GM optimizing its position by joining forces with Japanese producers. American Motors has done the same with the French auto manufacturer, Renault. Chrysler will continue its pattern of working with Mitsubishi, and Ford relies increasingly on overseas production centers when productivity and technology dictate.

In reality, the days of the domestic industry are over. No great company in any country is national in the old sense any longer. Nor will they ever again become so. While members of Congress may wring their hands over the Japanese threat to the U.S. computer industry, firms like IBM have for many years had major production, marketing, and sales units in all parts of the world. While there is surely a concern by IBM, General Electric, General Motors, and Eastman Kodak, for example, over competition from foreign sources both at home and abroad, the real concern is not that of parochial nationalism. The concern is over the factors in the United States that limit their effectiveness in producing as efficiently as possible in order to compete in world markets, including the United States.

The ease with which production moves from one country to another, to achieve advantages of greater productivity and market share, is not restricted to the large multinational firms. The image of corporate mobility is nowhere more misleading than to suppose that only the industrial giants are capable of shifting resources and personnel as would the general of an army to achieve a victory of increased sales at lower unit costs. The use of computers, easy transfer of technology, greater flexibility and availability of venture capital, and mobility of key personnel have given small business firms command over information, product design, alternative scenarios, and so on that are the means for developing international operations. Moving an industrial base from one country to another is no longer the province of the large company. It has become the springboard of success for countless small entrepreneurs. The governments of such countries as Singapore, Hong Kong, Taiwan, and South Korea have been especially facile in attracting the smaller, dynamic entrepreneur. They have done this by developing tax, regulatory, fiscal, and other government policies and postures that encourage easy movement of entrepreneurs across national borders. While protection of home industry is not unknown, the decline of such industries is viewed with less alarm than in the United States.

An example of this sort of phenomenon is that of the Zau brothers, Bernard and Ronny. Located in Hong Kong, the Zaus started Micro Electronics in 1964, producing rectifiers for Westinghouse. By 1981, Micro Electronics was making products for Mattel, K Mart, Sony, ITT, and Westinghouse. With abundant cash on hand in 1974, the Zau brothers financed a company in California's Silicon Valley. Ronny Zau talked an American engineer, Joseph Santandrea, into the venture, supported by several hundred thousand dollars from Micro Electronics. The new U.S. company, Monosil, now sends orders and hi-tech know-how to Micro Electronics. The Zau brothers own 42 percent of Monosil and recently shifted a part of the Hong Kong manufacturing plant to Canton, China. Bernard Zau sees the Canton plant as a long-term investment.[25]

More familiar to us are Sony's plants in California and Alabama, Honda's auto and motorcycle plants in Ohio, and Nissan's new truck plant in Tennessee. This is quite as common as U.S. production plants abroad. And of course Volkswagen produces autos in Pennsylvania. The four top Japanese electronics companies have production facilities in Britain. Fujitsu, the leading Japanese computer company, linked with Germany's Siemens, is now providing a helping hand to Britain's troubled state-owned computer company, ICC.[26]

The difficulty with identifying the national origin of a company is only exceeded by the difficulty of knowing who really makes the trademarked product. Olivetti's sleek portable electronic typewriter, the Praxis, is a Japanese product. The leading computer manufacturer in Germany, Siemens, sells Fujitsu mainframe computers under the Siemens name. Alfa Romeo has an agreement with Nissan to produce jointly 60,000 cars.

As we know, not only is industry mobile with regard to locating where it makes sense for market growth, but labor as well does the same if permitted and in some cases where it is not permitted. The guest workers in Germany, Switzerland, and other European countries were involved in a situation of benefit to both the guest worker and the host country. Illegal migrants from Mexico and other Latin American countries have flocked to the United States to fill a need for labor, but the conditions in the United States are less than optimal. There has been no real effort to develop a before-the-fact rationale for either permitting or halting the flow, unlike the European situation where the guest worker is part of a larger industrial policy.

An observer of this increasing internationalization of small and large businesses sees a phenomenon that can be viewed from two perspectives, much like a reading of *Gulliver's Travels*. One can appreciate *Gulliver's Travels* as a fine adventure story, of course. But Jonathan Swift really wrote it with much deeper observations on humanity in mind.

What we have is the fact that companies and individuals are doing business from many points, all over the world, to a greater degree than ever before. Flows of capital, personnel, and technology have increased substantially since the early 1950s at a pace well beyond any similar situation in modern industrial history. This, in turn, has had a major impact on our interpretation of one of the most fundamental concepts of economics, that of comparative advantage.

Underlying the whole body of economic theory concerning international trade is the concept of comparative advantage. Given the fact that different countries have different resources, location, climate, populations, and so on, each country can produce certain items more efficiently than other countries. Even if one country can produce everything better than any other country, it will still have a relative advantage in one or a few commodities where it will pay to produce only those rather than all.

A personal, rather than national, example helps to clarify this concept. If there was a brilliant surgeon who was not only the best surgeon in town but was also the best bricklayer in town, it would probably pay him to pursue his medical career full time rather than to install brick patios. Though he would have an absolute advantage over all surgeons *and* bricklayers, his best, most useful and lucrative choice would reflect his relative advantage as a surgeon. So consider Country A and Country B with the following resources:

	Country A	Country B
Iron ore	None	Large deposits
Coking coal	None	Large deposits
Oil	None	Large reserves
Textile industry	Large	Larger than Country A's
Skilled labor force	Yes	Yes
Population	Half the size of Country B	Double the size of Country A (very large)
Chemical industry	Medium	Large

Which country would probably have the lead in production of autos? It would appear that Country B is the one, since it has all the basics one would look for, including a large domestic mass market conducive to large production runs and economies of scale. But Country A describes Japan and Country B describes the United States! What is wrong with the principle of comparative advantage? Nothing.

The problem is that what we always thought were the critical variables or factors when discussing comparative advantage are no longer as critical as others have become. Thus, Japan, a resource-poor country in one sense is immensely wealthy in another sense. It is immensely wealthy in the sense of being a society well enough organized to manage its human resources in a manner best calculated to achieve its social and economic goals. True wealth exists in the ability to use resources, no matter what their origin, in order to achieve the objective of higher productivity.

We often confuse the presence of a natural resource, such as coal or iron ore, as the presence of wealth. Wealth is only real when the possibility of converting a resource from a potential into a reality does actually take place. A country may be said to have a potential for wealth, as is the case in many developing countries with ample resources for which there are markets, but really *is* wealthy only when the potential can actually be converted for real economic demand.

Given the increasing value of R&D, information and superior management techniques in a technological society, these factors are more nearly the basis for wealth than the sorts of natural resources the term "wealth" traditionally referred to. True wealth is more tied to an ability than to a thing. Thus, Japan, without most natural resources, is wealthier than many larger, apparently better endowed countries that lack the ability to use their own resources.

Both the Japanese government and Japanese industry see the need for access to information as vital to their economy. Hence MITI has a major, and well-financed, program acquiring information all over the world on matters pertaining to technology, R&D, markets, and new innovations and channeling it to its industries. The major Japanese firms do the same. In our modern society, as never before, information is a key resource. In a shared-capitalism model, the complementary relationship between industry and government operates beyond national boundaries.

Major governments understand that there is no clear division between politics and economics. Hence, prime ministers and ministries of economics are actively involved in seeking to obtain advantages for major firms, including multinational ones, based in their own countries for operations in other countries. I once served on the board of directors of a major U.S. firm involved in negotiating with a developing country for a production facility in that country. The potential market was very substantial, even for a $6 billion-a-year firm. While we were negotiating, the prime minister of a major European country was visiting the president of the developing country. Prior to and during his visit, the prime minister was presenting information and contract possibilities for a major firm in his country, which was competing with the U.S. firm. The prime minister saw his role as that of advancing the future of one of his country's major firms, since the foreign trade benefits would be substantial for his nation. It was only under great duress that the U.S. Department of State and the U.S. Department of Commerce could finally be convinced of supporting the efforts of the only U.S. company involved to even obtain an adequate hearing before the president of the country. The U.S. position, simply put, was not one that saw its government officials as being responsible for trying to help a U.S. firm to compete in a foreign country.

Perhaps the most sophisticated example of an awareness of the necessity to internationalize the perspective of using venture capital to national advantage came in a 1982 decision in Japan. An agreement signed in November 1982 provided Japanese money, in the amount of $200 million, from six Japanese banks to provide Mount Isa Mines Pty., of Australia, with capital necessary for a coal development project in northeast Australia. The banks involved are Bank of Tokyo, Long-Term Credit Bank of Japan, Taijo Kobe Bank, Nippon Credit Bank, Tokai Bank, and Sanwa Bank.

The $200 million credit, in both yen and dollars, is part of a $1 billion project. The project will initially result in an annual production of 4 million tons of steam coal and 2 million tons of coking coal by 1984, all going to Japan and other Asian nations. This not only provides a necessary further guarantee of an important source of fuel and chemicals derived from coal but it also further cements relations, and markets, for Japanese industry.[27]

Some U.S. business firms have been rather open about their internationalization of markets and products, perhaps sensing that business tends to follow logic more readily than politics. The most obvious example has been the Ford Motor Company's "world car."[28] Ford's European-made Escort is assembled in Britain, West Germany, and Portugal for sale in Europe and the developing countries. Its parts come from 17 different countries, including the United States. The rainbow of supplier countries is fascinating. Only a partial list and items include England, France, and Italy: cylinder heads; Germany: cable assemblies, brakes, clutch, distributor; Norway: muffler flanges; Spain: radiator and heater hoses; Switzerland: speedometer gears and undercoating; Canada: glass, radio; United States: hydraulic tappets; Japan: bearings, alternator, and starter.

This sort of "out-sourcing" has become increasingly common for all companies throughout the world. While it is understandable that the United States, far more isolated in its spatial relationships than European and Asian countries, secure in its large internal market and history of limited concern over foreign markets, has continued to view that it can deal with national industrial problems without an industrial policy of larger scope and sophistication, such a view is really untenable. The evidence before us should make it obvious that:

- An industrial policy that is international in its orientation is a must.
- Both public and private capital and implicit tax and fiscal policies must be perceived as moving beyond national boundaries to achieve national economic goals.
- Policies and legislation must reflect emerging international as well as national values. Perhaps the most significant area in which this problem is posed is that of our concern over monopoly or size of firm as it affects market control. The Sherman AntiTrust "philosophy," as reflected in the original legislation, no longer meets our industrial policy needs.
- The only way to compete with the social partnerships that produce effective economic competitors in Germany, Japan, Singapore, Taiwan, and others is to develop our own mechanism for teaming private industry, government, and labor.

Finally, the need to move away from economic growth policies that are primarily inward-looking, or largely concerned with domestic problems, grows out of other factors, factors of fairly recent concern. To begin with, though the United States could at one time consider "beggar-my-neighbor" policies such as tariffs, quotas, and other trade barriers and fear only limited retaliation, this is no longer a realistic option. Since 1970, export of goods as a share of the GNP has increased by more than 100 percent. The burden of protecting employment in a domestic industry by imposing import quotas or other barriers on competitive imports not only affects our consumers by increasing prices but retaliation by affected countries against U.S. export industries has an impact on the employment in those industries. It is simply not politically as feasible as it once was to help U.S. industries by discriminating against competition from abroad. The votes of senators and representatives from the state in which the protected industry is located is now increasingly opposed by congressional peers whose home industries may suffer as a consequence of foreign retaliation.

Of perhaps greater significance is the fact that as the nations that are the major sources of capital for the developing countries, including those of the Soviet bloc, have extended loans to these countries, unless these developing countries have a world of relatively free trade available to them, the loan countries become hostage to the borrowing countries. Repudiation of national debts by Mexico, Argentina, Poland, and Chile, among others, would have major consequences for the economies of the lending nations. Bank asset positions and the effects on reserves result in serious restrictions of domestic economic activities. Beyond the economic consequences, however, of these economic problems are the consequences of the political instability accompanying default. The major trading nations of the world simply have to curtail traditional patterns of behavior that, during periods of economic crisis, sacrifice international economic considerations for domestic goals. They now must be seen as so closely related that neither can be considered without the implications for the other.

Finally, the many nations with large populations that make up the developing segment of the world represent a potential for trade that can only be achieved by expanding international cooperation rather than resorting to restrictive trade practices. For the major industrial nations to succeed in their efforts to increase per capita output and wealth, loans and other forms of aid must be tied to policies and programs that are productivity-oriented. Time and experience have shown that developing countries are often those with the least susceptibility to the sorts of political and economic reforms necessary for a more productive economy and society. Only if the industrial leaders of the world develop increasingly effective mechanisms for cooperation in trade and employment matters, abjuring policies that provide gains for one nation at the expense of another, will they be able to provide leverage for the necessary economic and political reforms required in developing countries.

We must succeed in increasing the rates of economic growth of these nations because in the not-so-long run, it is their levels of demand that will help the advanced industrial nations to achieve and maintain stable levels of economic output. Though nations such as Japan and West Germany have enjoyed prolonged periods of economic health, there will be periods of recession, such as 1980–82. Even Japan's economic growth rate waivered during 1981 and 1982. Had there existed a healthy rate of growth among the developing countries, which were instead in positions of near debt default, an additional factor of demand might have alleviated the severity of the economic downturn in the United States and Western Europe. The long-run interests of the United States, Japan, West Germany, the United Kingdom, and other important trading nations call for a greater dependence on international rather than national programs to deal with national problems.

Even lacking retaliatory actions by foreign countries, protectionist policies will result in U.S. unemployment that offsets employment created by tariffs, quotas, or subsidies. This is so because of the automatic mechanism of the "floating" exchange rate that has prevailed since 1973. If a decision was made to protect the U.S. steel industry by imposing import quotas on foreign steel, the currency of the foreign countries affected would drop in value relative to the dollar. This is so because we would no longer need those currencies for steel purchases. But the dollar would appreciate or increase in its relative value against those currencies, automatically increasing the cost in these foreign countries of various U.S. exports. Thus, for every U.S. worker gaining employment through protection, another in a different industry on foreign sales would have his or her job imperiled. With floating exchange rates, using trade barriers to save one worker's job means putting another worker out of work.

A Nonadversarial Relationship Between Key Economic and Political Institutions

At the beginning of this chapter, Lee Iacocca, of the Chrysler Corporation, was quoted as saying "I think free enterprise, laissez-faire free enterprise died a while back." This statement was made in 1979, when Chrysler was requesting aid from the federal government. On July 22, 1981, while addressing an audience at the National Press Club, he reinforced his 1979 position: ". . . Adam Smith went out of style decades ago."[29] The sentences preceding these words are, perhaps, of even greater significance. ". . . we need a new management attitude in this country.

We need the flexibility to put a labor leader on the board, the foresight to develop new techniques of cooperation in the work place, and the wisdom to avoid the temptation of preaching doctrinaire free enterprise, when we know Adam Smith went out of style decades ago."[30] I would only disagree with the word "wisdom"; it should be "honesty." There are very few business leaders who when "preaching doctrinaire free enterprise" really believe in what they are saying. While there were many Adam Smith ties worn in Washington during 1980 and 1981, very few of their wearers would have enjoyed competing in the marketplace envisioned as idyllic by Adam Smith.

To return to a critical earlier point, in the United States and Great Britain we have two nations that have a frozen economic philosophy that has caused a major deterioration in our capacities to produce, compete, and grow economically. Other nations have maintained a flexibility that has permitted their economic institutions to change in a manner calculated to meet their ever-changing social, economic, and political goals. One of the best statements recognizing this reality came from Bernard M. Sallott, of the Society of Manufacturing Engineers. Sallott was discussing the records of technological and industrial progress in Japan and West Germany. His concern was over the usual notion that it was the economic aid given these countries by the United States that provided the key stimulus for their recovery and consequent effective competition with the United States for world markets. But Sallott came up with a statement that is all too rare in its honesty and insight and gets to the heart of our problem:

> It has been said, in the case of Japan and Western Germany who are our leading competitors today, that the reason they are is because in World War II we destroyed their industrial base, and therefore they were able to rebuild, using new technologies.
>
> We submit that's a partial reason; it is not the entire reason.
>
> World War II was over 35 years ago. If you look at the technologies in many of the basic industries in our competitor nations, you'll find them 20 years or less of age. What this tells us is that they rebuilt with newer technology, but then revised that also upward.
>
> By contrast, in many cases in the United States we are still using technologies that served us well in World War II.
>
> When the industrial base of those countries was destroyed—and I don't think this point comes through significantly—we destroyed something else. That was the institutional structure surrounding the industrial base that made it work.
>
> When the industrial base was rebuilt, Japan and West Germany were able to rebuild a structure better suited to what they were doing. This then enabled them to set national goals, to plan to their implementation, and to bring together, in a cohesive fashion, all the elements of their society.

> We have not done that. We had a system that for 200 years has served us well, in fact, extremely well. This was the competitive free enterprise system. But we wonder if perhaps that competitive free enterprise system has not gone over the threshold and gone into really, in some cases, a bitter struggle between the segments of our economy, those segments that should be working together. I think you can find many people who would support that.[31]

No economic or political ideology is immune for very long from the encroachment of the forces of change, not even the supposed monolith of Marxist socialism. As the Soviet Union continues to await the withering away of capitalism, but exists chiefly because of the availability of food and technology from the Western capitalist countries, the Soviet satellites that have done best are those that have managed to move away from the Marxist's prescription. Bulgaria, Hungary, East Germany, and Czechoslovakia have, in varying degrees, begun to meld central planning with a variety of free market mechanisms.

In 1979, Hungary was confronted by serious balance of payment problems with the West. It had paid out $1 billion more in various Western currencies than it had taken in. With a $7 billion debt to foreign bankers, it could ill afford such a drain, especially if it continued. Quickly, Hungary passed laws that permitted entrepreneurs such as building contractors and computer programmers to set up their own private businesses. It broke up giant trusts, such as coal, which were operating uneconomically, and threatened to shut down enterprises that did not show a profit. Hungarian officials had also begun to discuss the possibility of establishing a stock market or bond market so promising industries could raise capital. By the end of 1981, Hungary's trade deficit was eliminated and the country was running a slight surplus in its convertible currency accounts.[32]

East Germany has adopted the targeting strategy of MITI, working with growth industries, coordinating what are, in reality, industry goals with supportive government legislation, but using efficiency indicators not too far removed from a bottom-line profit. Bulgaria has moved away from fixed, arbitrary quotas for production to a system based on cost-effective models and balance sheet results. Poland, as we know, was halted in its efforts to remake its economic model so that it reflected the growing, difficult-to-conceal widening gap between a passé political ideology and the realities of a new economic order. The brutal austerity of the clampdown on Poland cannot forever stay the need for reform, unless the military might of the Soviet Union remains forever at the ready to enforce the rules of an outmoded system. Interestingly, as of this writing, only the willingness of its creditors of the West, the capitalists, to delay calling the overdue debt prevents Poland from defaulting.

Even the Soviet Union itself has been moving in the direction of a mix of state-dominated objectives and private-oriented mechanisms. In an article Thomas H. Naylor, of Duke University, commented on a recent trip in Russia:

> My stay in Moscow included visits with scientists in leading research groups spread over the Soviet Academy of Sciences, Gosplan and Moscow State University. They were using a wide variety of different state-of-the-art management science and computer-based modeling techniques. The research agenda, however, was always the same: evaluating the effect of decentralized, market-driven planning in the Soviet Union.
>
> The quality of this research was at least equal to that being produced by leading American corporations and graduate schools of business. The United States need not fear that the Russians will try to steal its management-science technology. They have already developed their own.
>
> One of the most interesting projects I saw was a computer-based management game to show the effects of flexible wages and incentives on worker productivity and absenteeism. Another project involved real-world experiments with a sample of Soviet industries to study the effects of alternative management systems and price-formation mechanisms on Soviet enterprises. Since my return from Moscow, two other leading Soviet research groups and a Polish group have contacted me about their work in this field.
>
> These efforts appear to go well beyond certain reforms of the 1960s that consisted of isolated and abortive attempts to introduce market-oriented techniques. First, the work observed in Moscow is widespread throughout the Soviet Union and other East European countries, including Czechoslovakia, Hungary, Poland and Yugoslavia. Second, this work is being done with the full knowledge of the Soviet government. Indeed, the Soviet planning agency, Gosplan, is one of the sponsors. To cynics who might claim that none of this is new, the answer is that it appears that someone in Moscow is listening to what these Soviet economists are saying.[33]

With the advent of the socialist government, in 1982, in France, the expectations for a radical move away from the previous government's reliance on market-force motivation were logical. But what actually transpired was quite different. A cooperative mixed form of shared capitalism evolved instead. Jacques Delors, economic and finance minister, has encouraged the growth of venture capital necessary for social objectives through the use of various devices relying on the profit motive. In order to encourage the use of private funds for starting new, innovative enterprises, the Finance Ministry has granted tax exemptions and encouraged businesses to use principal capital to generate growth via such exemptions. Also contemplated is a new division of the French stock market to help finance medium-sized business firms. The socialist government is busy pushing risk taking, with suitable monetary rewards via tax breaks, in order to achieve economic growth. It was put most clearly by Daniel Lebegue, adviser to Prime Minister Pierre Mauroy and one of the architects of the new French economy: "We don't want to stop people from making money. But we want them to be the most creative people, the ones who are taking risks."[34]

Capitalism, in its various forms, continues as the most effective way of bringing together the resources of a nation in order to serve the needs and values of that nation. But capitalism is a dynamic force. Perhaps the worst enemies of the capitalist system are those who propose to freeze it, chain it to a static philosophy. The best supporters of a capitalist system know that the core of capitalism is a motivation to achieve in an environment, political and economic, that takes into account the changing values and institutions of the larger society.

The evidence has long been in that the most effective model for capitalism is the one that brings the key institutions into a harmonious, cooperating relationship, not an adversarial one. In a way, the greatest capitalist of them all, commenting on a far different matter, the trust versus the individual, described where we are currently. John D. Rockefeller said, "The day of combination is here to stay. Individualism has gone, never to return."[35] The day of government, or industry, or labor going its own way has long disappeared from those capitalist countries that have been competing most effectively and sustaining levels of productivity necessary to sustain a healthy economy.

Though Rockefeller was at the opposite end of the spectrum from Theodore Roosevelt, they both shared this insight, but for different reasons. Roosevelt observed:

> A simple and poor society can exist as a democracy on a basis of sheer individualism. But a rich and complex industrial society cannot so exist; for some individuals, and especially those artificial individuals called corporations, become so very big that the ordinary individual . . . cannot deal with them on terms of equality. It therefore becomes necessary for these ordinary individuals to combine in their turn. . . .[36]

Roosevelt was referring to the natural growth of farm coops and labor unions. He then added the observation:

> Business cannot be successfully conducted in accordance with the practices and theories of sixty years ago unless we abolish steam electricity, big cities and, in short, not only all modern business and modern industrial conditions, but all the modern conditions of our civilization.[37]

Teddy Roosevelt's acumen was, almost 80 years ago, infinitely greater than that of many of the economists who have been advising our leaders in industry and government.

In the United States, Great Britain, Canada, and many of the developing countries, where the new model of shared capitalism has not developed, economic performance has lagged. Unless steps are taken to move in the direction of shared capitalism, the United States will continue to lag. In each country, we must take into account special needs, values, and characteristics as we move to a new model. No country can or should simply seek to duplicate or copy another. The Japanese took from the West what it needed, but kept much of what was of most value in its culture. The art of great innovation is to build on the shoulders of others but maintain a sense of integrity to one's own values in order to achieve the objectives without losing one's own identity. The United States did this in its Revolution, its Constitution, its industrial revolution during the 1860s, and at the turn of the nineteenth century. We are at a point where we must build anew.

Notes

1. *Chrysler Corporation Loan Guarantee Act of 1979,* Hearings before the Committee on Banking, Housing and Urban Affairs, U.S. Senate, 96th Congress, 1st Session, Part 1, November 14, 15, 1979, p. 641.

2. Herbert Stein, "Mr. Reagan Is a Tax Hike Hero," *Wall Street Journal,* August 27, 1982, p. 16.

3. *New York Times,* August 27, 1982, p. A10.

4. Ibid.

5. Ibid.

6. Ibid.

7. *Washington Post,* Washington Business Section, August 23, 1982, p. 3.

8. Ibid.

9. "4 'New Japans' Mounting Industrial Challenge," *New York Times,* August 24, 1982, p. 1.

10. "Make Way for the New Japans," *Fortune,* August 10, 1981, p. 177.

11. "4 'New Japans' Mounting Industrial Challenge," p. D5.

12. Ibid.

13. John Stuart Mill, *Principles of Political Economy,* 2 vols. (reprint ed., New York: Augustus M. Kelley, 1979), Book II, pp. 199–200.

14. Ibid., p. 243

15. James Maitland, Eighth Earl of Lauderdale, *An Inquiry into the Nature and Origin of Public Wealth,* 1st ed. (1804; reprint ed., New York: Augustus M. Kelley, 1962).

16. Daniel P. Raymond, *The Elements of Political Economy* (1823, reprint ed., New York: Augustus M. Kelley, 1964), vol. I, p. 45.

17. Ibid, p. 36.

18. J. F. Bell, *A History of Economic Thought* (New York: Ronald Press, 1953), p. 351. The perception, or interpretation, of Bagehot is best illustrated in Bagehot's writings on the abstract nature of political economy, *The Collected Works of Walter Bagehot,* vol. 11 (London: The Economist, 1978).

19. H. E. Striner, *Retraining as a National Capital Investment, Productivity Brief 10* (Houston, Tex.: American Productivity Center, February 1982), p. 3.

20. Ibid, p. 5.

21. Bureau of Labor Statistics, U.S. Department of Labor, USDL 83-248, *News,* May 26, 1983, p. 2.

22. H. E. Striner, "Regaining the Lead in Productivity Growth," *The National Productivity Review,* (Winter 1981–82): 5–12.

23. Peter F. Drucker, "Toward the Next Economics," in *The Public Interest,* special ed. (New York: National Affairs, 1980), pp. 17–18.

24. David Sarnoff, John von Neumann, et al., *The Fabulous Future* (New York: Dutton, 1955), p. 47.

25. *Fortune,* August 10, 1981, p. 178.

26. *Fortune,* November 30, 1981, p. 122.

27. *Wall Street Journal,* September 1, 1982, p. 19.

28. M. Anderson, "Shake-Up in Detroit: New Technology, New Problems," *Technology Review,* August–September 1982, pp. 56–70.

29. Lee A. Iacocca, "We Can Do It the American Way," Remarks on July 22, 1981, National Press Club, Washington, D.C., p. 17.

30. Ibid.

31. *Implementation of P.L. 96-480, Stevenson-Wydler Technology Innovation Act of 1980,* Hearings before the Subcommittee on Science, Research and Technology, Committee on Science and Technology, U.S. House of Representatives, U.S. Congress, 97th Congress, 1st Session, July 14, 15, 16, 1981, p. 168.

32. *Washington Post,* May 24, 1982, p. 1.

33. Thomas H. Naylor, *International Herald Tribune,* November 1, 1982, p. 4.

34. "This Is Socialism?" *New York Times,* November 1, 1982, p. A19.

35. *New York Times,* May 9, 1982, sect. 3, p. 1F.

36. John Morton Blum, *The Republican Roosevelt* (New York: Atheneum, 1972), p. 110.

37. Ibid., p. 117.

The New
Shared Capitalism
in the United States
===6===

What has been described in the preceding chapters concerning the German and Japanese experience and the new economic model is a form of capitalism that differs radically from what we are used to associating with this term. It is not the capitalism built upon the types of market forces that grow out of the narrow instincts of self-interest, in accordance with laissez-faire economics. It is a capitalism emanating from the instincts for cooperation, sharing of risks and a wish for a more secure society. In this capitalism we can bring all of our ample resources to bear for achieving growth rates and levels of economic output that raise the standard of living for all of our citizens at the long-term expense of none. Of course in a short-term situation, someone must give up something if another is to get more. But that worry has been the all-consuming concern of our economic and political thinking. It is the counterpart of the short-term management decision making we know we must begin to change. The concept of a "zero sum" does not appear in the Japanese or West German perspective of economic growth.

In his book *The Zero-Sum Society* Lester Thurow described as the ". . . heart of our fundamental problem"[1] the fact that though we are all in favor of more investment for economic growth, no one is willing to cut his or her own personal income in order to provide for the necessary amount of investment funds. As a means of illustrating this problem, Thurow related a story about his appearing before a group of Harvard alumni and asking, " 'Whose income were they willing to cut after they had eliminated government programs for the poor?' Not a hand went up." The problem, Thurow says, is that the solutions to our economic problems all ". . . have the characteristic that someone must suffer large economic losses."[2] Because we tend to veto the efforts of others who would cause a loss of income to ourselves, and we in turn are vetoed by others whose income we attempt to cut, the result is an economy with a substantial zero-sum element. Is there no way out of this problem in the United States? While Thurow sees the problem of allocating economic gains as achievable, he sees allocating losses as a problem that paralyzes our political processes.

This need not be the case. Among their many mistakes, the "supply-side" economists in the early 1980s made a spectacularly faulty assumption about the relationship between savings and investment, that savings would result *very quickly* in investments. Although savings do not necessarily generate investments overnight, they do provide the basis for investment at *some* future point.

What would happen if the Japanese tax treatment on savings were introduced in this country? What if up to $50,000 to $60,000 of bank deposits were exempt from taxes on interest, and, as would likely happen, available commercial bank reserves increased substantially? Since it is these reserves that provide the base for creation of new accounts, it would seem that a larger source of investment funds and venture capital would become available. In addition, the untaxed interest income would also be available for investment purposes.

But, one might respond, wouldn't government tax receipts be lower as well as sales in those industries whose sales are curtailed? Yes, but these could well be offset by tax income generated by the stimulus of higher investment levels over time and the new incomes generated by these higher rates of investment in plants, jobs, and so on. This in turn would lead to increasing consumption of goods and services.

There are many more, rather complex secondary and tertiary effects that could be followed through in an economic analysis of this sequence of events. But for the purposes of this discussion, suffice it to say that neither Japan nor Germany has apparently succumbed to the zero-sum sickness. There do seem to be antidotes, but—and here Thurow is absolutely correct—these antidotes assume that we must change *something*. The something is the set of institutional relationships that hinder us from seeing all of our key actors as critical components that must cooperate in our capitalist system.

Our objective must be to promote those forces that increase the size of the economic pie substantially enough, steadily enough, so that all share to a meaningful degree. The proof of the efficacy of this simple observation can be gained from our own recent economic history.

During the decade of the late 1950s to the late 1960s, when the buoyancy and growth of the U.S. economy was unparalleled, we heard little about the problem of sharing. The major emphasis was on the nature of the mechanism for sharing the product in the most effective way to achieve our national goals, such mechanisms as the Manpower Development and Training Act or the War on Poverty. It was during this period that our society was long-term goal oriented, since the economy seemed to guarantee that the means for achieving these goals would and could be available. Now the emphasis is less on long-term aspirations or goals and more on simple survival.

Though the 1958–68 decade was one of great achievement, it contained the seeds of its own undoing. Adversarialism, a move away from production management to financial management, excess pride of being number one industrially, easy granting of pay demands exceeding productivity gain, and lack of concern for human resource investment necessary to maintain a skilled labor force were some of the key deficiencies in our pattern of thinking and planning. Now we must change our form of capitalism. We must develop the sort of model referred to in the previous chapter. We must now build a system based upon the fact that though we are not capable of eliminating risk, we can develop a mechanism that shares the risks of a capitalist system in such a way that we minimize the waste of economic resources and maximize the potential and output of our resources. Shared capitalism is what has been working in Japan and West Germany; laissez-faire capitalism is what has been failing in the United States.

This chapter describes how to apply the model of shared capitalism in the United States. An easy response to this description may be that it is utopian and impractical. It is no more utopian than that which currently exists in those countries that have surpassed our economic record in recent years. If by impractical is meant that it requires significant change, then the only counter is to accept that we are ready to continue on as we have been for the last seven or eight years, in a morass of a poorly functioning economy. It is imperative that we accept the dictum "You can't be what you want to be by being what you are."[3] Progress is always based on constructive change.

The first major area of change in our national agenda for economic growth policies relates to human resources investment. There is where productivity starts. This is the basis for our system of value.

The Human Resources Investment Strategy

True job security lies in re-instating productivity as the purpose of governments and the practical goal of business.[4]

But productivity and job security are linked not only at the point of employment. Productivity and job security are linked in terms of employability. No matter how many job vacancies exist, if you do not have the

required skills you will remain unemployed. Employability in an industrial economy characterized increasingly by its high-technology characteristics starts with an adequate grade-school education. The combined
level of illiteracy and functional illiteracy in the United States is somewhere between 20 and 30 percent. In at least one specific instance, it is
more than 40 percent. A government survey in 1979 revealed that "forty-
two percent of recently surveyed black 17-year-olds were functionally illiterate."[5] For such individuals, even public service employment offers
little hope.

Based on a 1979 Ford Foundation report, William McGowan wrote
that about 25 million Americans cannot read at all and 35 million more are
functionally illiterate.[6] As McGowan comments, recent cuts in federal aid
to help deal with this problem only continue a several-decades-old record
of earlier federal inactivity. "Right-to-Read" programs instituted in both
Democratic and Republican administrations have received little real
funding commitment. In a world based more and more upon communications, the unemployability and low-productivity implications of illiteracy
are of major proportions. The impact on profits and costs to each of us is
equally serious. Mutual of New York Insurance Company "estimates that
70 percent of its dictated correspondence has to be redone at least once
because of errors. In 1975, a herd of prime beef cattle was killed acciden-
tally when a Chicago feedlot laborer misread a package label and gave the
cattle poison instead of food."[7]

The situation where jobs exist but not the people with matching skills
who can fill the jobs was cited by the Regional Planning Association of
New York as the area's chief industrial problem for the next 20 years.[8]
This problem exists throughout the United States and results in part from
poor primary and secondary school systems.

The most desperate problems of grade and high school education are
to be found in the large metropolitan centers like Detroit, New York, Chicago, and St. Louis. Yet these are the very cities with the most severe problems of inadequate funding. The St. Louis school system, with about
59,000 students, is typical of that of a growing number of large cities with
the increasingly difficult problem of providing a high quality of education
for its youth. Since 1976 the costs of education have risen about 63 percent
in St. Louis, but state aid only increased by 3 percent. By 1982 the school
board deficit rose to $26 million, but federal aid dropped by $12 million
and local tax revenue dropped by $2.4 million. Because voters voted
down a tax increase that would have helped the school system, school
officials were forced to lay off 24 percent of the system's work force. The
average size of classes rose by about 40 percent, and when schools opened
in September 1982, some classes had 75 students in them.[9]

The distressingly low educational quality of the students coming out of our public schools is manifested not only by poor job performance in industry but also in the military, the public sector's largest "employer." In a study done by the Congressional Research Service, Library of Congress, it was found that the proportion of below educational average personnel in the U.S. military has risen substantially between 1975 and 1981. There has been an increase in the percentage of volunteers with a low educational standard. The percentage of average and above average enlisted personnel has declined since the shift to volunteer forces. Under the volunteer system the proportion of blacks has risen substantially. The correlation between volunteerism, low incomes, inadequate educational preparation, blacks, and poor city schools is socially programmed.[10]

But the problem in the military also reflects the larger problem of a national shortage of skills. Given the increasing demands for highly trained and skilled workers in the civilian sector, the natural process of salary competition among firms also drains skilled personnel from the military. Air force aircaft, army tanks, and naval ships are out of operation because of too few skilled personnel available to operate or maintain them. In a typical situation in 1980, repeated many times since then in other services, a frontline ship was tied up in Norfolk, Virginia, because there were not enough sailors with the required skills to operate it.[11] The ship, the U.S. Canisteo, was unable to steam out of port on a critical assignment because the "skipper told his Navy superiors this would be unsafe because she has too few key people—such as chiefs, boiler technicians, and machinists mates—to steam safely for months at a time."

An internal navy study indicated in 1980 that the service was 20,000 short of the most skilled enlisted people, and even if their most ambitious goals for reenlistment were realized, they would still be 15,500 short in 1985. The solution was felt to be higher pay in order to compete with the private sector. But this is hardly a practical alternative in an economy where the shortage of these very skills is causing the private firms to increase pay levels on a constant basis. Only during periods of recession can the armed services look forward to any gain in competitive advantage. It is hardly worth saying that an adequate U.S. defense posture cannot be based on a state of continuing recession. It has been obvious to any individual following the employment scene that during any normal period of economic activity, mechanics, production engineers, tool and die specialists, computer maintenance personnel, and so forth, are in short supply. But even during periods of recession, the supply of such skilled individuals as computer maintenance personnel, laboratory technicians, health maintenance personnel, office machine maintenance personnel, and professional secretaries is inadequate to fill the demand.

At the professional level, we are confronted with a major shortage of personnel in most of the engineering and science fields.[12] American companies are recruiting people from Asia, the Middle East, and South America to deal with a shortage of technical professionals that emerged in the mid-1970s and is still with us even in the midst of a recession economy in 1982. According to the National Science Foundation, fewer American students are seeking advanced degrees in technical fields, opting to take high-paying jobs after graduation; foreign students take their places in graduate schools and then later fill the higher paying senior jobs in industry.

The Xerox Corporation estimates that 15 percent of its U.S. research staff is composed of foreigners; General Electric estimates 25 percent of its research personnel at Schenectady, New York, are alien residents; Intel, a major Silicon Valley manufacturer of computer components, estimates that fully 40 percent of its 500-person research staff is foreign. "We have one computer design group," said Gerry Parker, Intel's vice president of technology, "where eight of the ten members are Chinese nationals from Taiwan."[13]

Perhaps the worst aspect of this shortage of professionals in the engineering, computer science, and related fields is that we are in the midst of losing our preeminence in engineering and science education. In 1981, a study was published indicating that U.S. schools of engineering are being stripped of faculty because of industry shortages of such professional skills.[14] Inability to fill increasing numbers of faculty vacancies, larger numbers in classes, less research being done, lower quality of teaching, less variety of courses, increased teaching loads, greater reliance on graduate assistants for teaching—all are symptomatic of a major underinvestment in our science resources.

In addition to the human resources underinvestment situation, our unwillingness to invest in the capital equipment that today must be linked to the person in order to achieve productivity gains is also at an unbelievably low level. In 1980, Tokyo University added more computing power to its education programs than was then in place at the ten leading universities in the United States.[15] In 1982, most of the students at major U.S. institutions were still unacquainted with how to work with a computer. Students in schools of engineering, schools of business, and other components of a university where computers are closely tied to studies complained of inadequate computer facilities for a worthwhile learning experience.

Though all of the evidence from industry and government indicates severe shortages of workers for existing jobs, we really do not know the full extent of these shortages. The United States does not have, as most industrialized countries do, a system for acquiring information on job vacancies in the economy. The individual state employment services only have job-order information. That is, if a firm chooses to list a job as vacant with its local employment office for purposes of getting recruiting help, then we know about the job opening. But many firms do not follow this practice, for various reasons.

Hence, when economists say ". . . there simply are not enough jobs, good or bad, to go around,"[16] they really do not know this for a fact. This may be true during a recession, but during periods of high levels of economic activity the real problem could be that there are too few people with requisite skills to fill available jobs. I suspect that our changing definition of "full employment" really reflects this lack of information about unemployability versus unemployment. Since the late 1960s, when full employment was seen as existing when the unemployment level reached around 4 percent, by the late 1970s, this figure was held to be around 6 percent.[17] By 1982, some economists felt that 7 percent might be a better figure.

It does not take much stretch of imagination to conclude that with 60 million Americans who cannot read or write well enough to hold basic jobs, at least a small proportion of these people would be among the unemployed. Only 5 percent of the 60 million would be enough to account for the difference between 4 percent and 7 percent unemployed! A difference of these three percentage points accounts for 3 million unemployed.

A major part of the problem of dealing intelligently with the problem of those individuals who are unemployable is simply put: it is that of racism. Large numbers of Americans who are well educated, economically secure, and pride themselves on being fairminded on the subject of race, nonetheless address, or refuse to address, problems from a point of view clouded by subconscious racist perceptions.

This was once forcibly brought to my attention when I was addressing a group of senior business leaders on the subject of investing in retraining and basic education programs for the unskilled and unemployable in our work force. One of the executives reacted by raising doubts about the motivation and willingness of such individuals to take part in these programs. When I asked him for further details on what sorts of people he had in mind, he appeared reluctant to go any farther. I then asked if he meant blacks. Breathing a sigh of relief at having been rescued from offering this information on his own, he nodded affirmatively. "Yes," he said, "to deal with the inherent problems of motivating such people would be extremely costly and time-consuming, something we, as a nation, would not be willing to assume as a burden." I replied that it would certainly be costly to do what I proposed, but in all of my research and thinking about the problem of this group, I had only been able to come up with three alternatives, each of which was far more costly than the one I was recommending.

The first alternative was to continue to do what we are doing. Specifically, pay unemployment benefits, welfare, and accepting the loss to the GNP of tax income lost by these people not working. For each percentage point of unemployment, this cost the United States about $30 billion per year. In addition, there are some unknown, but probably huge, theft, property damage, police, and higher insurance costs growing out of the antisocial behavior patterns of the unemployables, who see themselves as aliens in their own land.

The second alternative was to build more jails and prisons to, essentially, warehouse these people. At a cost of $50,000 to $60,000 to build each cell, with its attendant facilities, plus the annual costs of food, clothing, equipment, security, maintenance, and heating, this surely must be significantly higher than any envisioned cost for retraining and skills upgrading.

Finally, I said, there is a third alternative. We could shoot these people. Not outright, of course, but by judicious instructions to police and jail guards that on the slightest pretext of resistance when being arrested, or in dealing with prison infraction, escalate the situation in some way so that the miscreant could be shot fatally. This, I said, could at least eliminate some of this population. But, I ventured, no one could really view this alternative as a civilized option.

At this point, I asked this business leader if he had an alternative I had not thought of which was more effective and less costly to our society than my program for adequate counseling and training, calculated to provide an unemployable person with a real job potential. And then I waited for an answer. And waited. The silence in the room was appalling. Typically, in such a situation, the socially graceful thing to do is for the speaker to go on to other matters or another question, in order to get the person off the hook. But I didn't. Finally, a quiet, sad response came: "I never thought of the problem that way."

The fact that many Americans have not thought of the problem "that way" continues to impose upon our economy a burden of major proportions. And for our society, it means an increasing sense of conflict, a growing imbalance in the sharing of the burdens and benefits of our output, and, perhaps worst of all, an erosion of our belief in our democracy.

Unless we undertake a massive commitment to an educational skills-training and retraining program, the United States will continue to have a hemorrhage of wasted human resources. The cost in dollars, as of 1982, is about $30 billion for each percentage point of unemployment, considering only the unemployment benefits paid and lost production and income taxes. But there is a larger figure, the cost in terms of higher wages paid to a limited supply of skilled workers redoing shoddy work and of course the social costs of large numbers of unemployed workers. Crime, property loss, more prison space, and law enforcement are a part of this cost. It all sums up to a significant loss of national economic productivity.

This problem of a shortage of skilled workers is not a newly recognized one, nor is it a local problem. Back in 1977, it had begun to attract serious concern in many quarters. By 1978, it was perceived by fairly conservative organizations as a problem of national scope. In a *Wall Street Journal* article the point was made that though labor scarcities existed in such numbers as to constitute an economywide shortage, there were no really effective training programs to deal with the problem.[18] General Dynamics, Boeing, Koppers, Litton, Data General, Fisher Scientific, among others, cited critical shortages of toolmakers, welders, design drafters, machinists, computer programmers, boilermakers, and electricians. In the service industries a similar situation existed for bank tellers, nurses, paralegal secretaries, clerical workers, and office machine maintenance workers. And this was at a time when the unemployment rate was 6 percent. It was also at a time when it became easier to redefine full employment at the 6 percent level rather than do something about training or retraining unemployed workers for vacant, well-paying jobs.

The situation is going to worsen. In the next decade or so, there is going to be a major increase in the demand for welders, mechanics, machinists, sheet-metal workers, carpenters, and various other skilled workers in heavy construction. The ever-recurring concern about technology eliminating jobs will once more be laid to rest by the growth of other sectors that call for human workers, not robots. What is the new growth sector? Nothing less than our very cities and community facilities.

Rebuilding America's Public Plant

While America has been caught up in a feverish concern about robotics, microcomputers, silicon chips, a fiber-optics telephonic system, and other niceties of a Buck Rogers world coming into real existence, we have literally ignored what is beneath our feet and in front of our eyes. Our bridges, water systems, roads, docks, and other public works are in increasing disrepair and will have to be rebuilt, expanded, and repaired. In a remarkable study of this problem, the extent of corrosion, disrepair, and undercapacity of our nation's public plant is about to reach truly emergency needs.

The nation's 42,500-mile Interstate Highway System, only now approaching completion, is deteriorating at a rate requiring reconstruction of 2,000 miles of road per year. Because adequate funding for rehabilitation and reconstruction was not forthcoming in the late 1970s, over 8,000 miles of this system and 13 percent of its bridges are now beyond their designed service life and must be rebuilt. Although the system constitutes less than one percent of the nation's highways, it handles over 20 percent of all highway traffic. Its further decline will adversely affect the national economy and the well-being of thousands of communities and individual firms.

The costs of rehabilitation and new construction necessary to maintain existing levels of service on nonurban highways will exceed $700 billion during the 1980s. Even excluding the estimated $75 billion required to complete the unconstructed final 1,500 miles of the Interstate System, the balance required for rehabilitation and reconstruction is still greater than all the public works investments made by all units of government in the 1970s. Since inflation in highway construction has averaged 12.5 percent since 1975 (doubling costs each six years), continuation of present investment levels will permit less than one-third of needs to be met in this decade.

One of every five bridges in the United States requires either major rehabilitation or reconstruction. The Department of Transportation has estimated the costs of this task to be as high as $33 billion. Yet in Fiscal Year 1981 Federal Highway Authorizations, only $1.3 billion was allocated to repair bridge deficiencies.

Estimates of the amounts required to rebuild the deteriorating roadbeds and rolling stock of the railroads of the Northeast and Midwest are not available. While economic necessity may compel reductions in CONRAIL trackage by as much as half, or total reorganization of the system itself, this will not obviate the need for rail modernization. Railroads will play a critical role in national efforts to reduce transportation, energy consumption and ship more coal to power plants to replace imported oil. This is a national issue of major importance. A viable eastern rail system is essential to the economic health of the western and southern systems since these regional rail systems can thrive only as part of a national network linking all markets and centers of production.

No reliable estimates exist of the investments required to modernize our ports, but numerous instances exist of harbor facilities unable to service efficiently world shipping coming to American docks. Vessels in some ports must wait for as long as a month to pick up their cargo.

The nation's municipal water supply needs will make heavy demands upon capital markets in the 1980s. The 756 urban areas with populations of over 50,000 will require between $75 billion and $110 billion to maintain their urban water systems over the next 20 years. Approximately one-fifth of these communities will face investment shortfalls, even if present water rates are doubled to produce capital for new investment. At least an additional $10–$13 billion beyond that generated by existing user charges will be required.

Over $25 billion in government funds will be required during the next five years to meet existing water pollution control standards.

Over $40 billion must be invested in New York City alone over the next nine years to repair, service, and rebuild basic public works facilities that include: 1,000 bridges, two aquaducts, one large water tunnel, several reservoirs, 6,200 miles of paved streets, 6,000 miles of sewers, 6,000 miles of water lines, 6,700 subway cars, 4,500 buses, 25,000 acres of parks, 17 hospitals, 19 city university campuses, 950 schools, 200 libraries, and hundreds of fire houses and police stations. Because of its fiscal condition, New York City will be able to invest only $1.4 billion per year to repair, service, and rebuild these facilities.

At least $1 billion will be required to rebuild Cleveland's basic public works—$250 to $500 million is needed to replace and renovate the publicly-owned water system; over $150 million is required for major repairs of city bridges; and over $340 million must be spent for flood control facilities. In addition to these expenditures, Cleveland must find additional funds to rebuild or resurface 30 percent of its streets, now in a state of advanced deterioration, and to reconstruct the city's sewer collection system, which frequently floods commercial and residential buildings.

Even fiscally healthy cities face large public works investment requirements. For example, Dallas must raise almost $700 million for investment in water and sewerage treatment systems in the next nine years. More than $109 million must be generated to repair deteriorating city streets.

Over one-half of the nation's 3,500 jails are over 30 years old. At least 1,300 and perhaps as many as 3,000 of these facilities must be either totally rebuilt or substantially rehabilitated in the 1980s. This construction, in most cases, is court ordered. Thus, it often takes legal precedence over most, if not all, other public capital expenditures.

Rural facility needs, as yet unknown, are the subject of a major survey by the U.S. Department of Agriculture currently underway.

Water resource development will require major investments in all regions of the nation in the 1980s. The agricultural base in the old "Dustbowl" will be in jeopardy toward the end of the decade unless new water sources can be developed. After the Second World War, vast underground water resources close to the surface were tapped for irrigation. Today, this area in the Texas and Oklahoma panhandles and surrounding states has over 10 million acres under irrigation (23 percent of the nation's total irrigated farmland). This irrigated production produces over 40 percent of the nation's processed beef and major portions of wheat, sorghums, and other crops that supply much of America's agricultural exports. The region's water source is being depleted. At present rates it will be gone by the year 2000. The reversion of the region's agricultural production back to low-yield dryland farming would have a devastating effect on the economies of six states. It would seriously harm the nation's balance of payments and ultimately reduce the value of the dollar in international markets. If this production is to be retained, major public works to bring surplus water from adjacent regions are required.

Even such water "surplus" areas as New England, Pennsylvania, New Jersey, and New York are in water crises, in part, because of the inadequacies of their water supply, storage, treatment, and distribution systems that become apparent in times in *(sic)* drought.

A large number of the nation's 43,500 dams require investment to reduce hazardous deficiencies. The Corps of Engineers has already inspected 9,000 of these facilities and found many of them in need of safety improvements. The funds to inspect even the balance of these dams have not been available. A majority of the dams that are potentially hazardous are privately owned and the dam owners lack the financial resources, willingness, or understanding to take remedial measures. Nor do the states have the legislative authority, funds, or trained personnel to conduct their own inspection and remedial efforts.

These are not isolated or extreme examples. They represent broad trends of decline in both the quantity and quality of virtually every type of public works facility in the nation. Unless these trends are reversed and soon—the number of public facilities in usable condition will fall to even more dangerous levels.[19]

Just using the limited sums of money called for in the incomplete listing of public investment needs in the preceding paragraphs, about *$90 billion per year* is required to maintain and upgrade such facilities during the 1980s. This minimal figure translates into about 2 million people who must be employed in order to produce and maintain these public facilities. On the basis of U.S. government research which relates direct expenditures for highways, for example, to all of the indirect industries affected as suppliers, each billion dollars generates about 24,000 jobs.[20] This figure is a minimal one, as it does not take into account the effects of the income multiplier or accelerator. Parenthetically, the research being done in this area has been eliminated by budget cuts in 1982. Data on the job-created effects of expenditures in the U.S. economy will no longer be available on an up-to-date basis.

As can be seen from Table 6.1, public works investment (PWI) has been declining steadily, in real dollars, since 1967. What this major study shows is that the national plant itself must be funded at levels that are only perceived by specialists. But the order of magnitude will soon be obvious to every citizen and every company by virtue of the fact that the daily doing of business will be increasingly affected.

An October 7, 1982, article of the *Wall Street Journal* (p. 32), properly titled "Crumbling America: Put It in the Budget," was concerned about

Table 6.1. Total (Residential and Nonresidential) Public Works Investment, Gross and Net, and Depreciation (millions of constant 1972 dollars)

Year	Federal				State and Local				Total Government			
	Gross Investment	Depreciation	Depreciation as Percent of Gross Investment	Net Investment	Gross Investment	Depreciation	Depreciation as Percent of Gross Investment	Net Investment	Gross Investment	Depreciation	Depreciation as Percent of Gross Investment	Net Investment
1957	3,571	5,395	151.1	−1,824	20,374	8,325	40.86	12,049	23,945	13,720	57.30	10,225
1958	4,364	5,039	115.5	−675	21,663	8,752	40.40	12,911	26,027	13,791	52.99	12,236
1959	3,783	4,679	123.7	−896	22,081	9,128	41.34	12,953	25,864	13,807	53.38	12,057
1960	3,787	4,335	114.5	−548	22,300	9,523	42.70	12,777	26,087	13,858	53.12	12,229
1961	4,424	4,058	91.7	366	23,988	9,929	41.39	14,059	28,412	13,987	49.23	14,425
1962	4,981	3,865	77.6	1,116	24,660	10,342	41.94	14,318	29,641	14,207	47.93	15,434
1963	5,784	3,963	68.5	1,821	26,799	10,780	40.23	16,019	32,583	14,743	45.25	17,840
1964	6,602	3,756	56.9	2,846	28,652	11,259	39.30	17,393	35,254	15,015	42.59	20,239
1965	6,872	3,829	55.7	3,043	30,281	11,775	38.89	18,506	37,153	15,604	42.00	21,549
1966	7,040	3,949	56.1	3,091	32,422	12,327	38.02	20,095	39,462	16,276	41.24	23,186
1967	5,911	4,056	68.6	1,855	35,041	12,933	36.91	22,108	40,952	16,989	41.49	23,963
1968	4,401	4,132	93.9	269	36,944	13,608	36.83	23,336	41,345	17,740	42.91	23,605
1969	3,684	4,170	113.2	486	34,749	14,277	41.09	20,472	38,433	18,447	48.00	19,986
1970	3,716	4,189	112.7	−473	32,741	14,902	45.51	17,839	36,457	19,091	52.37	17,376
1971	3,931	4,185	106.5	−254	31,882	15,510	48.65	16,372	35,813	19,695	54.99	15,538
1972	4,010	4,164	103.8	154	31,125	16,111	51.76	15,014	35,135	20,275	57.71	14,860
1973	4,128	4,138	100.2	10	31,135	16,712	53.68	14,423	35,263	20,850	59.13	14,413
1974	3,845	4,094	106.5	249	32,147	17,335	53.92	14,812	35,992	21,429	59.54	14,563
1975	3,482	4,026	115.6	544	30,680	17,997	58.66	12,683	34,162	22,023	64.47	12,139
1976	3,765	3,954	105.0	−189	27,510	18,571	67.51	8,939	31,275	22,525	72.02	8,750
1977	4,122	3,893	94.4	229	25,826	19,076	73.86	6,750	30,037	22,969	76.47	7,068

Sources: J. C. Musgrave, BEA, special tabulation; U.S. Department of Commerce, *A Study of Public Works Investment in the United States* (Washington, D.C.: 1980), pp. 1–63.

the problems growing out of not having a capital budget for the United States. Reflecting this author's own views, this form of budgeting was seen as essential in order to deal properly with the problem of growing investment needs in our public facilities. But one reference graphically related industrial productivity to the level of adequacy of public facilities: "Two out of every five bridges in the U.S. are seriously deficient. U.S. Steel is losing $1.2 million per year in employee time and wasted fuel re-routing trucks around bridges that can no longer support the weight of its vehicles." The same can be said for millions of other commercial vehicles, school buses, and government vehicles, which have to do similar "detour planning."

In the area of housing and community facilities, the United States has had a very low percentage of GNP allocated for such programs. As can be seen from Table 6.2, West Germany, France, and the United Kingdom have been between 300 and 900 percent higher in their allocations. We have been cheating ourselves. To fund these activities will be one major question; to find the skilled workers to fill the jobs will be another. And the skills directly involved in repairing or building bridges, roads, docks, transit sytems, water systems, dams, streets, public hospitals, parks, and other public institutions are only the tip of the labor force iceberg. Supplier industries such as steel, glass, concrete, wood, and tools will also be called upon for additional output levels needing skilled workers. The tragedy of our concern over technological displacement of workers is that the near future will call for a major increase in the very types of workers and skills we now see as being obsolescent.

Can we plan for what we will need to provide in the way of skilled workers, assuming certain levels of increased activity in these construction industries, both at the final and supplier levels? To a great degree, yes. But dealing with this problem will require a planning process we are not

Table 6.2. Public Expenditure on Social Services as Percentage of Gross National Product, 1978.

	France 1977	Germany	United Kingdom	United States
Social security and welfare services	17.0	18.8	11.9	10.0
Health	5.6	6.3	4.8	2.6
Education	5.9	4.9	5.6	5.8
Housing and community amenities	2.0	1.2	3.6	.4
Total	30.5	31.2	25.9	18.8

Source: National Accounts of OECD Countries 1962–1979, vol. II (Paris, 1981), Annex 1.

used to as a nation. This has begun to be recognized by industrial leaders. David T. Kearns, president and chief operating officer of Xerox Corporation, was concerned with the primacy of retraining the labor force as well as the development of a national strategy for dealing with the quality of the U.S. labor force.[21] Kearns ended a speech delivered before a meeting of the American business press by saying:

> Some experts say that the average lead time on retraining is 10 years. We are the only industrial country that does not have a national manpower strategy. I don't know if we need a formal policy. But it seems to me that we can start managing this change by recognizing that it's here—now. It is going to take a change of focus from unemployment to employment. And it's going to take the realization that retraining—not reindustrialization—is the answer.

The task of relating the effects of increased production necessary for our public plant to the supplier industries, and the manpower implications, is a task for which an ample set of economic tools already exists. Indeed, other countries have availed themselves of the best of all economic tools for understanding these industrial interrelationships and developing the requisite programs and funding indicated. This analytic mechanism is the input-output technique developed by Nobel Laureate Wassily Leontief. In an article on this subject, Leontief stresses the effective use the Japanese have made of this technique for determining the primary, secondary, and tertiary effects of increases or decreases in levels of economic activities, by various sectors. What has been developed to a high level in Japan and other major industrial nations is in the United States "assigned to a small team tucked away in one of the many bureaus of the Department of Commerce."[22]

The Japanese see this form of economic analysis as indispensable to government and business planning. In the United States industry hardly knows about the technique, and government sees it as an activity of minimal interest. It would be difficult to find many members of the various Presidents' Councils of Economic Advisors who have ever been involved in using the technique or understanding its value. Since it was developed by an American economist and first used in the United States, it could be seen as another one of our exports used by our competitors to eclipse our industrial performance.

A Manpower Strategy

I believe that our manpower strategy must follow the lead taken in Germany. Every American, employed or unemployed, should be entitled to a period of retraining, with an income stipend, to guarantee that our labor force will be sufficiently skilled, on a continuing basis, in order to meet the skills needs of industry and public institutions. As with the German program, the stipend subsidy should be inversely related to the last prior income so that low-skill trainees will receive the most encouragement to upgrade skills and increase income levels.

This strategy must be based upon a simple, logical fact of modern life. Just as a primary and secondary education was a necessary form of public support in order to provide the basic educational needs for the world of work up until the 1930s, reality now calls for a new, continuing form of investment in our human resources throughout life. If a 40, 50, or 60-year-old, can improve his or her work skills and thereby increase personal income, pay higher taxes, and increase our productivity, then for a society not to invest in this potential is nothing short of absurd. In Germany, France, and other Western European countries, such programs exist and can be looked to for legislative models.

This sort of manpower strategy must also include literacy training components. Past inadequacies of literacy training have to be dealt with, both at the grade and high school levels, as well as at the adult education level. Here the availability of computer-assisted learning techniques can, with amply available equipment, dramatically shorten the period for teaching reading skills.

What is most crucial in the design of this manpower strategy is that it be viewed as an entitlement. To build such a program on the basis of annual legislative hearings and appropriations is to guarantee its failure. The problem of short-term corporate planning is as nothing when compared to the short-term agendas of legislators, both federal and local. Investment in human resources must be viewed and understood to be long term. The yo-yo of annual appropriations is as inappropriate for this effort as it would be for a war for survival. Indeed, this is a war for economic survival and, as in all wars, the individual is at the center of crucial decisions and operations. As technologies, processes, and products change, so will the role of the individual worker and manager. As some industries grow in significance, others decline. The process is natural and calls for a continuing, calm analysis of the actual situations involved. Too often, the "Chicken Little" syndrome takes over, and we generalize what are specific situations in an illogical way.

In a paper in 1967 on this subject of changing technologies, I emphasized a few currently applicable points:[23]

> There is one additional elementary fact which must be considered when we conjure up an image of an overflowing horn of plenty enabling an ever-increasing outpouring of goods calling for less and less actual hu-

man inputs by 1984. This fact is that as the absolute numbers of production or blue-collar workers have grown less rapidly in our economy, there has been a sharp relative and absolute growth in nonproduction, nonagricultural workers. During the last decade or so, for the first time in our history this latter group of workers exceeded the number of production workers in the nation. In addition, ratios of supportive, maintenance, and similar types of workers to professional staff have changed radically. Crawford Greenwalt, President of E. I. du Pont de Nemours & Co., commented on this in 1955.[24] In 1938, there was one laboratory assistant to six professional scientists. By 1955, this ratio had changed to a one-to-one relationship. Support personnel in the health field have shown similar shifts. In one large hospital, the Boston Children's Hospital Medical Center, the number of personnel per patient has increased from three to four since 1960.[25] Interestingly, this occurred during a period of major purchases of capital equipment, which presumably represented an automation of services. But on a closer, more detailed examination of "automation" equipment, one discovers that an important portion represents new services, which in turn require more maintenance and supportive personnel. New open-heart surgery equipment doesn't replace anyone, except possibly the undertaker—but not forever! Computers displace, but in many instances create new uses and functions. There is still no really conclusive study on the net unemployment consequences of new technology. Technology displaces, replaces, and places. Returning to the medical field, the St. Francis General Hospital in Pittsburgh installed a new heart-lung machine, representing a new service. But this equipment called for the hiring of two technicians, a clerk, and two physicians.[26] New surgical techniques do the same. One new type of brain operation may require a team of 15 physicians and technicians, plus the new equipment. The equipment in turn calls for additional hours of maintenance, above and beyond original production personnel.

We get caught up in a simplistic cliché like "reindustrialization," which provides little help in dealing with the real, underlying problems of the economy. An adequate number of skilled individuals available to serve the changing need of industries, as they exist and change, is certainly one of these. A subset, a critical subset, is that of our scientists and engineers. Unless our investment in R&D and its human resources base is adequate, it will be difficult to achieve necessary levels of productivity gain.

R&D and Scientists and Engineers

The best indication of how a society establishes a priority, and how it changes its support, is to see how much of the goods and services pro-

Table 6.3.   National Expenditures for Performance of R&D, as
Percentage of Gross National Product

	United States	West Germany	France	Japan	United Kingdom
1961	2.73 (1.20)	N.A.*	1.38 (.97)	1.39 (1.37)	2.46 (1.48)
1962	2.73 (1.23)	1.25 (1.14)	1.46 (1.03)	1.47 (1.46)	N.A.
1963	2.87 (1.29)	1.41 (1.26)	1.55 (1.10)	1.44 (1.43)	N.A.
1964	2.96 (1.31)	1.57 (1.38)	1.81 (1.34)	1.48 (1.47)	2.29 (1.49)
1970	2.63 (1.50)	2.18 (1.96)	1.91 (1.47)	1.79 (1.77)	N.A.
1971	2.48 (1.46)	2.38 (2.16)	1.90 (1.33)	1.84 (1.81)	N.A.
1972	2.40 (1.44)	2.33 (2.13)	1.86 (1.35)	1.85 (1.81)	2.06 (1.48)
1973	2.32 (1.43)	2.22 (2.01)	1.76 (1.30)	1.89 (1.85)	N.A.
1978	2.23 (1.54)	2.37 (2.19)	1.76 (1.35)	1.93 (N.A.)	2.11 (1.47)
1979	2.25 (1.57)	2.36 (2.18)	N.A.	N.A.	N.A.
1980	2.33 (1.63)	N.A.	N.A.	N.A.	N.A.

*N.A.: Not available.

Source: Science Indicators, 1980, National Science Foundation (Washington, D.C.: U.S. Government Printing Office, 1981), Tables 1-3 and 1-4.

duced in the economy are allocated for a specific function. In Table 6.3 we can see, for a sample of years, the allocation of GNP for R&D by the countries of primary interest to us. The percentage figure in parentheses is the allocation for R&D by the civilian sector. The total percentage figure includes that funded by government as well.

During the years 1961–80, the allocation by the United States dropped by 15 percent, and for the latest years available the change in West Germany (1962–79) was an increase of 89 percent, in France (1961–78) an increase of 28 percent, in Japan (1961–78) an increase of 39 percent, and in the United Kingdom (1961–78) a decrease of 14 percent, almost exactly the same as in the United States. A second significant relationship shows that for the same periods in each country, the civilian R&D increased by 36 percent in the United States, increased by 91 percent in West Germany, increased by 39 percent in France, increased by 35 percent in Japan (1961–73), and remained about the same in the United Kingdom.

Apparently, these gross data show that in the United States and the United Kingdom government is far more significant as a source of R&D funding than in Japan and somewhat less so in West Germany and France. In the United States the government share of funding of R&D shifts between 30 and 60 percent of the total, a major amplitude of change. In the case of the United Kingdom, the range is 30 to 40 percent, West Germany 8 to 9 percent, France 23 to 30 percent, and Japan 1 to 2 percent. Given the fact that when the U.S. government spends between 30 and 60 percent of total R&D expenditures, it must have a major impact on the supply and demand for scientists and engineers, equipment, education, career planning, new products and processes, science plant investment, and so on. Since this government also varies its rate of expenditures by major changes in short periods of time (by 25 percent between 1964 and 1970), it is no exaggeration to say that the U.S. government is a major force for instability in our R&D picture.

The gross percentages tell only a very small part of the story, however. Of considerable significance to productivity gains are such questions as how much of our R&D is basic research, applied research, or developmental research. How much R&D is for defense as contrasted with R&D more directly related to increasing the potential for industrial productivity? Finally, the gross data do not deal with the very important questions of if we have a real R&D or science policy, and how we are organized to achieve the objectives of such a policy.

Basic, Applied, and Developmental Research

Basic research is concerned about fundamental, new knowledge, without a specific product or use as an immediate objective. Applied research is concerned with the use of available knowledge to produce a specific product or process improvement. Developmental research has to do with the further improvement of a currently existing product or process. In the long run, without basic research, the stream begins to run dry for new products or processes—that is, unless there is a strategy for utilizing the new basic research being done elsewhere in the world. Japan for many years followed a strategy of importing new basic research knowledge produced elsewhere and then applying it to the development of new products and processes. This is not simple to do. It calls for a carefully developed strategy and information acquisition process. It also calls for a very effective organization that stimulates the innovation process, which does not necessarily accompany a research process. The United States has never been a great importer of other people's basic research. We believe in "growing our own," though this may not necessarily be the most cost-effective alternative at all times.

Given the fact that the U.S. government funds R&D in a rather erratic manner, and given the fact that basic research is a long-term type of commitment, one would hope that most basic research in the United States relies on private funding sources. This is not the case. Close to 70 percent of all basic research done in the United States depends on federal funds. With the support of federal dollars, the basic research is actually done by industry, universities, and other nonprofit organizations. By a ratio of almost 3 to 1, universities do far more of the basic research than industry.

Table 6.4. Percentage of Gross Expenditures on R&D, by Source of Funds

	United States		Japan		West Germany		France		United Kingdom	
	Government	Business	Government	Business	Government	Business	Government	Business	Government	Business
1977	56	44	41	59	44	53	53	41	N.A.	N.A.
1967	67	33	37	63	42	58	65	32	53	43
1975	57	43	43	57	48	50	56	39	55	41

*N.A.: Not available.

Source: Science Indicators, 1980, National Science Foundation (Washington, D.C.: U.S. Government Printing Office, 1981), p. 217. Percentages are rounded. Totals are not necessarily 100 percent because other sources (funds from abroad, for example) are shown separately in the original data.

Hence, as federal funds for basic research go up and down, since 70 cents of every basic research dollar comes from government, educational and research programs at universities are significantly affected. In terms of constant dollars, total basic research in the United States increased substantially, about 48 percent during the period 1963–68. Growth was halted, and between 1968 and 1976 basic research decreased by about 10 percent. In 1978, a slight increase took place, and in 1981, total basic research, in constant dollars, was about 7 percent higher than in 1978.

In all of the countries we have compared, the government is a major factor in the direct funding of R&D, as seen in Table 6.4.

Funding of R&D is only the monetary counterpart of a more significant factor, the number of scientists and engineers actually engaged in R&D. As seen in Tables 6.5 and 6.6, the United States has been lagging when an important factor is considered. Depending on the nature of the perceived national defense situation, about 50 percent of all government R&D funds are related to defense. Since, on the average, the federal R&D expenditures account for about 50 percent of total R&D, about 25 percent of all scientists and engineers in R&D are probably in defense-related activities, with very little real spinoff for economic productivity.

These data tell only a very limited story about the human resource base for science activities. Indeed, these data are in many ways just the tip of an iceberg. The tremendous numbers of people who are the laboratory personnel, research support, secretaries, and research assistants do not figure in these numbers. Nor does the quality of education of such people show up in these data. Level of both general and advanced scientific and technical education is another important factor influencing a nation's scientific and technical capabilities. From a number of studies it appears that Japan, West Germany, and the Soviet Union have stressed scientific and mathematical proficiency in their secondary institutions to a much greater degree than have the United States and the United Kingdom. Sub-

Table 6.5. Scientists and Engineers Engaged in R&D per 10,000 in the Labor Force

	1965	1968	1970	1975	1977
France	21.0	26.4	27.3	29.3	30.3
West Germany	22.7	26.2	30.9	41.0	41.7
Japan	24.6	31.2	33.4	47.9	49.9
United States	64.1	66.9	63.6	56.4	57.7
United Kingdom	19.6	20.8	N.A.	31.3	N.A.

*N.A.: Not available.

Source: Science Indicators, 1980, National Science Foundation (Washington, D.C.: U.S. Government Printing Office, 1981), p. 217.

Table 6.6.   Scientists and Engineers Engaged in R&D (in thousands)

	1965	1968	1970	1975	1977
France	42.8	54.7	58.5	65.3	68.0
West Germany	61.0	68.0	82.5	103.9	111.0
Japan	117.6	157.6	172.0	255.2	272.0
United States	494.5	550.4	546.5	534.9	573.0
United Kingdom	49.9	52.8	N.A.	80.7	N.A.

N.A.: Not available.

Source: Science Indicators, 1980, National Science Foundation (Washington, D.C.: U.S. Government Printing Office, 1981), p. 217.

stantial proportions of the populations in Japan, West Germany and Russia have technical and scientific training superior to that in the United States.[27]

This would result in important potential gains in the labor force affecting productivity, at least in the cases of Japan and West Germany. In Japan and West Germany, as we have seen, national policies promote the training of scientists and engineers in greater numbers than are expected to engage in scientific and engineering professions; consequently, positions in industry and government, largely in the management areas, are often filled by individuals with excellent backgrounds equipping them to deal with computer technology, systems problems as well as problems related to innovation of new types of production equipment. In Japan, about half of all the civil service and industrial managers hold degrees in engineering or related fields.[28]

This is not to say that we in the United States should train our managers in government or industry as engineers. It is to say that backgrounds that provide a good grounding in science and mathematics along with a sensitivity to human relations and social institutions would improve on the types of training now given to our future managers.

In the area of applied and developmental research, the on-off pattern is a bit less marked than for basic research. Looking at Table 6.7 we find, first of all, that the levels of applied research in industry are well below those of developmental research. The latter is far less significant for productivity benefits. Second, we also find that during the period of the mid-1960s to the mid-1970s, there was little growth in applied and developmental research. This trend followed the pattern for basic research. For a decade, there was little or no growth in the R&D activities of the United States.

Given the fact that the R&D efforts of Japan, West Germany, and France have been growing more rapidly than those of the United States, not only in terms of proportions of GNP allocated but also in terms of ratios of scientists and engineers to the labor force, does this necessarily

Table 6.7. Industrial R&D for Basic, Applied, and Developmental Research Activities, in 1972 Dollars (millions)

	Total	Basic	Applied	Developmental
1960	15,297	547	2,954	11,796
1961	15,733	570	2,851	12,312
1962	16,237	692	3,469	12,076
1963	17,622	728	3,428	13,466
1964	18,569	755	3,573	14,241
1965	19,077	796	3,575	14,706
1966	20,256	813	3,704	15,739
1967	20,725	796	3,687	16,242
1968	21,116	778	3,785	16,553
1969	21,094	712	3,787	16,595
1970	19,756	659	3,747	15,350
1971	19,081	615	3,556	14,910
1972	19,552	593	3,514	15,445
1973	20,106	597	3,620	15,889
1974	19,915	608	3,731	15,576
1975	19,263	581	3,640	15,042
1976	20,435	620	3,869	15,946
1977	21,403	651	4,045	16,707
1978	22,103	685	4,178	17,240
1979	23,104	730	4,371	18,003
1980	24,103	761	4,595	18,747
1981	25,216	796	4,797	19,623

Source: *Science Indicators, 1980,* National Science Foundation (Washington, D.C.: U.S. Government Printing Office, 1981), p. 277. 1978–79 data are preliminary; 1980 and 1981 data are estimates.

mean that the United States must eventually be displaced as the leading scientific nation in the world? After all, we do still have the largest numbers in terms of total expenditures and total personnel. The answer to this very legitimate question depends on several things. To begin with, turning the R&D spigot on and off means a lot of waste. Stopping and starting projects, breaking continuity of efforts, training and retraining personnel and teams are all counterproductive. In addition, after enough of such discontinuities, it would be surprising if the really good scientists and engineers would want to work on government-sponsored research. Many such people, and even some R&D-oriented companies, have steered clear of government R&D projects.

An excellent example of a far more rational, and probably effective, means for achieving the growth of critical research needs and scientific personnel is that of France. On June 30, 1982, the French National Assembly passed a law funding nonmilitary R&D over the next five years so that an annual growth of funds, in constant francs (thus eliminating the erosion aspects of inflation), of 17.8 percent will be achieved. In addition, on the human resource side, funds to increase the research labor force by an annual rate of 4.5 percent will be allocated, again in constant francs. In the United States support of nonmilitary R&D has decreased consistently as the rate of inflation erodes the purchasing power of the research dollar.

Not only are the physical and biological sciences being targeted, in the form of growth industries and what might be termed growth problems such as energy, pollution, and resource conservation, but the social science areas are also being targeted. In an effort to produce a more meaningful dialogue between science and society, the new French law also provides significant funds in the humanities and social sciences. As we in the United States well know, the use of more automated production techniques such as robots, the worker-displacement effects of new industrial processes and technologies, the problems of retraining cause very real personal trauma and general social unrest. The new French law specifically allocates funds for research to help forecast such problems and how best to equip workers and the French society to deal with them. Basically, what we are talking about is crisis avoidance. Knowing that problems inevitably result from the application of new technologies, it is only intelligent to take steps to deal with them. This is in sharp contrast to recent economy moves in the United States that eliminate data and information produced by the U.S. government upon which much industrial and social science research is based. Such "economies" only guarantee a lessening national ability to think and act rationally on the matters dealt with by the government surveys and data.

In a story covering this development, what is equally fascinating is the tell-tale title the *New York Times* used.[29] Our simplistic, adversarial orientation even causes our journalism to cast events as either-or. Science, thus, in this article is seen implicitly as either laissez-faire or socialist. As a matter of fact, as the article itself states, research would be decentralized, dispersing it from R&D efforts now heavily concentrated in Paris to many areas in France, and many nongovernment representatives would be involved in policy and administration concerning this new effort. A major effort would be made to have researchers move more freely among academic, industrial, and government laboratories. In addition, special emphasis would be on aiding the rapid growth of innovative enterprises. This last item reflects the same approach already described as a part of the German stratagem for fostering the growth of small and medium-sized firms in key industrial, hi-tech areas.

What is involved is not a "socialization of science," in some sense of "socialism"; what is involved is a sharing of risks in order to catalyze activities and an increase in the supply of human resources necessary to achieve economic growth and productivity. In order to minimize the risk of becoming less competitive in world trade, less understanding and effective as a society in coping with major industrial changes, and less educated as a nation in understanding the forces for change, the French have begun to organize, as well as fund, its R&D relationships differently.

How we organize to achieve national goals is probably of even greater significance than how much we decide to spend in achieving them. The problem in the United States is not that we "throw dollars" at problems; the problem is we do not spend enough time considering how to set goals and then translate those goals into effective organizational models and strategies. Our science policies, "wars on poverty," and so-called manpower programs have all suffered from this debility.

Under the French approach, the policy will not only be to increase the national R&D effort, achieving a goal of 2.5 percent of GNP spent for R&D in 1985, but also effecting a different relationship between government and industry. The law that was passed in June 1982, was presaged in 1981. In a *Business Week* article the chief government official concerned with this new direction was quite explicit about the intent: "We want to create a partnership between government and industry. We want to do with the nationalized companies what the Japanese do with private enterprise—create a synergy."[30]

Shorn of the political rhetoric, the new "socialist" government is organizing in a manner that is not so much socialist as it is a shared capitalism. "It may seem paradoxical, but socialism is giving autonomy to companies" was the observation of one of the chief advisers to Pierre Dreyfus, minister of industry.[31] Dreyfus is the man who as chief executive of Renault built the nationalized auto company into a worldwide competitor. To muddy the waters of our simple, or rather simplistic, and neat division of economic institutions into capitalist or socialist, the nationalized Renault is now involved in a major joint venture with American Motors Corporation, our very own AMC, producer of that most American of American cars, the jeep.

Organizing for R&D

When we look at a comparison between market, or laissez-faire, capitalism and shared capitalism in the context of R&D and economic productivity, the United States is a paradox. For that sector of our economy where we have had the most sustained high level of productivity, we have followed a shared capitalism model since the 1860s. I am referring, of course, to agriculture. As I said earlier, beginning with the Morrill Act of

1862, a partnership has existed between the private and public institutions of this country concerning agriculture. Based upon grants of federal land, the Morrill Act established the public educational institutions that became the source of scientists, R&D, cooperative research, and innovative farming practices that produced, and continues to produce, the most productive agricultural economy in the world. The results are not limited to agriculture. The work of Selman Waksman at Rutgers University, College of Agriculture, in the 1930s and 1940s produced one of the early antibiotics, streptomycin. This land-grant college and its major research and educational products are typical of the host of similar institutions produced by a law passed during the Civil War.

In addition to, and beyond, the land-grant college system is the U.S. Department of Agriculture. Traditionally led by conservative Americans, no other department, outside of the Department of Defense, compares in using the model of shared capitalism. From this department, through its counterparts in every one of the states, is a relationship that looks to cooperation between government and the private farmer, or corporate agribusiness firms, in order to maximize agricultural productivity and output. Experimental farms supported by public funds, the county extension system for stimulating innovation and use of new technologies, tax benefits to stimulate better practices and use of capital—the list is long and well known. The only close comparison would be that of the relationship between defense agencies and the private companies producing for our defense needs. But the comparison is, in many ways, a poor one. The defense example lacks the long-term, in-depth aspects of the agricultural situation.

For the most part, the partnership between the public and private sectors in R&D is an on-off one, with what might best be called "passive" stimulants. Though we have a number of institutions—the National Science Foundation, National Institutes of Health, National Academy of Sciences-National Research Council—these agencies only rarely become involved in true partnerships with relevant private institutions. Only NIH approaches such a relationship in its programs in the health field. The others do studies and provide limited grants and fellowships to affect the supply of R&D professionals and direction of research. There is almost a total absence of the sort of involvement that is calculated to stimulate new industries, products, or technologies. The closest approximation to this comes via defense contracts to stimulate new products or processes. In this instance, for example, air force procurement has had an important effect on robotics, but hardly of the sort that a MITI type of operation can produce.

U.S. policies tend to be of the passive, noninvolvement type, best typified by the patent process. But even here, a supine patent policy, assuming the traditional adversarial role, is very different from one that sees national productivity as worthy of a joint venture between the private and public sectors. For example, the traditional posture of the U.S. government in the patent field is that when a private company performs research for the government, any resulting patents are public property. This is based upon both a philosophical point of view and an economic perspective. The former views equity as demanding that public funds not provide a basis for individual enhancement. The economic perspective sees a situation where the new knowledge being made available to all will stimulate many to produce rather than just one. One might think that so obvious a set of desiderata would preordain that all patent policies of all nations mirror this enlightened view. No so. In Japan, government funds for R&D can result in an exclusive patent for the company doing the research. Varying degrees of this approach hold true in most industrialized nations.[32]

Lest it be misunderstood that these countries pursue patent policies that favor the larger institutions to the neglect of the individual, some patent policies, for example, that of West Germany, prohibit a company from seeking agreement from an employee regarding patent control by the company. In West Germany, the employed inventor has guaranteed rights and control of his or her invention.

What is at stake in the United States is a set of assumptions that appear to be equitable but in reality may be neither equitable nor effective in stimulating the processes of invention or innovation. And this arises primarily because we approach the patent as a public versus private property right. It has to be approached not only as a private or public property right but also as a realistic productivity situation. For example, if a government agency asks a company with a long history of research in a field to do a specific piece of work on a specific product, and as a result of this contract the company comes up with a patentable product, the usual stance is that this patent is public property. There may be exceptions, but only under unique situations. But the work done for the government might represent only a miniscule addition to the years of earlier research by that company.

The policy of public money-public patent guarantees that very few firms with the most background will be eager to be involved in a marginal piece of government work that could jeopardize years of earlier work on a problem. The results could be most inequitable. For years this situation has been a major bone of contention, and a force for limiting the availability of some of the best researchers in private industry for important government work. In addition, from the economic point of view, the general policy of public money-public patents by no means guarantees there will be many "takers" of this new knowledge. Especially when large investments in plant, equipment, and labor are necessary to exploit a patent, many companies will be leery of such an effort unless there is a guaranteed period of protection for a recovery of investment. This is not sinful; indeed, this is what a patent is all about.

A shared-capitalism model starts by asking how can we achieve output and productivity gains by sharing risks in a rational manner. A patent policy should be designed for these purposes. There are ample examples of how this has been achieved by other countries.

Beyond this sort of passive role that a patent policy plays to stimulate R&D and innovation, there are mechanisms that can more actively bring together the public and private sectors. The spectrum of such mechanisms can start with industrial standards. The problem of industrial standards is little understood and of little concern to most people. But it has important implications for export industries. Among the industrial countries of the world, only the United States has no set of industrial standards. In every other country, the standards that relate to products and processes are set by cooperative arrangements among government, industry, and other relevant representatives, such as public, academic, and labor. Safety codes, materials, and metric versus British are all involved. U.S. exports are affected by our lack of uniform, clearly understood standards. Rate of innovation, quality control, ease of market entry are all affected by this problem.

Since the late 1960s, the U.S. Congress has had a bill before it to deal with this problem, but it has not acted. It should, but only with the involvement of industry and public representatives and only in a nonadversarial spirit.

In the field of industrial technology, there should be a targeting of those areas where, over the next ten years, unless important progress is made, the United States will be negatively affected in productivity gains. In such cases, specific long-term research contracts as well as product development contracts should be given by the federal government to produce the required new knowledge and new products. Joint boards composed of government, industrial, and public member representation should be the mechanism. In some cases universities may be the site of such activity; in others, it may be private firms or consortia of firms and universities. The key is flexibility to achieve the desired result, the increase in productivity. Science, technology, and innovation should be linked. Though each of these three areas is self-standing in one sense, they have very little in the way of productivity benefits unless the organization of their relationships is geared to economic growth and productivity gains. Organizing to achieve this has the precedent of agriculture in the United States, MITI in Japan, and the science and innovation programs in West Germany.

The chief factors that must be involved are:

1. Linkages between the key partners. If a research program is set to affect a specific industry, and the sponsor is a public agency, the program should involve the public agencies that are relevant, the representatives of the industries to be affected; and relevant research personnel from other institutions likely to be affected, for example, universities and foundations in the field.
2. Informal discussions that are long enough to surface most "hidden agendas" and achieve a sense of complete idea sharing.
3. A set of achievable goals and criteria for performance evaluation.
4. A mechanism for continued involvement and feedback about the operation of the program.
5. Reactions by the responsible operating authority to suggestions from the continuing group.
6. Periodic reports on rates of progress and suggested changes.

A very important ingredient for success will obviously be the choice of participants. The programs that have brought industrial leaders, government officials, and other relevant representatives together in Japanese and West German efforts have usually sought a blending of seniority and knowledgeability. Political appointees without really relevant experience or ability are obviously wasted seats.

Whether it be an effort to support research by direct funding by government of private research or direct research by a government organization, the same principles should apply. The development of a tax policy to stimulate research or the use of new technology should follow the same guidelines.

Mechanisms for organizing more efficiently for R&D and innovation could be cooperative industrial research associations, government laboratories and dissemination centers, or special consortia established on an ad hoc basis to meet special needs. None of these organizational mechanisms has been used to any great degree in the United States, although they have been used in Western Europe and Japan. In the past, not only the Department of Agriculture but the U.S. Bureau of Mines was active in using imaginative methods for organizing efforts to affect relevant areas of research and technology. The early support of the Bureau of Mines had an important impact on mining technology. Joint efforts with industry as well as schools of mining are a worthwhile model with which to reacquaint ourselves.

In the R&D, technology, and innovation areas, shared capitalism has one of its greatest potentials for achieving productivity gains of significance. The reason is that this is where most of the changes in patterns of output, production efficiency, and new products start from. Achieving the sharing of responsibilities, funding, and risks at this juncture is where you build the highest probability for affecting the overall economic system.

Money, Gold, Budgets, and Banking

When one gets into the area of money, gold, banking, and budgets, one is confronted by what can appear to be truly puzzling phenomena. Reality often appears unreal, and vice versa. We understandably look for clearcut messages or clues in any effort to comprehend a complicated subject. But seeking simplicity in complex relationships is often not only impossible but counterproductive. For example, it is surely sensible to assume that a nation cannot owe more than the entire economy is capable of producing. This surely must be the equivalent of a company on the verge of bankruptcy. In 1946, however, the total national debt of the United States exceeded the gross national product by well over 20 percent.

During the last decade or so the media are full of tales of woe about the federal debt and its burdensome impact on the economy. But if one looks at Table 6.8, it is obvious that since 1967, the total debt as a percentage of GNP has fallen by 15 percent, from 40 to 34 percent. In 1950, total U.S. debt was 90 percent of GNP. Looking at this relationship from a slightly different perspective, that is, the annual federal deficit as a percentage of GNP, during the period 1972–81, the figure has gone from a low

Table 6.8. Federal Interest-Bearing Debt As Percent of GNP (1950–81)

	A U.S. Gross National Product ($ billions)	B Total Interest- Bearing U.S. Public Debt ($ billions)	C B ÷ A (%)
1950	285	257	90
1967	799	322	40
1968	873	344	39
1969	944	351	37
1970	992	369	37
1971	1,077	396	37
1972	1,185	425	36
1973	1,326	456	34
1974	1,434	473	33
1975	1,549	532	34
1976	1,718	619	36
1977	1,918	697	36
1978	2,156	766	36
1979	2,413	819	34
1980	2,626	706	35
1981	2,922	996	34

Source: Economic Report of the President, 1982, derived from Appendix B, (Washington, D.C.: U.S. Government Printing Office, 1982).

of three-tenths of 1 percent in 1974 to a high of 4 percent in 1976. The rate in 1981 was 2 percent, unchanged from 1980.

The reasons for relating budget deficits and national debt to the GNP grow out of the fact that in the final analysis the ability of the federal government to repay debt must rest on its taxing power. Taxing power is related to income of the nation and the ability to pay taxes levied. In addition, if debt assumes too large a proportion of the national wealth, it must result in impacts on investment, inflation, and the private capital market. The level of debt is highly significant, but to understand the significance of debt is even more significant. We have to be able to sort out reality from myth, or newspaper headlines that are more calculated to sell newspapers than clarify an issue. Just as the debt (bonds) of most U.S. companies goes up along with their sales and growth, so also does the national debt with the growth of the U.S. economy. What is more meaningful to ask is what is the purpose of debt. Will it add to our national wealth in the long run?

As we have seen, a problem in many cities now exists where bridges in disrepair can no longer accept truck traffic. Trucks have to follow detours, going out of their way, sometimes for many miles. Costs in time, gasoline, drivers' salaries, and depreciation on equipment are usually passed along to the consumer. Would it not be more sensible to repair the bridge? Probably. But if local tax revenues are inadequate or a local law forbids raising taxes above a certain arbitrary level, the only alternative is a local bond issue, or going into debt. Is debt bad in this case? Some think so, in which case the trucks must keep detouring and consumers will pay for the additional costs for a self-imposed drop in productivity.

Having been confronted by double-digit inflation during the late 1970s and outset of the 1980s, many people were caught up with the idea of gold as a source of stability. How nice it would be to have a dollar "as good as gold." A gold standard does not stabilize anything except the price in dollars we must be prepared to pay for gold. If we were on a gold standard, should the Soviet wheat crop fail disastrously, the Soviets would probably have to sell some of their gold stocks in order to obtain foreign exchange so they could buy wheat. The United States would have to buy Soviet gold in order to prevent the price of our standard (gold) from falling. To do this we would either have to increase taxes or increase the supply of money. In one case there would be a deflationary impact, in the other there would be an inflationary impact. Neither provides a stable economy, contrary to the "gold bugs" who were proposing a return to the gold standard in the late 1970s and 1980. Even when we had a gold standard, the dollar was not stable or prices steady.

The comparisons the gold bugs use are the perfect sample of statistics that lie. While they are correct in claiming that the price level in 1913 was the same as in 1882, they neglect to tell you about what happened in between. The price level fell 47 percent in 1882–96 and then rose about 42 percent between 1896 and 1913. While on the gold standard, recessions were longer and periods of recovery shorter than since we have been off the gold standard. But there is an aura about the idea of a gold standard that captures the imagination and our desire for some immutable, ever-present standard for our monetary system. There isn't one. We, in our ability to think, judge, and act, have to provide that stability and standard.

What about money and budgets? Aren't they straightforward, unambiguous? No. They, too, are creations of our intellects. We really do live in the sort of world Lewis Carroll described in *Alice in Wonderland*; words mean no more and no less than we intend them to.

Let us start with money. What is it? It is usually defined as those types of assets that an individual or corporation or any institution can use in a commercial transaction. So its characteristics are liquidity and universal acceptance. In addition, most governments also mandate that by law at least certain types of money must be accepted as legal tender. That is, no ifs, ands, or buts, this ten-dollar bill with Alexander Hamilton's visage on one side is *really* money. But there are lots of things that some people accept as money that others do not. I may choose to accept payment for an item I may sell in a form not usually regarded as "money," for example, stocks or bonds. The moment I accept them, they are money. While I keep them locked in a safe deposit box they are not. A check is surely money! Only if it is accepted. As an out-of-towner in New York or Chicago, I am often, and rudely, reminded of this by bank tellers who refuse to cash my Washington, D.C., checks.

If you look at the Federal Reserve System's definition of money, you come across money forms you have never seen and probably never will—Eurodollars, money market mutual fund shares, term repurchase agreements, overnight repurchase agreements, savings bonds, bankers acceptances, and such catchalls as commercial paper. Only the components called M1, M2, and M3, are the usual money forms we refer to when we talk about affecting the supply of money. But some items not in these categories, such as bankers acceptances, commercial paper, and savings bonds, are certainly near enough to money for most practical purposes to be used as such. And they are. This semichaotic situation obviously makes it difficult to envision money in some simple, straightforward sense. As Irving Kristol put it well in a *Wall Street Journal* article, referring to monetary policy:

> Here, it must be said, confusion reigns supreme, and I confess to being no less confused than the next man, or the next woman, or the next banker. Indeed, my confusion may be the more acute, since I have spent

these past weeks diligently consulting people who are supposed to have an expert knowledge of this arcane area.[33]

Earlier in this work, we discussed the improbability of a realistic application of the so-called theory that sees the control of the quantity of money as the key to economic stability. It is certainly hard to control what is difficult to define.

Budgets pose a different type of problem. We can define them, but we really use different types of budgets in order to achieve different effects or understanding about what is happening in an economy.

The federal budget has been the subject of debate and confusion for many years. As a matter of fact there really wasn't a federal budget in the modern sense until the Budget Act of 1921. Until recent years, the federal budget was an "administrative budget," that is, it only included what might be called current expenditure and income operations. Programs like unemployment insurance, retirement and social security benefits, the interstate highway program, and the federal employees retirement program did not appear in the federal budget. The effect was that there was a considerable difference between real expenditures and income as contrasted with what was conveyed by the federal budget. This was changed, and we are now on what is called a consolidated cash budget. This does not mean, however, that all expenditures or income related to the federal government's activities are included in the budget. There is a collection of items called "off-budget," none of which is to be found in the regular budget. In recent years the amounts have varied around $14 to $25 billion. Off-budget items include military assistance, farm income stabilization, area development, mortgage credit and thrift insurance, energy and housing assistance, and aid to higher education. Most of this off-budget financing is done through the little known Federal Financing Bank (FFB), which provides financial intermediation services for federal agencies; for example, FFB buys title to direct loans made by federal agencies.

Given the $20 billion or so off-budget items, isn't a federal budget of about $800 billion at least 98 percent accurate? Not really. Of course this depends on how one defines accuracy. But if the object is to understand how the budget reflects the role of federal expenditures and income in the economy and how the budget can be used by the government to help the economy to grow or maintain its health, then the matter is far more complex.

The unified cash budget is neither comprehensive nor rational as an economic device. All it does is measure the inflow and outflow of dollars. Because it does not account for off-budget items, it does not achieve this goal completely. Beyond this, however, there are other discrepancies that would be viewed as horrifying by any business accountant. The federal government has a very large loan program, or loan guarantee program. In 1980, this totaled more than $600 billion. The value of the interest subsidy is about $27 billion. If this were added to our budget it would increase the deficit level.

But there is another side to what is *not* counted, happily. In the private sector these types of items would show up as asset increases and offset deficits. The federal government has a number of investment functions, such as strategic stockpiles, petroleum reserves to offset another OPEC crisis, and various other capital assets. The value of such investments in 1981 came to almost $150 billion. With consistent inflation, the value of these assets tend to increase. This increase in federal assets does not show up as an offset to a budget deficit either.

Finally, the national debt itself is affected by the rate of inflation. Though the debt increased in 1981 in terms of 1981 dollars, given the rate of inflation, in terms of real dollars there was no increase in the national debt. Since about $80 billion in interest rates on the national debt has a built-in impact growing out of high market interest rates, there should be an offset of most of this, since the roughly $80 billion increase in national debt reflected current dollars, not constant dollars. Put another way, the national debt is affected in exactly the same way as our family debt during an inflationary period. As inflation and incomes go up, past debt costs us less to pay off. Everybody knows that; but the understanding seems to halt at the federal debt. So just as we smilingly adjust for how much easier the three-year car loan is to pay off as the dollars mean less, the value of the federal debt shrinks in its drag effect. This amount should be reflected as an offsetting gain in our budgeting procedures.

Given these types of adjustments, which could easily be rationalized, whether a federal budget is in deficit or surplus depends on what you think should be included or excluded in the budget process. And that really is at the heart of what the federal budget should be. The federal budget, unlike the budget of a private business firm, was never envisioned as a mechanism for producing a bottom-line profit, or surplus.

In 1967, a special presidential commission reported to the president of the United States on reforms of the budget and budget process. The commission was made up of political conservatives and liberals, business leaders, economists, and former government officials. In the report, the commission stated:

> The budget is the key instrument in national policymaking. It is through the budget that the Nation chooses what areas it wishes to leave to private choice and what services it wants to provide through government.[34]

The budget is the national statement of purpose. It should be the force that directs our policies on taxes, money supply, and resource use—not the other way around. The problem is that very few people in the nation really understand what the budget is all about. The same commission understood this problem well when it cautioned: "Wise fiscal policy and wise choices for individual Federal programs depend, in the final analysis, on public and congressional understanding of the budget."[35]

Unfortunately, very few citizens are sufficiently well enough informed about the federal budget to ensure that they are not misled by the cynical rhetoric and misinformation about the budget and its effects on the economy. Simplistic homilies and fatuous generalizations about the similarity between family budgets and the national budget are not merely misleading, they are destructive of our ability to set a sound economic course.

All of the threads involved in budgets, money, and the economy come together in the banking system. This is the engine that powers the economy. At the head is the Federal Reserve System, the central bank of the United States. The primacy of the Federal Reserve System, or "Fed," grows out of the fact that it can dictate how much of each depositor's savings the bank can use as loans, how much the banks themselves must pay for loans from the central bank, and, if the Fed wishes, how much the interest rate can be affected by the Fed's selling or buying of securities in the market.

The reserve ratio, that is, how much of each dollar of deposits the private bank must hold as a reserve, has a tremendous impact on the level of profits a bank makes. If 20 cents on each depositor's dollar must be held as reserves, this leaves 80 cents available for loans. Since each loan is usually in the form of a checking account, the loan results in payments to others for products or services, these recipients become deposits in turn. Since only 20 cents on each new dollar of deposits must be kept as reserves, the original deposit of one dollar can create five new dollars of spending power in the economy. Each loan produces interest income for the bank of deposit.

Thus, the commercial banking system is one of the most important means of producing new money. Only Federal Reserve policy can affect this rate of creation of funds. What the Fed defines as prudent depends upon the particular philosophy of the Board of Governors, which in turn is heavily affected by the particular economic philosophy of the chairman. If the chairman is a supporter of the quantity theory of money, then the Fed attempts to maintain a steady, and very limited, rate of growth of the money supply. This policy is followed, as was the case between 1979 and 1981 and most of 1982, no matter what happens to the rate of interest, levels of unemployment, or economic growth.

In addition, since the Federal Reserve System is an independent agency, established by act of Congress, it often follows a policy, which is calculated to offset an administration's fiscal policy, that the Fed believes is in conflict with sound economic goals, as defined by the Fed. Unlike most other major industrial nations, our fiscal and monetary policies are in the hands of the Federal Reserve System and the Treasury Department, two competitive agencies that often pursue different approaches for the economic well-being of the nation. It is our adversarial system built into the realm of budgets and banks. It is not only unconnected to productivity gains in the economy, it often subverts productivity to the attainment of questionably useful interest rate levels or stocks of money.

All of the foregoing about money, gold, budgets, and banking seeks to make two points. The first is to demonstrate that financial arrangements and institutions are artificial and not some independent fact of life. The experiences in Japan and West Germany show what can be done where the financial institutions are made to perform in order to achieve the goals of economic growth and productivity gains. We have come to accept the dominance of financial institutions over economic performance. Federal budgets, Federal Reserve policy, and banking practices are geared to the wrong criteria of performance if they are not designed to provide for an efficient use of our nation's resources growing out of increased productivity, regardless of what the interest rate may be or the rate of growth of the supply of M1 or M2 or M3.

In the mid-1980s, with U.S. rates of interest almost double those of Japan, it is the U.S. that is in economic trouble, not Japan. But as we have seen, Japan tailors interest rates to achieve economic growth and productivity. The 2.5 percent unemployment level in Japan testifies to the bankruptcy of the U.S. policy of accepting unemployment levels 400 percent higher than those in Japan in an effort to lower our interest rates. There should be a better way to achieve a healthy economy and we should be able to do so.

The second point has to do with financial matters and the separation of our fiscal and monetary policies. As long as the Treasury Department and the Federal Reserve are cast in the roles of adversaries, it will be impossible for the United States to achieve an ability to use financial institutions to gain the objectives of sufficient economic growth and productivity gains. This separation almost guarantees a continuation of irresponsible behavior on the part of each, but for different reasons. The Treasury Department policy will tend to reflect, and be handmaiden to, the political philosophy of the executive branch and blame financial instability on Federal Reserve policies. The Fed will represent the economic philosophy of the board and most of all its chairman. Failures to restrain inflation, interest levels, or increasing unemployment will be blamed on the policies of the Treasury Department. Only by bringing the Federal Reserve, the nation's central banking system, into the same house as the

Treasury Department will we be able to develop an effective set of consistent, articulated financial policies geared to the goals of economic growth and productivity gain.

What must be built is a structure of federal budgets set to achieve annual rates of economic growth of 3.5 to 4.5 percent and productivity gains adequate to support those growth levels. Financial policies must relate to fiscal policies. Both fiscal policies and financial policies must view their objectives as being geared to productivity gain.

A new Department of Finance would become the central focus for relating interest rates, intermediation, bank reserves, money, and stock and bond issuances to the needs of new, productivity-oriented industries, as well as general economic indicators of inflation and employment levels. Lowering interest rates by increasing unemployment by several million people and reducing plant output to less than 70 percent of capacity is hardly the mark of an effective capitalist system. Solution by crisis is no solution, it is a tragic waste for all concerned, business executive as well as blue-collar worker. A capitalism based upon rational economic relationships and goals related to increasing productivity and a sharing of the risks to produce desired outcomes is where we must now direct our energies. The difficult question is how to begin to move away from the current situation in the direction of this new type of shared capitalism.

Notes

1. Lester C. Thurow, *The Zero-Sum Society* (New York:Penguin Books, 1981), p. 110.
2. Ibid.
3. First heard in a Xerox Corporation presentation on productivity.
4. *The Economist,* December 26, 1981, p. 9.
5. *Wall Street Journal,* January 11, 1980, p. 12.
6. William McGowan, "Iliterasee att Wurk," *New York Times,* August 19, 1982, p. A27. This same figure of 60 million appeared in a *New York Times* article on September 16, 1982, p. B6, quoting Barbara Bush, wife of the U.S. vice-president. The problem of defining illiteracy is a difficult one. The official U.S. Office of Education estimate is that less than 1 percent of the adult population of the United States is illiterate. So little direct interest seems to exist on this question that the U.S. Office of Education uses UNESCO data as its source. There are two studies which have been looked to as helpful, carefully researched efforts to determine the level of adult illiteracy in the United States. The first is a study supported by the Division of Adult Education, U.S. Office of Education, in 1971, and done by the University of Texas at Austin. Published in 1975 by the University of Texas under the title *Adult Functional Competency: A Report to the Office of Education Dissemination Review Panel,* this study showed that because of a lack in read-

ing skills, between 14 and 24 percent of the U.S. adult population did not have the ability to function effectively in our society. The second study, *Adult Illiteracy in the United States*, by C. St. John Hunter and D. Harman (New York:McGraw-Hill, 1979), was supported by funds from the Ford Foundation. This study estimated that about 60 million adults in the United States lacked sufficient reading comprehension skills to function effectively in our society.

7. McGowan, "Iliterasee Att Wurk."

8. McGowan, "Iliterasee Att Wurk."

9. *New York Times,* September 5, 1982, p. 37.

10. "Manpower: Most Urgent Problem for the Military," *New York Times,* July 21, 1981, p. B20.

11. "Supership Docked for Lack of Crew," *Washington Post,* April 12, 1980, p. 1.

12. "Foreigners Snap Up the High Tech Jobs," *New York Times,* July 5, 1981, p. F13.

13. Ibid.

14. Frank J. Atelsek and Irene L. Gomberg, *Recruitment and Retention of Full-Time Engineering Faculty, Fall 1980,* Higher Education Panel Reports, no. 52, October 1981 (Washington, D.C.:American Council on Education).

15. *Industrial Growth and Productivity,* Hearings before the Subcommittee on Industrial Growth and Productivity, Committee on the Budget, U.S. Senate, 97th Congress, 1st Session, December–January 1981, p. 95.

16. Thurow, *Zero-Sum Society,* p. 203.

17. "Jobs, Jobs Everywhere," *Time,* May 29, 1978, p. 29. Henry Wallich, a governor of the Federal Reserve, insisted that the United States was at full employment though the unemployment rate was 6 percent.

18. "Help Wanted," *Wall Street Journal,* October 16, 1978, p. 1.

19. Pat Choate and Susan Walter, *America in Ruins* (Washington, D.C.:Council of State Planning Agencies, 1981), pp. 1–4.

20. Robert Ball, "Employment Created by Construction Expenditures," *Monthly Labor Review,* December 1981, pp. 38–44.

21. "Too Late to Reindustrialize," *Christian Science Monitor,* July 20, 1982, p. 23.

22. Wassily Leontief, "What Hope for the Economy," *New York Review,* August 12, 1982, p. 33.

23. H. E. Striner, "1984 and Beyond: The World of Work," paper delivered before the American Psychological Association, 75th Anniversary Convention, Washington, D.C., September 2, 1967. Published by W. E. Upjohn Institute for Employment Research, October 1967, pp. 4–5.

24. David Sarnoff, John von Neumann, et. al., *The Fabulous Future* (New York: Dutton, 1955).

25. *Wall Street Journal,* August 21, 1967, p. 1.

26. *Wall Street Journal,* August 24, 1967, p. 8.

27. *Science Indicators, 1980,* National Science Foundation (Washington, D.C.:U.S. Government Printing Office, 1981), p. 5.

28. Ibid., p. 7.

29. "Seeking Technological Gains, the French Socialize Science," *New York Times,* August 15, 1982, p. 8E.

30. *Business Week,* November 23, 1981, p. 94.

31. Ibid.

32. J. Herbert Hollomon, "Policies and Programs of Governments Directed Toward Industrial Innovation," in *Technological Innovation for a Dynamic Economy,* ed. Christopher T. Hill and James M. Utterback (New York: Pergamon Press, 1979).

33. Irving Kristol, "The Trouble with Money," *Wall Street Journal,* August 26, 1981, p. 22.

34. *Report of the President's Commission on Budget Concepts* (Washington, D.C.:U.S. Government Printing Office, October 1967), p. 11.

35. Ibid.

Conclusions
===7===

I hope that the reader shares some of my beliefs about the nature of our economic problems and what must be done if we are to deal with them. What are these beliefs?

The first is that we can control our economy in order to achieve our economic and social goals. Our intellectual abilities, our judgment, our values, these are the key factors for achieving our aims; we are not held hostage by natural forces of the marketplace. We can change the institutional framework within which we live and function. If we are sufficiently open to this recognition and willing to alter the ways in which we design our production systems and institutions, we can improve our economic environment. Even without most economic resources, this can be done. The Japanese economy is living proof of this. After all, what else have they had except determination, well-educated people, and a way to blend them into an effective, competitive economy?

Second, our world is complex and must be grappled with on that basis. Simplistic solutions only reflect lack of understanding. In our society this seems painfully the case. In a recent article this position was very well put: "The truth seems to be that in moments of crisis those who try to speak with some awareness of complexity are likely to be disabled politically. A depressing thought."[1]

Although Howe was referring to the environment of the 1960s, it could just as well be applied to the more recent years of the Carter and Reagan administrations. We sought simple, quick, pat solutions for terribly complicated problems. We were deluded by slogans that held out quick relief to burdensome troubles of big government, big business, big unions, and big social problems. The word "big" signified little of their complexity, only that they were very troublesome. We sought to deal with them with little or no change in our institutions, personal habits, and

167

values and with an unwillingness to consider that our basic, traditional perceptions of solutions might be wrong. It has not worked.

But, paradoxical as this might seem, this has really been a necessary exercise. It has been most unfortunate, indeed tragic, for those who have had to suffer for what has been, in reality, a very costly educational process. If we have not learned lessons from this tragedy of unemployment, family deprivation, social conflict, and underproduction in our industries, the tragedy will be all the greater.

Finally, the nostrums and fantasies of supply-side economics, Laffer curves, and equally illusory visions of easy solution by Keynesian models have all gone their way. We are in a new world. New approaches, new coalitions, and new methods are called for. Where will the leadership come from and what should be proposed? What sort of grand scheme should we seek to develop? There are at least six key aspects of this new perspective.

1. The time has come for a new coalition that recognizes that management and labor must lead the way. Government in the United States should not lead. Indeed, it cannot.

2. Government, industry, and labor are inextricably bound together as joint partners in our economy. Each must be seen in a complementary relationship, not an adversarial or superior-inferior relationship. Each serves vital needs for the other.

3. Private and public policies must focus on gearing fiscal, monetary, and human resources policies to achieving gains in productivity. No one of these policy areas can be developed without an analytical relationship to the other two.

4. At the core, our most significant values, economic and social, center on our people. Productivity policies must relate to the benefits to be derived by the individuals who make up our society. Achieving this goal will go a long way toward achieving the economic goals of high levels of demand, adequate saving rates, and an efficient labor force.

5. Size or scale of industrial operation or joint efforts by companies should be judged on the basis of contribution to economic growth rather than an outmoded antitrust policy. Being big or small does not of itself imply goodness or badness. The society as a whole depends upon effective, efficient use of resources not on the size or scope of the company. Competition should be encouraged, but success should not be penalized.

6. Just as economic institutions must be flexible, so also must ones in government. Not only must new agencies be developed for specific new functions but old ones must be eliminated as their utility disappears. In addition, terms of office must be changed if necessary. Certainly no term

of two years is sufficient for a member of Congress to become familiar with major issues and be able to develop significant legislation. A two-year term guarantees that maximum concern will be with electioneering and public posturing rather than public service. Rigor mortis in government can offset even the most dynamic growth in managerial and labor effectiveness and efficiency.

The New Coalition

Since the mid-1970s, an increasing number of business and labor leaders have learned that wages, profits, and competitive position are related to productivity. Hundreds of these leaders from our largest unions and companies have visited plants in Japan and seen how dependent the manager and the worker are on each other. Most of the industrial giants in the United States have major production centers in other countries where management and labor are in an environment emphasizing harmony rather than conflict. Many U.S. companies have operations in West Germany and Sweden, where worker representation on boards of directors is customary. These companies have perspectives that have changed dramatically from those held a decade ago. In the early 1980s, unions have begun to understand, and act on, the necessity to gear wages and work practices to the goal of higher productivity levels in order to continue to compete with foreign producers. This is not to say that all managements and all unions have moved in this direction, far from it. But a significant number of major firms and unions have done so.

Steps can now be taken by those leaders of major corporations and major unions to establish a Joint Productivity Council (JPC), an independent organization to provide guidance to government, companies, and unions on policies affecting productivity. Training programs, safety regulations, tax policy, monetary policy, procurement practices, QC Circles, wage policy, and inventory practices would be some of the areas of likely concern.

The JPC would be the perfect vehicle to consider problems from industrial standards to environmental regulations as they affect productivity, export markets, and work conditions. The major gain would be that the JPC would conduct continuing discussions and analysis in an environment of mutual labor-management concern rather than in an adversarial, legislative-hearing environment, usually conducted after major problems creating sharp antagonisms have surfaced.

I believe that a significant number of industrial and labor leaders are ready for this sort of coalition. As I have said, common experiences in other countries show that this is not only feasible but it is also effective. In addition, both industry and labor have come to understand that government simply does not have the ability, or motivation, to deal effectively with a problem until it reaches the crisis stage. Too many agendas, too many foci of power, and too little time to legislate intelligently operate against rational well-thought-out solutions.

The economic crisis of the 1977–82 period has produced a more mature, insightful leadership in business and labor. An organization based upon a coalition of these interests could provide needed guidance, which is pragmatic in its orientation, for private and public policies. Indeed, an effective JPC could well eliminate many areas of unnecessary public intervention.

A JPC is suggested rather than the use of already existing organizations. This is so because of the need for as much freedom as possible from prior images, positions, or personnel. The JPC should be as unencumbered as possible in its venture into this new terrain.

Partnerships of Government, Industry, and Labor

Just as there has been a counterproductive set of adversarial relations among government, industry, and labor, so also have there been built-in adversarial relationships among government agencies. Both types of conflict situations have to be dealt with.

Within the executive branch, departments that represent special interests are only legitimate as long as they do not subvert overall economic growth and productivity gains to narrower interests. The interests of labor and commerce are not sufficiently protected only by having separate departments. There are other alternatives where both interests can be protected while better serving the larger interests of the nation. Any one expert in the affairs of Washington and the federal bureaucracy knows full well that the reorganization of the army and navy after World War II into a single Department of Defense did not eliminate their abilities to lobby effectively for special interests. The Department of Defense framework did, however, improve significantly the possibilities of a more systems- and efficiency-oriented means for achieving better interservice relationships and use of resources.

The Departments of Labor and Commerce are now two empires fighting for turfs and protecting jurisdictions that can only be dealt with intelligently within a broader framework. Minimum wages should not solely be within the bailiwick of labor; they impact on industrial hiring and training practices. Likewise, regional development or small business practices have considerable implications for questions of migrant labor laws. Government agencies may live in concrete abodes, but their organizational "houses" should be much more flexible and relate to the merging complexity of issues.

In the other area of relationships among government, business, and labor, there have to be clear, rhetoric-free understandings about what each sector must do. Government, and only government, can act for the whole society in areas of industrial safety, law, large-scale education, and security. Meaningless generalities about "getting government off our backs" are nonsense. Criticism of counterproductive regulation should be supported. But adversarial language used only as a debating ploy really does not move our society ahead. The only real way to achieve a lessening of such sophomoric hyperbole, as well as getting government to understand how much industry and labor can contribute to better legislation and regulatory procedures, is to develop a different set of processes than now exists for involving government, industry, and labor.

Every executive agency and every legislative committee should have subcommittees from the JPC sitting in as advisory bodies. In the executive agencies, these JPC subcommittees should be present as far down into the structure as the JPC and agency head agree upon. They should be present, however, at least two levels down in a major agency. These subcommittees would function strictly as advisory groups, discussing, analyzing, and reacting to all major contemplated legislation or regulations.

Obviously, these JPC subcommittees would bring back to the parent organization a sense of the problems as seen from the position of government. This would in turn promote industry and labor reactions, some of which could lead to ameliorative changes in labor or industrial policies and practices or a more frank, better informed series of hearings before congressional or executive agencies.

The principle is simple. All parties to a problem should be involved in such a way that all relevant positions are understood and evaluated fairly. But unless all parties are present, how can this be achieved? This also holds true in regard to management and labor. To what degree would corporations and unions or other labor groups benefit by a mutual participation in both corporate and union decision making? Probably greatly. But this cannot be legislated meaningfully unless the institutional setting is supportive. Worker participation in German companies was a gradual achievement and only became law decades after it was viewed as acceptable in certain major industries. Social values must work their will. A successful JPC could over the years achieve a level of cooperation, trust, and commonality that might well provide the acceptance of worker-management co-involvement in each other's organizations. But that is for the future to determine. We are far from a pragmatic possibility now. A JPC would itself be a major, highly effective step for producing a more harmonious and cooperative environment within which management, labor, and government would operate for mutual benefit.

Integration and Articulation of Fiscal, Monetary, and Human Resources Policies

Government fiscal, monetary, and human resource policies are developed by separate agencies of government as though each is a self-contained entity. They are not. Fiscal policies have an impact on interest rates that in turn affect savings and investment rates, thus creating problems that are often finally deposited at the doors of the Federal Reserve System. The actions triggered by responses of the Federal Reserve System can in turn affect levels of industrial activity through the availability of money, thus creating consequences for the labor force and employment levels.

As indicated previously a partial solution is to bring the Federal Reserve, as our major source of monetary policy, into a formal relationship with the Treasury Department. Both would then be forced to develop tax and monetary policies against a backdrop of overall fiscal constraints hammered out by the annual budget process. But this has little or no impact on relating fiscal and monetary matters to industrial output as it is translated into labor force effects. A device exists for this purpose but has been little used in the United States.

Enough was thought of the development of the economic technique called input-output analysis to award a Nobel Prize to its conceiver, the American economist Wassily Leontief. This technique permits following through to the employment level the results of projected effects on industrial output of various factors, including tax and monetary measures. Other countries have used this valuable economic tool in order to determine where economic problems could likely arise and prepare measures to offset them. We have yet to do the same.

This tool, utilized by the appropriate congressional offices and executive agencies, could bring together under one format, on an industry-by-industry basis, the linkages among fiscal, monetary, and human resource policies. The Congressional Budget Office and the Office of Management and Budget would be the most logical monitors of such efforts in their respective branches.

Beyond this, it is time that the federal budget be recognized for what it was originally intended to be. It is nothing more and nothing less than the proposed program of the federal government and the anticipated means for financing the program. The budget has an obvious, important effect on the overall economy. But depending on various accounting practices, separation of capital from current items and how assets are seen as being created by federal activities, one can as easily have a deficit as a surplus in many years. If, instead of a consolidated cash budget, as is used by the federal government (but not by most state governments), a budget separating capital from current items was established, there would probably have been no deficit shown in the fiscal year 1983 budget, as was anticipated in 1982. In mid-1982 on the basis of a consolidated cash budget a deficit of approximately $150 billion was anticipated. But over $155 billion in that budget was for items of a capital investment nature. That is, this $155 billion expenditure was for the nation's "plant and equipment" and would produce long-term payoffs necessary for economic growth and productivity.

A consolidated cash budget creates a misperception in that capital, self-liquidating items are placed on an equal basis alongside items such as procurement of oil filters for a motor pool vehicle. Other countries have been able to develop budgeting practices and public discussions about proposed budgets that generate much more light than heat. We usually achieve the reverse, mostly for partisan political motives.

The budget should differentiate between long-term investment programs, quality-of-life programs, current administrative operations, and other meaningful categories. The public should be educated to these differences so that an intelligent response to proposed budget changes can result. The budget of the United States should be seen not only as a statement of economic objectives but also as an educational vehicle that clearly states what the federal government will be investing in and providing current operations expenditures for in order to achieve clearly understood objectives for economic growth, social welfare, security, and productivity gains.

The budget must be related to the achievement of productivity increases and an adequate level of economic growth. These two components are really the bottom line. Deficits and surpluses are only vehicles for achieving these twin objectives, which are the only meaningful hallmarks of a healthy economy.

Human Resources Investment

In Western Europe there is an overriding concern with the individual. This was best put in a remark by a senior vice president in one of the largest companies in West Germany while we were lunching together. He said that in the United States managers and workers were often on a first-name basis, but he observed that neither really cared about the other. In

West Germany, he said, first names were rarely used, and formality was the rule. But each really was concerned about the other. This is certainly so in Japan. It is also true in many U.S. companies but is not the rule.

The human being is what our society is really about or should be about. Much of the lack of worker loyalty, hostility between social groups, and antisocial behavior grow out of a correct perception that most often we really do not care about each other's plight. An individual living in a neighborhood with broken sidewalks, torn-up streets with few street lights, and poor garbage collection is correct in assuming that the power structure in the community does not really care about him or her. Such a person is smart enough to know that talk is cheap, but paved streets cost money and call for sacrifice.

The result is a corrosive set of social relationships and mistrust. Caring is only genuine if it is translated into a meaningful act. If we do not act, we do not really care. It is interesting to recall Chancellor Schmidt's remark about caring for, and employing, the guest workers in Germany. Tourists in most European cities have trouble knowing, when they are walking in an area, which houses are those of low-income residents as opposed to middle-income residents. This is not so in the United States.

Conflict and social tension are only remedied by practical evidence of the larger society's real sense of concern. Really decent schools, adequate housing, streets and sidewalks in good repair are all the sorts of evidence that the low-income groups look for. It is really quite understandable. Table 6.2, which shows the proportion of GNP spent on housing and other community amenities, tells the story. And a society that accepts 20 to 30% illiteracy is not a society really concerned about the economic plight of its less advantaged citizens. Unless we become more concerned, and soon, the costs of unemployment benefits, welfare, crime, property damage, and insurance will continue at rates well above those in other countries. The only alternative to investing in human resources is to invest in more courts, prisons, welfare, and doorlocks. This hardly benefits productivity.

We must not only invest adequately in these areas, we must also insist on quality. The curricula found in most of our primary and secondary schools compare poorly with those in Japan, West Germany, France, and, yes, the USSR. Sciences, languages, and mathematics are largely absent in our curricula. Federal, state, and local educational authorities are to blame. Federal and state funds must be used to exert pressure on local systems to provide a level and type of education needed if we are to produce a labor force capable of supporting a productive economy. Federal and state funds for teacher training and retraining will be called for and must be available.

An adequate level, sustained over a decade at least, of funds for R&D is a necessary part of our investment in human resources. At least 3 percent of the GNP should be budgeted by the public and private sectors for performance of R&D. This level of effort will require an expansion of our efforts to provide a sufficient number of scientists and engineers and the faculties to train them. Given the fact that the markets for skills change periodically, a national program that provides all citizens with the right to public retraining education, just as is the case for primary and secondary education, is a must. The German version of our GI Bill for all their citizens has proven the practical worth of this approach. For us to ignore what is working in Germany and France along these lines is tantamount to refusing to deal with our labor force problems even though a solution is available.

Which Is Better, Big or Small? Which Is More Desirable, Lower or Higher Productivity?

Nothing better exemplifies the ease with which public policy in the United States has been able to deal with the most complicated problems by simplistic legislation than in the case of monopoly and antitrust situations. Growing out of the battles between the agricultural interests and the great railroad companies in the late 1800s, the Sherman Antitrust Act was passed in 1890. It sought to minimize undesirable aspects of the large trusts and mergers of that period. In the more than 90 years since its enactment, no law has been more difficult to apply, with the possible exception of the Prohibition Law, which was finally repealed.

Monopoly, big, small, and so on, are highly relative terms. But certainly there can be no doubt that such companies as IBM, GM, and AT&T are big by any standards. All of these companies have been the concern at one time or another of the Antitrust Division of the Department of Justice, IBM as recently as the 1980s. With few exceptions the antitrust laws were found either so difficult to define in terms of real market control or so difficult to apply on a pragmatic basis that they have probably had little effect over the long run. In some instances where bigness has a potential for market mischief, no doubt the presence of the various antitrust laws has served to curtail such potentials. But could not the same results be achieved without substantial losses that accrue in terms of productivity benefits foregone because of antitrust laws? I believe so.

The Western European countries and Japan have been able to curtail economically undesirable concentrations of industry or the results of excessive size of firm without losing attendant benefits of large-scale production and joint corporate ventures. For many years special cartel courts in Europe, specially equipped by training, dealt with this problem in a more effective manner than the regular court system in the United States.

In Japan the ministry entrusted with antitrust problems must work closely with MITI in order to determine the cost-benefit trade-off of antitrust as compared with overall productivity and economic gains.

Given the myriad regulations, both federal and state, concerning collusion, misleading advertisement, mislabeling, as well as the sensitivity of government that now exists to the sort of outrageous business practices that triggered passage of the antitrust law, it would seem that a "midcourse correction" is due in this area. This is certainly indicated when we recall that giants like GM, Chrysler, U.S. Steel, and General Electric are literally fighting for their lives because of the intensely effective competition coming from foreign shores. If these giants are not free to manipulate markets and prices for their self-protection in their home market, there surely must be some concern about the reasons for still looking to a Sherman Act as a primary source of protection from these companies.

The cost of such legislation is high. Not in the sense of enforcement, but in the sense of lost productivity gains. Shared R&D, joint ventures to achieve economies of scale, pooling information or innovative processes—all have the potential for major gains in productivity. But they are illegal under current laws. Similar regulations restrict companies from expanding into activities that are related but could possibly cause broadening of a firm's power base. The acquisition of one oil company by another oil company is not inherently "evil." It is only an evil if it runs counter to achieving a net social and economic gain. Many years ago the courts established the rule that mere size alone was not inherently a violation of the antitrust laws, but the burden of proof is still largely on the shoulders of industry and tends to discourage growth or market control beyond some vague point. Sherman's Sword of Damocles is hardly conducive to industrial activities that may not only gain lower unit costs, large overseas markets, and the potential for more employed but may also gain an antitrust suit.

Legislation in this area must be reexamined in the light of modern industrial structure, international competition, and the mechanisms for economic growth and productivity gain. Doing homage to an antiquated concept embodied in an obsolete law is hardly conducive to the creation of an investment, production, or R&D environment to help U.S. industry to compete with European and Japanese industry. Surely we have gleaned some ways since the 1890s for combining ways to preserve an environment for competition while not penalizing the society by eliminating productivity gains that can only be achieved in an environment of industrial cooperation and rational industrial growth.

To return, then, to the question of which is better, big or small. The answer is, "It depends." If national productivity gains can be shown to have a high probability of increase by virtue of increasing size of firm and cooperation among firms, then no antitrust legislation should prohibit this effort. If such is not the case, and what is more likely are such negative results as declining productivity and economic growth effects, the law should tend to limit its causes.

Institutional Change and Government

In the earlier brief statement on this point, the suggestion was offered that the period of two years as the term for those in the House of Representatives is too brief. The reason was that most significant legislation affecting the economy could neither be designed nor tested in so few years. In addition, the pressures for reelection foredoom most reasonable efforts to design legislation in an intelligent manner. It makes no sense to theorize about potentially effective economic programs if the term of office is so brief as to limit the ability of Congress to deal effectively with the design of new programs.

The role of government is crucial to the operation of an economy and society. Deregulation for industries did not result in Elysian Fields for effortless romping through an unfettered market. Especially if they still had to compete with competitors supported by other governments. Long-term, high-cost capital equipment investments are not so easily made when many insecurities attend. This is no new insight. Our first secretary of the treasury, Alexander Hamilton, knew of this when he supported the development of a tariff system, public transportation, and other public investments he felt necessary to help to develop U.S. industry. Hamilton was no liberal or socialist. He had a keen sense, however, of the assets and liabilities of a market economy.

In the conflicts between new technologies and the need to provide a civilized environment in which to live, the role of government has necessarily expanded enormously. In some cases the result has not been salutory for productivity and economic growth. In others it has. We really do have to distinguish between these two cases and not get caught up in limiting both while dealing ineffectually with the latter. Ill-conceived efforts to cut budgets and save money have often resulted in penny-wise and pound-foolish outcomes.

Three cases will, I hope, suffice in illustrating how easily we can be led into counterproductive situations.

The first case: "There is no free lunch." How true, and how appealing this sounds as we try to cut back on the use of public funds where we feel that people simply are not trying hard enough to improve their own lot. But we rarely use this cliché in reference to government.

In a sensitive and well-written article, George F. Will made this point.[2] Will was commenting on industry's wish to weaken the restrictions on lead additives in gasoline, in order to cut costs of production. He made the point that by releasing 600,000 tons of lead into the air, given the high metabolic rates of children, this was leading to a form of lead poisoning that causes mental retardation, brain damage, anemia, seizures, hyperactivity, and death. Since industrialization had started in the 1860s, lead in the environment had increased 200-fold. Each tank of gasoline sends two ounces of lead into the air. Four percent of our children, under the age of five, now have excessive levels of lead in their blood. But that figure, Will points out, is misleading in a way.[3] "Shaker Heights and downtown Cleveland do not share equally. The percentage of black preschoolers with excessive lead levels is six times that of white preschoolers. Other studies indicate excessive levels in one-fifth of black children from low-income families." The lead not only comes from gasoline fumes, it also comes from lead-based paint. Pre-1950 housing has 100 times more lead than is now permitted. The combination of old housing and living downtown, in traffic-congested areas, results in 20 to 25 percent of lead-poisoned black children. The loss of federal funds, and an inadequate tax base or concern at the local level, have resulted in less screening of ghetto children and treatment.

Now, here comes the "free lunch." By not spending money to eliminate excessive levels of lead in gasoline, by not replacing paint in old tenements, do we save money, do we have a "free lunch" for government or the society? No! The results are measurably lower levels of IQ, mental retardation, increased hospital costs, and eventually, of course, higher crime and property destruction rates.

> Any childhood disease that threatened affluent children as lead poisoning threatens poor children would produce public action faster than you can say "Swine Flu." As things are, government spends upwards of $1 billion annually on children with lead poisoning, 80 percent on special education for the learning-disabled. Conservatives dissolve in admiration for this insight: "There is no free lunch." It means: someone must pay for anything that costs . . . society shall pay (for example, with slightly higher energy costs) for reducing lead use; and society shall continue to pay a lot (for injuries to its human capital) if it does not reduce lead use.[4]

Losses in productivity are obvious, medical and social costs instead of well people are the result, and are paid for by all of us.

The second case: An evaluation of the two-year post–Job Corps experience of graduates of the program, compared with a control group of similar young adults who did not pass through the program, indicated that the cost-benefit ratio was quite favorable. That is, the average program cost per trainee was $5,070 while the posttraining income increase for only two years following graduation from the program was $7,343—a 45 percent benefit over costs.[5] The trainees were what are classified as "severely disadvantaged."

One of the early program cuts under the Reagan administration was the Job Corps. When the new president entered office, 44,000 trainees were enrolled. This number was reduced to 32,000 for fiscal year 1982. A further proposed cut in fiscal year 1983 sought to lower the number of trainees to 22,000. This second reduction envisioned a budgetary "saving" of $85 million. But given the cost-benefit ratio of a 45 percent gain, the "saving" to society would have been nonexistent! The budget "saving" would have cost society about $123 million in lost income and productivity, or $38 million in net lost income. But this is a conservative figure. There is no easy way to determine what other costs, such as crime, welfare dependency, property damage, and insurance costs, will also result.

The third case: This has to do with the well-accepted facts that in the midst of our revolution in technology, science and industrial innovation, information, data and rapid communication are essentials for economic performance. The chief source of information, of all sorts, in the United States is the U.S. Census Bureau. No private agency or firm has the ability to collect as much data about as many things as this government agency.

With increasing budget cuts of various government operations, programs in the Census Bureau were also curtailed. Hence, some surveys were eliminated and the results of others became later and later in their availability. The costs of these "savings" are rarely seen. Most people are even unaware of these costs. But the victims are often surprising ones.

Because of budget constraints, the findings of the 1980 Census are very slow in emerging, and some services that were promised to data users have been canceled. Many people and organizations bear the brunt of these "savings," and the costs that result from these "savings" are interesting. Land development companies in Orange County, California, are still having to use information from the 1970 Census in an area that has grown so fast that some communities are vastly different from what they were then—in incomes, education, life styles, and family size. Business decisions are being made on the basis of obsolescent data. Mistakes will cost money, affect profits, and undoubtedly result in higher prices.

Companies that supply demographic data to business firms concerned about the location of new outlets, branches, or franchises, now find that late census data is slowing down the opening of such facilities. From McDonald hamburger outlets to Chase Manhattan branches—all are affected. Because of budget cuts, one of the tabulations eliminated by the census was 1980 data by ZIP codes. Commercial users such as Sears,

Roebuck, national magazines, and other major retailers have had to form their own consortia to compute the ZIP information, from census computer tapes, at a much higher cost.

Most of what the Census Bureau provides is used by industry, various levels of government (including state and local), educational institutions, and private citizens. Because of that shared use, no one has been able to come up with a better way of paying for this universally used information than by tax dollars. By slowing down the availability of data, or cutting it out completely, the "savings" usually result in higher costs or lower productivity or both. Government can only cut back on this activity at the expense of our economic efficiency. Indeed, there is no free lunch!

In a way, the "free lunch" analogy also applies to activities that are directly or indirectly supported by government, but where little or no productivity results from such support. Indeed, in many cases the results are really negative productivity. No better example exists than in the case of bank loans for the purpose of corporate mergers that waste economic resources and achieve no real economic benefits. The Federal Reserve acts as a regulator of the commercial banking system. By virtue of reserve requirements, rediscount rates, and open-market operations, it regulates the supply of money. Beyond this, it also utilizes various regulations to impede or stimulate credit, depending on the state of the economy. To permit credit or loans for merger purposes where there are no economic or productivity benefits to be derived should not be viewed as an acceptable banking practice. Suitable regulations to circumscribe such use of investment funds should be developed.

In addition, in concert with various government agencies and the proposed Joint Productivity Council subcommittees, specific industries should be targeted for special productivity grants or loans, with interest rates well below the market rate. The establishment of this interest-rate schedule would be the responsibility of the Federal Reserve and would be set at levels calculated to stimulate needed R&D, development, or production calculated to result in long-term productivity gains in the specific targeted industry.

This targeting should not be perceived as a device reflecting a so-called liberal or conservative policy or philosophy. It must be viewed as a necessary mechanism for achieving industrial growth, higher real income, and increasing share of market through the judicious and logical use of investment funds. Though some will undoubtedly criticize this control of investment decisions by the private banking system, it is hardly a prudent use of depositors funds to stimulate unproductive merger activities and thereby lessening the sums available for more rational, useful types of economic ventures. Unfortunately, the debates over such matters too often grow out of stances taken as liberals or conservatives rather than as intelligent citizens concerned with the effectiveness of our economic institutions.

The continuing debate between the so-called liberals and conservatives seems to focus on two issues: social justice and wealth. But, as we have been learning, without wealth the means for achieving social justice simply do not exist. Wealth is the product of a society that has been able to harness its people and physical capital so they, together, can produce more. Sharing in the use, as well as the results, of our capital in order to achieve a more productive economy and society is what we must now focus on. All of our institutions must be involved.

Industrial Policy in the United States

Since 1981, there has been an increasing interest in the United States in the development of an industrial policy. The reasons grow out of the fact that, as has been shown earlier in this book, Japan to a large degree and West Germany to a lesser degree have since the end of World War II marshalled their resources around a set of economic objectives and national goals. Public and private organizations have worked closely together, planning to achieve national, corporate, and labor goals. Industries with potential have had risk lessened by government. Obsolete industries have been pushed out of existence but with the path of exodus made easier by special tax help and retraining of workers. The roles of MITI and the Ministry of Finance in Japan are seen by many in the United States as paragons of what industrial policy can do to stimulate industrial growth, high productivity, increasing market share, and low unemployment.

By mid-1983, the public media and halls of Congress were caught up in discussion and debate about how the United States could develop its brand of industrial policy. Some suggested a new federal department that would combine the interests of the old Department of Commerce with broad new responsibilities for stimulating trade and markets abroad; others suggested a council, or councils, which would guide the president and/or Congress in targeting changes in antitrust statutes, tax policies, subsidies, and research and development, among other things, all calculated to help develop new industries or aid old industries to become more productive and competitive. Such efforts are helpful, but tend to ignore several salient features of our society and culture that force us to go farther than these models, which are designed to lead from the top.

Foremost among those, in this writer's mind, who have put forward constructive and realistic strategies for developing coherent, effective industrial policies are Felix G. Rohatyn and Robert B. Reich. Drawing on an all too-rare combination of conceptual insights and pragmatic business experience, as a senior partner with the New York investment banking firms of Lazard Freres & Co., Rohatyn has fully comprehended the need for a permanent public source of loans, tied to a quid pro quo of productivity gain and industrial growth from the private loan-recipients. Financing must be accompanied by internal changes if an industry is to improve its competitiveness. In the case of emerging industries, financing must be joined to clear and persuasive evidence that the organizational structure, leadership and market potential offer high probability of a competitive, high-productive operation.

Professor Robert B. Reich, in his recent work,[6] building on earlier research with Ira Magaziner,[7] moves the industrial policy argument away from the simplistic notion of targeting special industries, hopefully by some super-agency or collection of seers, for government help, and builds a position based on a concept of the fundamental shifts which have taken place in our society, both in our economic and political activities. His thesis, that our social policies must combine both economic and political values is central to any future industrial policy which will increase our nation's competitive ability. But of even greater immediate significance is Reich's observation that the transformation of our nation's economic institutions, moving away from mass manufacturing to flexible manufacturing, places a premium on the wise use of our human resources. And that wise use calls for a program of investment in our people. They are the final, base resource. The industries that should be supported by an industrial policy must be those which simultaneously offer the highest productivity and have a long-term human resource investment policy. The emerging economy of the 1980's, according to Reich, must be based upon technologically-driven products and processes.

Industrial policy, as conceptualized by Rohatyn and Reich, brings together institutionalized risk capital in the service of an economy serving the twin masters of greater material wealth and a more pervasive sense of social justice. Achieving such a goal is remarkably close to what has been sought in West Germany and Japan since World War II. But, too often, a simplistic approach to a U.S. industrial policy has ignored the cultural differences which must force the U.S. to follow approaches far different from those followed in other countries.

The social partnership of West Germany and the consensus of Japan are based upon a heritage of shared responsibility and traditions of mutuality. Our history and values have been based on individualism and a highly varied population, varied in religion, color, country of origin, history, and values. Singleness of purpose, which is critical for an industrial policy, is more difficult to achieve in the United States than in Japan or

West Germany. It can only be done by developing mechanisms such as have been suggested in this study, that is, by bringing together industry, government, and labor at lower levels in order to plan and work on how to achieve mutually desirable goals that are clearly of national significance. Advisory committees to the president and Congress must both lead and draw from these joint groups. Any new federal departments responsible for industrial policy formulation and operation must work with and depend upon the Joint Productivity Council discussed earlier. The JPC subcommittees become an increasingly larger network that establishes links of understanding, mutuality of purpose, translation of legislative intent into pragmatic performance, and feedback on what is truly happening in the field.

The United States simply cannot, and will not, look to a superagency or super advisory committee for "marching orders" on industrial policy. Our industrial policy must follow two tracks, which in reality is what happens in Japan. Our problem is that we have chosen to perceive Japan's industrial policy as being contained only within the walls of its ministries buildings. It is not. MITI could not exert its effective leadership were it not for the web of relationships, mutuality of trust, and understanding by industry, government, and labor of each other's concerns, needs, and problems. It is this web or network that we must "manufacture" by new types of organizations, such as the JPC, if we hope to develop a basis for industrial policy.

Finally, an industrial policy cannot operate unless contiguous policies are also operating. It does no good to design R&D programs, tax policies, and cooperative marketing arrangements to stimulate an exciting new industry if the nation's school system is turning out a high proportion of graduates who are functionally illiterate and mathematically inept and cannot provide the necessary supply of skilled people for such industries. The report in 1983 of the National Commission on Excellence in Education quite correctly sees our nation "at risk" because of the mediocrity, to be charitable, of our education system. Unless we address this problem and develop an adequately funded comprehensive education and training system, no industrial policy will work.

The time has come for us to accept and deal with the fact that there are no simplistic, short-term solutions to such major problems as productivity, world trade, or developing an industrial policy. Leaders in industry and labor have begun to recognize that the search for simple, short-term solutions and goals has led to an increasing inability to compete effectively. Our economic policies must be based on longer-term goals and relationships, reflecting the real world, which is complicated and does not yield to solutions grounded in wishful thinking or nostalgia and fantasy. Political leaders must grasp this nettle. As a nation, we will continue to be ill-served if they do not.

In reality, the old concept of the private sector or the public sector is over with. Passé. We should recall the wry advice given by Benjamin Franklin to his co-signers of the Declaration of Independence on July 4, 1776, "We must all hang together, or assuredly we shall all hang separately."[8]

Notes

1. Irving Howe, "The Decade That Failed," *New York Times Magazine*, September 19, 1982, p. 78.

2. George F. Will, "The Poison Poor Children Breathe," *Washington Post*, September 16, 1982, p. A23.

3. Ibid.

4. Ibid.

5. John L. Palmer and Isabel V. Sawhill, *The Reagan Experiment* (Washington, D.C.: Urban Institute Press, 1982), p. 260.

6. Robert B. Reich, *The Next American Frontier*, Times Books, 1983, NY, NY.

7. Robert B. Reich and Ira Magaziner, *Minding America's Business*, Harcourt, Brace, Jovanovich, 1982, NY, NY.

8. John Bartlett, *Familiar Quotations*, 15th ed. (Boston: Little, Brown, 1980), p. 348.

Epilogue

Since the 1930s, probably stimulated by the conflicts of ideology brought on by the Great Depression and the apostasy of Franklin D. Roosevelt (as seen by his social stratum peers), we seem to want to catalog those who write about social and economic problems as either conservatives or liberals.

For those readers who may wonder about the author, the label of progressive has been chosen. If conservatives are those who seek to retain old institutions and feel a hankering for some real or imagined "good old days," the liberals are often seen as those who, presumably, seek to abolish or uproot institutions they feel pose obstacles to achieving their goals of economic and social justice.

It seems to me that while there are certainly some institutions that must be abolished if we are to gain the socially desirable results being sought, these are probably rare instances. For by far the larger number of instances, what I believe is more desirable, more effective in the long run, is to seek to improve, redesign, and reorient our basic institutions to accommodate our changing values and desires. It would appear that this is certainly the case with most people in the United States. If there is any peculiarity about our nation it is that most among the lowest income groups, blacks and the newest arrivals from Spanish-speaking areas really believe in what the large majority of us agree upon as the American Dream. Very few of the minorities are clamoring for a communist, socialist, or fascist society. They are really hoping for a bigger share of what the overwhelming majority of Americans would agree America is about. What is amazing about most of the so-called disadvantaged, low-income people in our country is their continued wish to see American goals of equity, fair-income shares, a better life for their children, decent housing, a business or a decent job, translated into a reality.

For a brief few months while our nation celebrated its two hundredth anniversary, we seemed to come together. We have drifted apart since. Unless we realign our institutions into a more effective form in order to achieve the goal most of us want, a capitalism that benefits all, it is unlikely that this nation will be able to sustain, much less achieve, its dream.

Appendix A:
Quantity Theory of Money

In terms of a reality-oriented approach, Milton Friedman's focus on the supply of money as *the* critical factor for economic stability is highly questionable. Unfortunately, too many noneconomists throw up their hands in despair when monetary theory is discussed, pro or con, since they understandably feel that the subject is too technical and convoluted for their intelligent involvement in the discussion. Nothing could be less true. One only needs to comprehend the fundamental concepts of this theory to question it, as many do.

The quantitative theory of money has a long history, long before the advent of Friedman. The heart of the theory is in the equation

$$MV = PT$$

whcre

M = Quantity of money (demand deposits plus all currency in circulation).

V = Velocity of circulation of money, or the number of times for any set period, say a year, the average dollar is exchanged.

P = A price index or general level of prices.

T = Number of transactions made in an economy during a specific period. Physical output is the indicator used.

Hence, this relationship establishes a truism, something that is true by definition. Whether it is of any use in dealing with problems of inflation, the interest rate, and prices depends on a set of assumptions. The real question is how realistic are the assumptions.

The initial assumptions made by the early economists who developed the quantity theory of money are:

- The velocity of money is constant. Hence, from year to year the number of times a dollar changes hands in transactions is constant.
- Transactions, or sales, are always taking place in an economy where there is little unemployment of resources, including people. The economy is functioning at full capacity.

Given these assumptions, the only item that can affect prices is the supply of money, M.

We know that the velocity of money does indeed change. In the depths of the Great Depression, the velocity was around 2.5. In 1980, it was around 6. The number is derived by dividing the dollar value of our gross national product by the volume of all currency in circulation and checking accounts (or demand deposits) for each year. Velocity depends on many things. Wage increases are, of course, an obvious item. Less obvious, and more difficult to quantify, is the investment or consumption psychology of the consumer or the businessperson during periods of inflation, threat of war, political instability, or a sense of changing political times.

We also know that the economy does not operate in such a fashion as to guarantee a level of full employment of all resources, including people. Since the quantity theory of money evolved prior to the 1930s, the Great Depression certainly upset the assumption of T, number of transactions during a specific period, being based on full employment. This assumption was logical if based on the model growing out of classical economic theory—that is, free competition, no control of prices or markets by major producers (or not for long), full information about all prices and commodities by the consumers, no involvement by government in the economy, and the control of all economic decisions by "natural forces of the market." In brief, it is the old trolley-car syndrome: If my grandmother had wheels she would be a trolley car. But she doesn't and she isn't!

The supply of money undoubtedly does have an impact on price levels and inflation. But so do many other things. Unless we can understand how many things are involved, and how people react in their expenditure patterns in the short run as well as over longer periods of time, merely looking at the supply of money is not only not helpful, it can be positively misleading. We still do not have a quantity theory of money that contains a realistic appreciation of all of the forces that are involved, including political forces. Such governments as Chile and Great Britain, which chose the Friedman approach to price stability, were gradually forced to abandon the use of the quantity theory of money to stabilize prices. The reasons are obvious. The levels of unemployment, lack of growth in GNP, and political instability force a retreat before the theoretically perfect surgical technique left a dead patient on the operating table.

Modern monetarists, led by Friedman, hold that an unvarying rate of growth in the money supply, say 3 to 5 percent per year, would be the best way to achieve economic growth and price stability. The market, left to itself, with this sort of steady, predictable rate of money stock growth, would be the best way to guarantee a healthy economy. The Federal Reserve System is the vehicle for achieving this. It was, Friedman holds, improper Federal Reserve policy in the early 1930s that created the Great Depression. There are many more economists who have studied the causes of this great economic debacle in far more detail who would hold otherwise.[1] Like his view of the quantity theory of money, where one factor is seen as the only major one, so also in the case of the high complexity of the economy of the United States in the early 1930s, the Federal Reserve System is chosen for the role of the key factor leading us into the Great Depression.[2] Would that the world of economics was that simple! As seen in the chapters on West Germany and Japan, a successful set of economic policies does exist, but not based upon a simplistic version of reality.

Saving the most significant weakness of the quantitative theory of money until last, we are confronted by the difficulty of defining M, money. Here, to the noneconomist would seem to be the simplest task of all. It is the most difficult. M, as we have seen, is composed of demand deposits plus currency in circulation. This is what, also termed M-1, M-2 and M-3, is defined to include other types of money such as money-market funds, time deposits, etc. Given our imagination and penchant for arriving at new arrangements when it suits our economic needs, it turns out that the neat categories of M-1, M-2, and M-3 do not admit to the clarity ascribed to them for the purpose of applying the quantity theory of money, where M-1 is key. Money as we have defined it keeps changing! Commenting on this state of affairs, the president of the Federal Reserve Bank of Boston said it was impossible to measure the money supply "with any kind of precision."[3] This comment by Frank E. Morris was made in noting "that a recent acceleration in M-1 was the result of a buildup in interest-bearing checking accounts, even though much of the money in these new NOW accounts represents savings that would normally be included in M-2. Similarly, some people use their money-market funds as checking accounts, yet the Fed includes these funds in M-2."[4]

Morris is not alone in his concern for defining money so that the quantity theory of money can be translated into a tool with some degree of precision. Anthony M. Solomon, president of the Federal Reserve Bank of New York, takes the position that setting targets for money growth will become increasingly difficult. He feels this to be so because as new regulations calculated to serve the needs of the financial markets emerge, they tend to blur further the differences between "transaction money" such as cash and "near money" such as savings accounts.[5]

Though economics is often referred to as the dismal science, its groping for scientific precision in such artifices as the quantity theory of money can almost be amusing. For example, in a letter to the editor of the *Wall Street Journal* on June 28, 1982, Milton Friedman complained that the 10.4 percent rate of growth in M-2 for six months was dangerously high. Since over 80 percent of M-2 consists of the sort of deposits that pay interest, if the average rate of interest was around 13 percent, that fact alone would account for a 10.4 percent rise in M-2. Only by tampering with the interest rate could that increase in M-2 be denied. But that sort of action is forbidden to a doctrine of monetary theory. An interesting economic catch-22! This observation was made by Alan Reynolds, vice president, Polyconomics, Inc., in his letter to the editor of the *Wall Street Journal*, on July 7, 1982, p. 21.

Finally, a *Business Week* article commented on an analysis by two economists with Merrill Lynch, Pierce, Fenner and Smith of two recent studies of monetary policy by two different Federal Reserve banks.[6] Though the studies were for roughly the same period, 1970–81, and most of the same countries were covered—the United States, Great Britain, West Germany, Canada, France, Italy, and Japan—the conclusions were opposite. The Federal Reserve Bank of St. Louis study found a high correlation between a steady, controlled rate of growth of the money supply and economic stability. The Federal Reserve Bank of Boston found the opposite to be the case. The best advice on this situation came from the two Merrill Lynch economists, Donald E. Maude and Robert A. Schwartz: "Any dogmatic approach toward monetary policy should be treated with a good deal of skepticism."[7]

Finally, any effort to understand the role of the money supply as it affects domestic price levels must look beyond the domestic economy and domestic institutions. With differential international rates of demand for money, and different levels of short- and long-term interest rates between countries, it is obvious that any effort to define and control money must be on an international basis. Thus, as was happening in 1981–83, with an increasing world-wide demand for dollars, the Federal Reserve should have allowed a rate of growth that accommodated domestic demand as well as rate of growth in the U.S. money supply that was calculated to meet the increasing foreign demand for dollars. Not doing so had to exert an upward pressure on interest rates. Conversely, with a drop in the international demand for dollars, the Federal Reserve must shrink the money supply based on both domestic *and* foreign needs.

Central banking activities and policies can not be pursued with domestic factors as the sole source of guidance. Indeed, if all central banks were to do so simultaneously when all countries were confronted at the same time by a rise in price levels, the "normal" domestic policy of contracting the money supply of each country at the same time could produce a devastating decline in world-wide economic activity. The quantity theory of money, indeed the typical monetarist approach, offers little to deal with such problems. The differences and resulting confusion between countries of how M1, M2, etc. are defined, are such as to cause the Tower of Babel to pale in any comparison.

Notes

1. Still a classic on this sad period of our economic history, and eminently readable, is Broadus Mitchell, *Depression Decade*, vol. IX, Rinehart Economic History Series (New York: Rinehart, 1947).

2. Milton Friedman, *Capitalism and Freedom*, (Chicago: University of Chicago Press, 1962), p. 38.

3. *U.S. News & World Report*, July 26, 1982, p. 65.

4. Ibid.

5. Ibid.

6. *Business Week*, August 30, 1982, p. 12.

7. Ibid.

Appendix B:
MITI

Between December 3, 1980, and January 28, 1981, the Subcommittee on Industrial Growth and Productivity of the U.S. Senate Committee on the Budget held hearings. In the printed volume that summarizes these hearings, published in 1981 by the U.S. Government Printing Office, material was submitted by the Japanese Ministry of International Trade and Industry (pp. 245–55). In this rather detailed statement, the ministry presented an outline of its contemplated policies for the 1980s. No secret blueprint guides Japanese industry. No confidential set of plans indicates where priorities for industrial achievement and social goals are to be established, and aided in gaining them by policies and programs joining private and public sector efforts and resources. The tone of cooperation is set in the introduction.[1]

> In the 1980s Japan will be increasingly called upon to contribute to the harmonious development of the international community as positively as is comparable to its international status. Japan will also have to cope with the problem of the growing scarcity of energy resources. Appropriate policy is needed to deal with these tasks and problems. It will be more difficult for Japan to fix its course in the 1980s, yet it will be essential to select the right course.
>
> The essential task for the Ministry of International Trade and Industry is to set up guidelines that the people, business sector and government can follow in their concerted efforts to overcome the difficulties of the present decade and to open the way for a new age.
>
> MITI has directed its policies in conformity with two reports submitted by the Industrial Structure Council: "The Industrial Structure in Japan" in 1963, and "The Vision of MITI's Policies in the 1970s" in 1971. Currently, the council has submitted its report entitled, "The Vision of MITI Policies in the 1980s," whose outline is given below.

Setting the stage, MITI offers its general impression of what is happening to the United States as an industrial power and the increasingly close relationship between economic and political goals. To MITI, mercantilism is no mere subject for historical study, it is the present and future.

The political and economic stability of the world throughout the most part of this century has been rhetorically called Pax Americana in an analogy to Pax Britannica referring to the Peace of Europe in the 19th century. Although the U.S. remains the preeminent world power, its relative status is declining. Militarily, the bipolarization of the two superpower blocs—the U.S. and Soviet Union—will continue, while politically and economically, the world will experience further transition toward a multipolar and multifaceted structure, causing an intensification of political and economic instability.

The 1980s should be a period of cooperation among developed nations, while developing nations will have a stronger voice in the operation of international politics and economics. In addition, the oil producing countries of the Middle East are expected to be more influential, controlling the supply and price of oil. The politics and economics of China, now appearing to gradually liberalize its society, and the East-West relationship may also contribute to the further multipolarization and complication depending upon their evolutions.

On the other hand, interdependence among nations is expected to deepen further in the coming decade. Politics and economics will become more closely related with each other, making the world even more complex.[2]

How does MITI see Japan's near-term future, and what goals must it now set in order to deal with problems it perceives in that future?

After successfully rebuilding its war-torn economy in the '50s, Japan developed heavy and chemical industries in the '60s, and added new dimensions and leverage to its economy by developing knowledge-intensive industries in the '70s. Today, Japan accounts for 10 percent of GNP of the world, even though Japan has only 3 percent of the world's population and 0.3 percent of the world's land. Though on a stock basis Japan is still behind industrialized countries, on a flow basis, its per capita national income has reached 90 percent of that of the United States, exceeding the average of the EC countries. On the other hand, in view of unstable world energy situation, the heavy dependence on foreign supplies of energy—89 percent of its total energy requirements—now casts serious problems upon the future Japanese economy.

Since the Meiji Era, Japan has struggled to achieve a level comparable to that of Western countries by modernizing and developing an industrial society. Japan today has achieved the goal it set for itself. Yet immediately after the fulfillment of that goal comes the turning point. Japan in the 1980s will have to seek new directions and face new challenges.[3]

The goals MITI sets in order to deal with these problems are as follows:

The Japanese economy has attained the national goal of the past hundred years, reaching the level of Western industrial nations. It is time for Japan to establish new national long-term goals and to envisage the course to reach them. We propose the following three national long-term policy goals.

(1) Contributing positively to the international community.
(2) Overcoming the limitations of natural resources and energy.
(3) Attaining co-existence of dynamism of the society and the improved quality and comfort of life.[4]

Taking just one of these goals, that of overcoming the limitations of natural resources and energy, we can see how MITI translates a general orientation to a problem into broad guidelines that serve two critical purposes. The first is to induce an allocation of vital resources in the private sector in order to achieve the specified goals. The second is to state the nature of the government's commitment, be it financial or otherwise. For example, in the excerpt that follows, in (1) (a)–(c), (3) (a) and (b), (4) (a)–(c), and (5) (a)–(b), the research and development areas are delineated. Here are the foci for the 1980s for targeting the new technologies and industries. These targets support the Philosophy statement. But what is the role of the government to be? What can industry look to MITI in its "pledge" of resources to reduce risk and share the developmental burdens? The answer, under New Phase in Policy on Technology, is clear. In section (2) (b), MITI indicates what actual activities government will launch on its own— no guesswork about this. But in sections (3) (a)–(c), MITI also makes clear that R&D budgets will not only be raised in absolute amounts but also as a percentage of GNP, in spite of "expected deficit in the national budget."[5]

In looking at the following excerpt what is of further significance is that MITI makes quite clear that the principal role of government policy in technology is to help the private sector move away from its dependence on imported technology and begin to develop its own sources of creativity and innovation. If MITI succeeds, the 1980s will see the end of Japan as a "copier-improver" and its emergence as a "creator-innovator."

Philosophy

(1) Technological innovation is a source of progress for Japan as well as the world. Great expectations are therefore placed on technological innovation providing the key to the solution of various problems in the 1980s. Japan must strive to develop its creative capacity and contribute, as an innovator, to world progress.

(2) As technological development is a means of attaining economic security by strengthening a country's bargaining power, Japan must stand on the ground of technology.

(3) The now prevalent apprehension is that technological progress is about to stagnate. In the 1980s, however, the following types of technological efforts will be made (a) new application and combination of existing technologies, (b) flowering of new technology resulting from a new application of science and technology, and (c) the preparation for the next generation's epoch-making technological innovations expected in the years after 1990. If these efforts are successful, the economy and society are expected to move into a new, prosperous stage.

Objectives of Technological Development in the 1980s

The principal tasks for technological development to be stimulated by economic and social necessities in the '80s are the following:

(1) Energy:

(a) Energy-saving technologies such as magneto-hydrodynamics (MHD) power generation, highly efficient gas turbines, fuel cells and a waste heat recovery system.

(b) Alternative energy technologies such as nuclear power, coal, solar energy and geothermal energy.

(c) New energy technologies such as nuclear fusion for commercial application in the 21st century.

(2) Improving the Quality of Life and Community Facilities:

(a) Social systems related to personal and community life including a medical information system.

(b) New energy-saving housing systems and artificial ground for intensive use of land.

(3) Knowledge-Intensive and Innovative Technologies:

(a) Knowledge-intensive production systems equipped with microcomputers, and upgraded resource-saving and energy-saving technologies.

(b) Innovative technologies such as new materials, optical communication, VLSI (very large scale integrated circuit) and laser beam technology.

(4) The Next-Generation Technologies:

(a) In the field of life sciences: treatment of cancer, genetic manipulation, investigation into a photosynthesis process and its application for food production.

(b) In the field of energy: nuclear fusion and MHD power generation.

(c) In the field of data processing: applying newly discovered principles such as the Josephson effect.

(5) Among the above themes, particular emphasis must be placed on three areas.

(a) Development of technologies inventing new materials,

(b) Development of technologies, applying a large-scale system including those for alternative energy sources.

(c) Development of technologies related to a social system, including that in the field of personal and community activities.

New Phase in Policy on Technology

The principal role of the government policy for the development of technology is to encourage development efforts in the private sector. In the past, the Japanese industry achieved brilliant results in improving and applying imported technologies. In the '80s, however, it will be essential for Japan to develop technologies of its own. For this purpose, it is necessary to systematically pursue policies with an emphasis on the following three points.

(1) Development of Creative Technologies:

(a) Switchover to "forward engineering": Now that it has become increasingly difficult to find specific goals of development of imported technologies, Japan needs to press ahead with projects for the research and development of original technologies through trial and error and the accumulation of basic data.

(b) Training of personnel capable of achieving technological breakthroughs.

(c) Establishment of a system to encourage taking risks and squarely facing new challenges.

(2) Systematic Promotion of Technology:

(a) Technological developments must be promoted by presenting a "Long-term Vision for Technological Development," which identifies the priority goals for technological development, as well as systems for development and funding.

(b) In the area of energy-related technologies and in other pressing areas requiring a large amount of development funds, the government must launch national projects on its own initiatives.

(3) Increased Allocation of Research and Development Funds:

(a) Efforts must be made to increase the budget available for research and development of technologies.

(b) The share of government expenditures for R&D in total R&D expenditures is in the order of one-third in Japan, compared with around a half in Western industrialized countries. This share should be raised in spite of the expected deficit in the national budget.

(c) Recognizing that research and development of technologies are the nation's best interest, the government must make every effort to find a new source of funds for financing such projects.[6]

Finally, supporting a central theses of this book, the primacy of investment in human resources, the final statement of national purpose by MITI is specially significant. Not only because of its support of what is perceived by this author as a key aspect of a new U.S. economic policy but also because of the level of deterioration to which we have permitted the U.S. educational system to sink.

Progress is hindered by external and internal constraints: external constraints concern energy, the environment and international relations; in-

ternal ones, human wisdom and attitudes, and social systems. Although
we need considerable efforts to overcome the difficulties anticipated in
the 1980s and to achieve the promise of the future, we are convinced that
the nature of the Japanese people will bring success.

Education has played a vital part in the process of Japan's modernization. In order to foster the qualities needed in the 1980s and beyond—
creativity, individuality, and internationalism—education is expected to
play an even more important role. The period when we made progress
by applying and improving existing ideas has already come to an end,
and a period of creativity and initiative will begin. Japan must formulate
an industrial civilization based on its own culture and the creative
knowledge to be applied for industrial uses. It must protect the security
of the nation's welfare, improve the quality of life, and provide respect-
able image in the world community.[7]

Japan overcame many difficulties in the 1970s through an intensified
use of knowledge. While this will continue to be important, penetrating
insight and good judgment are essential to cope with the problems of the
1980s crowded with uncertainty. The 1980s must become an "Age of Vi-
talized Human Potential," that is, the age when obstacles and problems
are to be overcome through full utilization of creative knowledge.

Notes

1. *Industrial Growth and Productivity,* Hearings before the Subcommittee on
Industrial Growth and Productivity Committee on Budget, U.S. Senate, 97th Congress, 1st Session, p. 245.
    2. Ibid.
    3. Ibid., pp. 245–46.
    4. Ibid.
    5. Ibid., p. 251.
    6. Ibid., pp. 250–51.
    7. Ibid., pp. 254-55.

Index

About the Author

HERBERT E. STRINER (Ph.D. and Maxwell Fellow in Economics, Syracuse University; M.A. and B.A. Rutgers University) is University Professor of Management and Economics, College of Business, American University, Washington, D.C. His career has included teaching at Syracuse University, research at Johns Hopkins University, the Brookings Institution, Stanford Research Institute, and the W. E. Upjohn Institute for Employment Research. Prior to his current faculty position, he was for six years the dean of the Kogod College of Business Administration, American University.

Professor Striner has authored more than 70 articles and four books, among which are *Continuing Education as a National Capital Investment* and *Local Impact of Foreign Trade—A Study in Methods of Local Economic Accounting* (with W. Hochwald and S. Sonenblum). He has served in government, both in staff positions and as a presidential adviser. Since 1980, he has served as a consultant on productivity to numerous private corporations and several foreign governments.